D1326087

I LEAP OVER THE WALL

At the age of twenty-one, Monica Baldwin, daughter of Prime Minister Stanley Baldwin, entered one of the oldest and most strictly enclosed contemplative orders of the Roman Catholic Church. Twenty-eight years later, after a prolonged struggle with her vocation, she left the convent. But the world Monica had known in 1914 was very different to the world into which she emerged at the height of the Second World War. This is the account of one woman's two very different lives, with revealing descriptions of the world of a novice, the daily duties of a nun, and the spiritual aspects of convent life. Interwoven with these, as the author is confronted with fashions, politics and art totally unfamiliar to her, are the trials and tribulations of coping with a new and alien world.

I LEAP OVER THE WALL

A RETURN TO THE WORLD AFTER TWENTY-EIGHT YEARS IN A CONVENT

MONICA BALDWIN

LARGE
PRINT

First published in Great Britain 1949
by
Robert Hale Limited

First Isis Edition
published 2016

The moral right of the author has been asserted

A catalogue record for this book is available
from the British Library.

ISBN 978–1–78541–132–8 (hb)
ISBN 978–1–78541–138–0 (pb)

Published by
F. A. Thorpe (Publishing)
Anstey, Leicestershire

Set by Words & Graphics Ltd.
Anstey, Leicestershire
Printed and bound in Great Britain by
T. J. International Ltd., Padstow, Cornwall

This book is printed on acid-free paper

With love and gratitude to
Mary-Eula Draper Blair
who has shown me what friendship
between America and England can mean

INTRODUCTION

I am not the first member of my family to leap over a wall.

Nearly four hundred years ago, my ancestor, Thomas Baldwin of Diddlebury, leaped to freedom from behind the walls of the Tower of London, where he had been imprisoned for taking part in a plot for the escape of Mary Queen of Scots.

His name, with an inscription and the date "July 1585" can still be seen where he carved it on the wall of his cell in the Beauchamp Tower. Later, he added a motto to his coat-of-arms, *Per Deum meum transilio murum* — "By the help of my God I Leap over the Wall".

It has been the family motto of the Baldwins ever since; but the wall that I leapt over was a spiritual and not a material obstacle.

In 1914, my cousin, William Sparrow, who disapproved of my entering the convent, wrote to me:

" . . . Knowing you as I do, I can safely predict that it will be with you as with another fair and foolish female, whose unwisdom caused her to languish long behind prison walls. Your End will be your Beginning. I commend these words, with those of the family motto, to your meditation. Taken together, they may suggest a course of action in years to come . . . "

In the following pages I have tried to describe what happened when my cousin's rather ambiguous prophecy was fulfilled. It is a rash and foolhardy undertaking, in the circumstances, for I really know nothing about anything, except, perhaps, what goes on behind "high convent walls".

My only excuse is that so many, and such different kinds of people, have urged me to attempt it.

Some of them said to me, "Because of your past environment, your angle is unusual. It should interest people. You ought to write about it."

Others simply bombarded me with questions. It is chiefly on their account that I have embarked upon this book. Some of the remarks made to me revealed such fantastically wrong ideas about nuns and convents that I began to feel something ought to be done to put the monastic ideal in a truer perspective for those who know little or nothing about it.

So I have tried to write accurately and fairly about life in a strictly enclosed convent, as I myself experienced it. To do this it was necessary to describe not only the wonderful and exalted spiritual ideal which inspires that life, but also certain aspects of it which, for various reasons, may perhaps leave something to be desired.

2

I do not feel that I have done my subject justice. If, however, these pages help to straighten out even a few of the curiously crooked notions which so many people still appear to retain about convents, I shall be well satisfied.

One fact I must make clear from the outset. I describe the religious vocation from the point of view of one who had no such vocation. The alternative title of this book might well be *Impressions of a Square Peg in a Round Hole*.

Cornwall
February 1948   MONICA BALDWIN

CHAPTER
ONE

(1)

Leaps over walls — especially when taken late in life —
can be extremely perilous. To leap successfully, you
need a sense of humour, the spirit of adventure and an
unshakable conviction that what you are leaping over is
an obstacle upon which you would otherwise fall down.

My own leap was taken on October 26, 1941.

On that day I left the convent, where for twenty-eight
years I had lived in the strictest possible enclosure, and
came out again into the world.

In reality, it was not necessary to do any leaping,
either of walls or of anything else. As soon as the
customary formalities were ended, the doors were
opened and I simply walked out.

The story of what led me to do this might be
interesting: this, however, is not the place for it. This
book deals with what happened after the convent doors
were closed behind me and I stepped out into a world
that was just beginning its third year of a new and
particularly devilish kind of war.

Naturally, everyone whom I consulted assured me that
I could not have chosen a more unsuitable moment for
my exodus. What with clothes coupons, food rationing,
travelling restrictions and the appalling rise in the cost

of living, how on earth — they asked — did I imagine I should ever be able to cope?

I looked at all this, however, from another angle. Just because the world appeared to be in such a crazy turmoil, I felt that it was exactly the background that I required. Everybody was rushing round doing unprecedented things. Old standards had already been swept away. How easy it would be to plunge into the seething waters of the war deluge and splash about unnoticed, listening, looking about, experimenting, learning about things, till the floods died down! Afterwards — always provided that anything of the universe still remained to be lived in, which just then seemed unlikely — one might perhaps start trying to construct a life.

In my opinion, it would have been far more difficult to adjust oneself to the comparatively ordered rhythm of the pre-war world.

My sister Freda came to fetch me away, rather appropriately, on a cold and frosty morning. She brought with her an atmosphere of faint disapproval and a suitcase containing the clothes into which I was to change before finally going forth into the world.

The crescendo of shocks which awaited me began abruptly with my first introduction to up-to-date underwear. Frankly, I was appalled.

The garments to which I was accustomed had been contrived by thoroughgoing ascetics in the fourteenth century, who considered that a nice, thick, long-sleeved "shift" of rough, scratchy serge was the right thing to wear next your skin. My shifts, when new, had reached almost to my ankles. However, hard washing and much indiscriminate patching soon stiffened and shrank them until they all but stood up by themselves. Stays, shoulder-strapped and severely boned, concealed one's outline; over them, two long serge petticoats were lashed securely round one's waist. Last came the ample habit-coat of heavy cloth, topped by a linen rochet and a stiffly starched *barbette* of cambric, folded into a score of tiny tucks and pleats at the neck.

So, when my sister handed me a wisp of gossamer, about the size and substance of a spider's web, I was startled.

She said, "Here's your foundation garment. Actually, most people only wear pants and a *brassière*, but it's cold to-day so I thought we'd better start you with a vest."

I examined the object, remembering 1914. In those days, a "nice" girl "started" with long, woolly combinations, neck-high and elbow-sleeved, decorated with a row of neat pearl buttons down the front . . .

Next came the modern version of the corset. It was the merest strip of elastic brocade from which suspenders, in a surprising number, dangled. I thought it a great improvement on the fourteenth-century idea. The only drawback was that you had to insert your person into it serpent-fashion, as it had no fastenings.

What bothered me most were the stockings. The kind I was used to were enormous things, far thicker than those men wear for tramping the moors and shrunk by repeated boiling to the shape and consistency of a Wellington boot. The pair with which Freda had provided me were of silk, skin-coloured and so transparent that I wondered why anyone bothered to wear the things at all.

I said firmly, "Freda, I can't possibly go out in these. They make my legs look naked."

She smiled patiently.

"Nonsense," she said. "Everyone wears them. If you went about in anything else you'd collect a crowd."

By this time it had become clear to me that the generation which affected the transparencies in which I now was shivering must long ago have scrapped the kind of garments I had worn as a girl. I wondered what they had done about the neck-high camisoles with their fussy trimmings of lace and insertion and those incredibly ample, long-legged white cotton drawers.

The answer turned out to be an airy nothing called "cami-knickers", made, apparently, of cobweb. I felt my teeth beginning to chatter as I put it — or should one say "them"? — on.

One further shock awaited me.

An object was handed to me which I can only describe as a very realistically modelled bust-bodice. That its purpose was to emphasize contours which, in my girlhood, were always decorously concealed was but too evident.

"This," said my sister cheerfully, "is a *brassière*. And it's no use looking so horrified, because fashions to-day go out of their way to stress that part of one's anatomy. These things are supposed to fix one's chest at the classic angle. Like this —" she adjusted the object with expert fingers. "There — you see the idea?"

The worst problem was my hair.

For twenty-eight years it had been cropped convict-wise beneath the incredible system of headgear exacted by the Order to which I belonged. As a foundation, a "snood", or long narrow strip of linen, was wound two or three times round the head. Over this, a close-fitting cap — rather like those worn by bathers — was pulled down to the ears. A piece of fine cambric, called a "tip", was then bound tightly across the forehead and tied at the back with strings. Next came the "head" — a kind of wimple — which covered the head and ears. It was gathered in closely at the neck and then frilled out as far as the shoulders beneath the starched *barbette*. Over this was pinned an erection of black cashmere which fell, gable-wise, on either side of the head to just above the elbows. Between this and its lining of starched white linen was a double cardboard stiffening with strips of cotton, fortified with yet more starch. Finally, the veil proper — of thin, black material, rather like ninon — was mounted on the underveil and firmly secured with pins. Eight thicknesses in all! In summer it was apt to give one a headache. The wonder, of course, was that, having worn it for so many years, I had any hair left at all.

For about two months before my exodus, however, I had allowed my hair to grow. The result was that my head now resembled that of a moth-eaten golliwog. My sister, foreseeing this dilemma, had been inspired to bring me an admirable hat. Though neither toque, beret nor képi, it combined the advantages of all three. I drew it on now, a little apprehensively. Perhaps the effect may have been a trifle raffish; however, it concealed my elf-locks very satisfactorily.

Now we were on the threshold.

As I crossed it, two thoughts occurred to me. One was that the door which at that instant was being locked behind me was not a door but a guillotine. And it had just chopped off from me, utterly and irrevocably, every single thing which, for twenty-eight years, had made up my life. Henceforward I was a being without a background. And no one who has not actually experienced that sensation can know how grim it is.

The other thought flashed in upon me with the urgency of a commandment:

Thou shalt not look back!

And I knew instinctively that, if I wanted to keep my balance on the tight-rope stretched before me, I must slam the door behind me and keep on looking straight ahead. Otherwise I should have to pay the penalty.

I crossed the courtyard and went out into the pale October sunshine.

For good or ill, I had leapt over the wall.

(2)

Before I go further, I must explain why I found it — and still find it — so extraordinarily difficult to acquire that wideawake, all-alert attitude which is essential for any kind of success in the world to-day.

I had not been more than a few hours out of the convent when I realized that I didn't know even the first thing about modern life. I had forgotten the value of money; I knew less than nothing about clothes; I had never even heard of the authors, athletes, film-stars, politicians, whose names were in the news. My standards were all pre-1914. And even these had been badly blurred by the passage of time. In fact, if Providence had not blessed me with a sense of humour, the thought of the masses of information which I had to assimilate might well have made me defeatist before I had begun to fight.

The most difficult thing to deal with was my own interior attitude.

For twenty-eight years I had lived with my outside turned inwards. Now, swiftly and violently, I had, so to speak, to reverse engines and start trying to live with my inside turned out.

Let me try to make this clear.

Most people imagine that girls go into convents because of an unsuccessful love-affair. Possibly some do; but they are the rare exceptions. I myself believe that most people become nuns because they belong to one or other of two classes.

The first and smaller class consists of those who are naturally devout. Marriage does not particularly attract them. They like saying their prayers (as opposed, perhaps, to praying); they love a quiet, well-ordered existence, with heaven as its goal. They do not make the best nuns, but they certainly lead good lives and quite often arrive at a surprising degree of holiness.

The second class is the larger and the more interesting. It consists of the people who enter convents less because they themselves choose to do so than because they are chosen by God. These are the real "vocations". Some spiritual adventure has happened to them: some vital encounter has taken place between their souls and God. They know, beyond all possibility of doubt, that God is not just some vague, remote, spiritual ideal, but a living Person. They therefore become possessed by a kind of burning hunger and thirst for God, which only he himself can satisfy.

To those who have never had this experience, such an idea will probably seem fantastic. But the fact remains that you cannot read the lives and writings of the saints and mystics without repeatedly coming up against the assertion that, even in this life, it is possible for the veil to be lifted and for the human soul to enter into what is, literally, a conscious, experimental contact with God. And those who have experienced this contact declare unanimously that it can only be described as a foretaste of the bliss of heaven.

This being so, it is not really so very surprising that when this craving for contact with God becomes fierce and urgent, as it undoubtedly does in certain people, they are ready to trample underfoot the world and everything in it, if by that means their longing can be satisfied.

It is, of course, for this type of person that contemplative convents primarily exist. They are organized, down to the very smallest details, with one object in view — to provide for those who live in them the kind of life which will best enable them to attain their end.

12

The discipline to which religious subject themselves is extremely rigorous. God, lovelier than any dream, is pure Spirit; therefore, if contact is to be established, the counter-attraction of the senses must be overcome. You can't be completely wrapped up in God (and he is a jealous lover) unless you are unwrapped-up in what this world has to offer you. In convents, this process of unwrapping is effected by a system of remorseless separation from everything that is not God.

All intercourse with the outside world is reduced to the absolute minimum. The same applies to visits and letters, which the Superior is free to censor or suppress, as she thinks fit. Newspapers and secular literature are prohibited. In fact, one lives — as far as is humanly possible — oblivious of what goes on outside the convent walls.

I myself became a nun only a few months before the invasion of Belgium in 1914. The war brought many sensational happenings to the community; but beyond those in which I was necessarily involved I knew next to nothing of what was going on. Now and again a nun would be sent for by Reverend Mother and told that some relation had been wounded or killed; but I can't remember reading a single newspaper during the whole four years. Then, one day, bells were rung and Reverend Mother announced to us that the fighting was ended. Afterwards we went to the choir and sang the *Te Deum* in thanksgiving. That, for me, represented World War Number One.

So much for exterior separation. The interior separation cut deeper still.

Almost the first thing that the Mistress of Novices explained to me was the importance of being exact about even the smallest details of the Rule. She said, "You must give up your own tastes and habits and allow the Rule to mould you according to the pattern of the Order to which you belong."

As I was extremely lively and much attached to my own way of looking at things, I found this difficult. And it was some time before what are called "The Rules of Modesty" managed to transform my worldly manners into a "religious" exterior.

Among other things, these "Rules" decreed that when walking you might never swing your arms. Instead, your hands must be kept meekly clasped together at the level of your waist. This was "religious". To hurry was another breach of decorum. You were obliged to take short, measured steps, head bent just a little forward and eyes invariably cast down. Even had a bomb exploded just behind you, it would have been more perfect not to look up. In fact, this "custody of the eyes" was considered so important that to raise them, even for a moment, without strict necessity, in choir or refectory, was a minor breach of Rule.

The idea behind all this rigorous guard of the senses was that distracting thoughts interrupt the unbroken application of the mind of God. This, of course, is the ideal of the contemplative, as the fourteenth-century author of *The Cloud of Unknowing* knew full well, when he wrote, "Thou art the further from God that aught is in thy mind but only God".

One day my Novice Mistress said to me "God is a Spirit; that is why he can only be apprehended spiritually. Of course, he is everywhere — but not everywhere to us. The only place where we can really get into vital contact with God is in the centre of our own souls."

I asked her exactly what was meant by the "centre of the soul".

She explained to me that it was the very deepest, innermost part of you: the central core of your personality.

Later on, when I began to read spiritual books — Tauler, Blosius, Père Surin, St. Teresa (how I disliked St. Teresa!), Father Baker, St. John of the Cross — I discovered that it was in this "centre of the soul" that the real adventures of the spiritual life took place. The difficulty, of course, was how to get there.

According to the Mistress of Novices, there was only one way. She called it "recollection". It consisted in shutting off from the mind everything external, so that it might be free from all distracting thoughts. The mind was then able to enter into itself by "introversion": in other words, to concentrate itself upon its own highest — or, if you prefer it — deepest part.

The technique of recollection was quite simple. You just had to go on and on, emptying your mind of thoughts and images, so that your faculties were kept free from the memory, thought and desire of everything but God.

Once a fortnight, all the novices had to go to their Mistress for a short private interview. If you had difficulties about anything, you could ask questions and have them explained. Your faults were also pointed out to you, sometimes with a good deal of severity.

I disliked these little interviews quite intensely and, as often as not, came out from them feeling as though my soul had been scrubbed with prickly-pear.

My questions were nearly always about "recollection". I think my Novice Mistress must have grown tired of answering them, for one day, instead of talking to me, she gave me a little book to read. It was called *Of Union with God* by Albertus Magnus. I still think it one of the most wonderful books ever written on the spiritual life. The author — a man of one idea — insists that the end and aim of all the contemplative's labours is "to withdraw the powers from the memory, love and thought of what is below and to fix them upon God, reposing with him in the centre of the soul".[1]

---

[1] Elsewhere he explains that "it is of the greatest importance that what has been seen, heard, done or said, should not leave any traces in the imagination. Neither before, nor at the time, nor afterwards, should we foster their memories or allow their images to be formed". And in order to arrive at this emptiness of the mind, he advises, "Bar the doors of thy senses, and dwell therein, guarding thy heart against all images and shapes of earthly things . . . draw thy powers inwards and thence lift them up to God".

Later, I discovered that Père Surin, the greatest of the Jesuit mystics, went even further. He insists that nothing so helps to dispose the soul for prayer as the long-sustained effort to preserve oneself from what he calls "*le défaut de la multiplicité*". This, he explains, springs from all distinct and particular knowledge acquired from contact with exterior things.

One should, he declares, train the mind to raise itself rather to what is *universal*, and to be content with such knowledge as is general and *indistinct* (cf. Surin, *Catêchisme Spirituel*).

Obviously, one couldn't go on concentrating for years upon this kind of interior attitude without its doing something to one's mentality. What it did to me was to develop an inward habit which was as diametrically opposed to that induced by, for instance, Pelmanism, as can be conceived. Instead of observing, remembering, deducing, reflecting, my whole energy was employed upon effacing from my memory every kind of impression almost before it was received. Indeed, as a novice, my custody of the eyes was so rigorous that I must have been a menace to the community, for I remember constantly bumping into people who happened to be coming my way.

Of course, the result of all this was, that when I returned to the world and was forced to sit up and take notice of what was going on — with the utmost rapidity and violence on every side — I nearly went crazy. There was just no means of relaxing, even for an instant, from the desperate effort to do what I'd spent my whole life as a religious in trying not to do. Even now, after nearly eight years of effort, I have not achieved it. I doubt if I ever shall. I'm still unobservant, and the life-long habit of "emptying the memory" of everything one has seen or done, makes it all too easy to forget.

(3)

I had received two kind and most heartening letters when I told my family that I was leaving the convent. One was from my uncle and aunt *à la mode de*

Bretagne, the Stanley Baldwins, who told me that of course I must come straight to them. The other, from A.B., my mother's sister, insisted that from now onwards I should look upon her house in Sussex as my home.

But before I went anywhere or did anything, I just *had* to go where shops were and buy the necessities of life.

I dreaded the ordeal of shopping. All sense of the value of money had left me. I hadn't the vaguest idea what to buy. I didn't know which shops to go to, or even where they were to be found. My sister had promised to help me, but she was working in the Censorship and leave was not easy to get. A day and a half was the utmost she could spare me. I had a feeling, too, that she wasn't greatly enjoying this business of launching me. The sooner I was able to stand alone, the better she would be pleased.

I had hoped to spend a few days at her flat, to get advice about the endless problems that beset me. Unfortunately, the friend with whom she then lived suddenly developed Conscientious Objections to People Who Came Out of Convents, and flatly refused to let me spend even a night beneath their roof.

This was rather a blow.

My sister told me she didn't feel able to do anything about it, because she cared for the friend more than anyone else on earth.

Finally it was arranged that Freda and I should cram our shopping into that afternoon and the following morning. I was to spend the night with an aunt and uncle who lived in London, and go down to A.B. in Sussex the following day.

So, feeling top-heavy, self-conscious and slightly indecent in my short skirts, transparent stockings and high-heeled shoes, I allowed my sister to shepherd me and my suitcase into a Green Line bus.

We spent the journey up to London struggling frantically with the coupon problem. How I was going to rig myself out with the number of coupons available, we could neither of us imagine. Our list contained only the starkest necessities, but even with the extra coupons which generous friends had provided, it still looked as if sections of my person would have to remain bare. I began seeing visions of myself like the Emperor in Hans Andersen's story, clothed in lovely fresh air instead of lingerie.

The power, speed, noise and general ruthlessness of London overwhelmed me. I suppose my twenty-eight years behind protecting walls made this inevitable. I felt like a small and dithering mouse that had strayed in among the turbines of some gigantic engine-room.

I was completely dazed.

Freda started by whisking me off to a hairdresser, where she superintended the transformation of my elf-locks into an Eton crop. This gave me the beginnings of self-confidence and I began to feel more capable of facing what lay ahead.

After that, we set out on a hurricane shop-raid. We dashed up Oxford Street for shoes and stockings. We whirled into Debenham's to buy a suit. We raced to Shaftesbury Avenue where a Bessarabian friend of my sister's (at least, I think she was a Bessarabian — she certainly looked like it) had a dress shop. We tore like tornadoes to I know not how many places for blouses and lingerie. We flew back to Bond Street for hats. And a last rush up Regent Street was only prevented by the tiresome discovery that the shops were about to shut.

Several months later, when questioned about my first impressions of London, I replied that what I had seen depressed me. London was changed almost beyond recognition. Many of her familiar landmarks had been rebuilt. Her blitz-wounds were still fresh, and in several places the wreckage had been so severe that I had stood still, appalled before such frightfulness.

There were signs of war everywhere. For the first time I saw barrage balloons, decontamination centres, air-raid shelters, sirens, blast screens, trenches, black-out precautions and all the rest. I was impressed by the contrast between shop-windows as I remembered them and their present, heavily-boarded condition, with only small panels of glass let in to display the scanty wares behind.

The change in the shapes of the cars and buses struck me as most peculiar. They looked rather as if they had been fattened up, like ducks. They had lost their angles (this, my sister told me, was "stream-lining") and they carried their bodies so low that they almost dragged on the ground. This earthward tendency reappeared in the children's perambulators, which I remembered as large, luxurious cradles swung high up between enormous slender wheels. The odd little sturdy low-wheeled push-cars that contained the modern infant struck me as too quaint for words.

A thing that puzzled me was the frequent recurrence of large, tangerine-coloured balls on white poles at the edge of the pavements. These, said Freda, were Belisha Beacons. Not knowing who or what Belisha was, I wondered why . . .

I was much impressed by the tidy way that the traffic kept stopping at regular intervals, apparently of its own accord. When Freda showed me the traffic lights winking miraculously from emerald to ruby and back through orange-amber into emerald again, I was spellbound. So much so, indeed, that, standing enchanted before this lovely spectacle in Piccadilly Circus, I was nearly done to death by a passing taxi. I suppose I richly deserved what the driver said to me, but I remember that, as I listened, I realized that here at least was something in London that had not changed.

The shops left me speechless. The larger ones had been rebuilt; their size and splendour made me think that they must be Government offices or luxury hotels. Not so their contents. I was, of course, prepared for the war-time shortage of everything; what staggered me was the appearance and behaviour of the personnel. Gone were the frock-coated myriads of shop-walkers who had once thronged one's path like obsequious black-beetles; gone the satin-gowned moddoming ladies with swishing trains and incredible coiffures. Instead, a few rather disdainful elderly women and

21

scornful blondes in their teens had taken over. Their costumes were as unorthodox — at least, according to pre-1914 standards — as their behaviour, and it was just the hardest thing in the world to get them to take any notice of you at all. Occasionally, however, if you were really persevering, you might induce one of them to pause for a moment in her conversation with a friend. But even then it required the exertion of almost hypnotic powers on your part before she would condescend to sell you some fantastically high-priced substitute for what you actually required. The older ones treated you with condescension: the younger, with unconcealed contempt.

And nobody ever said "Moddom" to you at all.

The Londoners, on the whole, gave me a lot to think about.

To begin with, the "leisured classes" — as I remembered them — had completely disappeared. I've never been able to discover what has become of them. Like Atlantis and the Dodo, they have simply vanished away. In their place, London was thronged by what looked like the lower-middle and working classes — a vast multitude with strained faces and tired, blitz-haunted eyes. There were foreigners everywhere. One heard French, Polish, Russian, Czech, American in streets and buses. There were also an astonishing number of Jews. The few men in circulation struck me as very much the same as those I remembered twenty-eight years ago. Their trousers were baggier and some of them wore a new kind of baby toothbrush moustache. I noticed one youth wearing quite the most hideous garment I had yet encountered — a pair of elongated knicker-bockers, ending off about half-way down the leg. I pointed this out to my sister in some excitement. She murmured, "plus-fours". I had no idea what she meant.

With the women, however, things were different. The type had altered. When I left the world, Lily Elsie and Gladys Cooper had set the beauty standard: rounded faces; large, melting eyes, soft mouths and low-piled hair. But these women appeared to belong to a different civilization. They had narrow faces, high cheek-bones, wide, heavily-painted mouths and slanting eyes. Their chins jutted. Their noses were strong and short. Their hair — invariably waved or curled — hung loose on their shoulders. And most of them had terrible, claw-like, purple-painted nails.

Among their faces I noticed a curious similarity. Their features differed, but their expressions were the same. It suggested that the same environment had moulded them; that they thought the same thoughts, looked at, listened to and were influenced by, very much the same things.

Oddly enough, I believe that what most impressed me on that first astounding day was the spectacle of London without her railings. It was almost like seeing Queen Victoria without her clothes. And not only the parks, but the sacrosanct squares and the fronts of the houses were all now flung open to the vandal incursions of children and dogs.

Lately I have begun to revise a good many of my opinions; my first impression was, however, one of profound dismay. The disappearance of those railings seemed like a rather sinister portent of things to come.

(4)

My sister parked me finally at Portland Place, where I was to spend the night with an uncle and aunt.

Their house had been damaged when the B.B.C. nearby was bombed, and the ballroom and drawing-room were uninhabitable. Rolled-up carpets and stacks of furniture were dimly visible in the shadowy light from boarded windows; brocaded hangings showed, torn and blackened by blast and smoke. A depressing spectacle.

My aunt and uncle were kind to me: nevertheless, I could not help feeling — as I was to do later on with so many of my relations — that my return to the world was not greeted with unmitigated enthusiasm. Oddly enough, it was just those who had reproached me most bitterly for Going In in 1914 who expressed the sternest disapproval of my Coming Out in 1941.

Some people are curiously difficult to please.

After dinner, somebody turned on the wireless.

My first impulse was to fly from the room, shrieking "Witchcraft!", for the gramophone had been in its earlier and most excruciating stages when I went away. However, I controlled my emotions and was rewarded by rather an odd little coincidence.

It so happened that the last music I had listened to on the night before I left my home for the convent had been the haunting Tchaikovsky waltz from *Eugen Onegin*. It had always enchanted me and I had imagined that something sombre, almost fateful, lurked in those slow, downward-running octaves with which the melody is so subtly interwoven near the end. And now, after all those years, here it was, waiting to greet me on the threshold of the new world into which I was about to step. Out into the room it poured, billowing about me and over me in wave after wave of wild, romantic music, stirring me strangely and awakening poignant long-forgotten memories.

I listened, wondering that, at my age, such music still had the power to unlock the secret places in my heart.

Anyway, it was considerate of the Powers That Be to supply me with such an attractive signature tune.

It was, I suppose, inevitable after the austerity of a monastic[1] cell that the room in which I was put to sleep appeared to me, despite the blitz damage, almost palatially luxurious.

A nun's cell is so small that there is only just room for herself, a tiny chest-of-drawers and a *prie-dieu*, one

---

[1] Abbot Gasquet points out in his *English Monastic Life* that it is incorrect to apply the word "convent" exclusively to houses of nuns. The term "convent", "monastery" or "abbey" can be applied to any house of either monks or nuns. The use of the word "convent" for a religious house of women is of quite modern origin.

25

chair, a minute folding table and a hard little bed. I remember, as a novice, how much difficulty I had in getting accustomed to the rough woollen sheets, which — incredible as it may seem to modern notions of hygiene — were washed only once a year.

There is no washstand; instead, a small earthen jug and basin stand in a corner on the floor. Bare boards and plain whitewashed walls intensify the atmosphere of austerity. No one may enter your cell except the Superior, or, should you fall ill, the nun who holds the office of apothecary.

The cell is always a place of silence. Drawers, doors and windows must be opened noiselessly. Outside in the dormitory, white-habited figures move up and down like shadows. Not a sound must break the stillness — neither the sound of voices nor of passing feet.

And now, here I was, tucked into a nest of pillows in a down-soft bed between delicately fragrant linen sheets. And the room was large and high, with tall wide windows; and there were pictures on the walls, and mirrors everywhere. The thick pile rugs struck a note of rich and satisfying colour; and for washing there was a great, deep, blue-veined marble basin, into which hot and cold water cascaded from elegant and highly-polished taps. In the convent I had been used to going to bed by the light of a tiny oil-filled lamp like a small glass ink-pot, with a wick that could only be manipulated with a pin. Now I found an amber-shaded electric reading-lamp at my bedside; and there were switches which set other lights burning miraculously in various parts of the room. I leaned back, marvelling at the luxury of my surroundings. It seemed almost like a page out of the *Arabian Nights* . . .

I have always felt that the moment when first you wake up in the morning is the most wonderful of the twenty-four hours. No matter how weary or dreary you may feel, you possess the certainty that, during the day that lies before you, absolutely anything may happen. And the fact that it practically always *doesn't*, matters not one jot. The possibility is always there.

Even in the convent, I almost invariably experienced this rather childish thrill on first awakening. It helped me to bound out of bed when the calling-bell clanged ruthlessly at a quarter to five a.m. And nobody who hasn't tried it can imagine quite how disinclined one feels for bounding at that uninspiring hour, especially in winter, when one's sponge is a frozen fossil and one has to smash the ice in one's water-jug with the hair-brush handle before one can wash.

I myself was once appointed to do the calling for a time, which meant getting up half an hour earlier than the rest of the community. It gave one an odd, ghostly feeling to tiptoe about all alone in that long, dimly-lighted dormitory of sleepers; one was almost afraid to break the night's tremendous silence and set in motion the complex machinery of another long monastic day.

After ringing the heavy iron bell, it is the Caller's duty to go round from cell to cell, opening each door just wide enough to hear the answer when she utters the morning salutation of *Deo gratias*. It always amused me to study the different reactions of the various nuns to this stern command of duty. Most of them were already splashing by the time I got to them; but a few — one knew instinctively which they would be! — needed quite a volley of *Deo gratiases* before they could be persuaded to grunt a sleepy answer from beneath the clothes. The really heavy sleepers were apt to be tiresome. Sometimes you had to stand, saying *Deo gratias* at their doors till you were nearly hoarse.

Once a dreadful thing happened. After a more than usually lengthy effort to elicit an answer, the Caller got worried and entered the cell to investigate. To her horror, she found a corpse lying stiff beneath the bedclothes. The nun had died from heart-failure during the night.

I woke up in my unfamiliar surroundings with a new and vague sensation of peace that deepened gradually into one of definite content. I think it arose from my realization that what I had believed in when I leapt to what — for me — was freedom was truly worth my faith. I had no regrets, no anxiety about what lay before me. In fact, I felt like an explorer on the verge of setting out. I was full of the spirit of adventure and of enthusiasm for whatever might lie ahead — an attitude of mind which still seems to me as surprising as it was fortunate, in view of the rather soul-shattering happenings of the previous day.

(5)

Freda came with me to Victoria. Here we parted, pressing cheeks, while she kissed the air for reasons connected with lipstick. And for the first time I found myself really on my own.

I was terrified. The knowledge that I should have to change twice during the journey, not to mention coping with porters — or no porters, which might be even more annoying — filled me with alarm. Freda had warned me that, owing to precautions in view of the possibility of invasion, one could not see the names of the stations. I wondered how on earth I should know when to get out. And didn't one have to tip porters? I had forgotten to ask how much one ought to offer, and hadn't a notion what they would expect.

I opened my purse. Unfortunately, what I found there only raised fresh problems. To begin with, instead of the nice, bright, golden sovereigns that I remembered, I found dirty banknotes and some tinny-looking florins and half-crowns. (The old five-shilling pieces, my sister had told me, were no longer in circulation.) There were also some twelve-sided coins which were entirely new to me. The silver threepenny-bits of my youth, it appeared, had gone for good.

I studied my fellow-travellers. There were some soldiers, rather red about the ears and smelling of beer and hot khaki, and two or three hatless young women with padded shoulders and purple nails. All had cigarettes between their lips. This startled me. I had never seen a woman smoke in a railway carriage before. Their skirts were of a shortness which still shocked me a little; but then, my own were, after all, nothing to boast about, if it came to that.

I looked out of the window. The Sussex countryside was ablaze with the glory of autumn — orange, cinnamon, olive, rust-red and fairy gold. On the horizon, the soft green shoulders of the Downs curved mistily. Flights of birds wheeled suddenly and swiftly, then disappeared into the clear pale sky. Somehow, however, I have never felt the peculiar spell of Sussex which has caught and held so many of my kinsfolk and their relatives. Time was when Rottingdean, Burwash, Steyning, were alive with Burne-Joneses, Baldwins, Ridsdales, Howards, Kiplings, and Mackails. I thought of them, wondering about the gaps that must have occurred among their ranks and of which, in most cases, I was ignorant. I had been gone so long that, like Rip Van Winkle, I did not know what I was going to find.

On the whole, I got through my first journey rather better than I had expected. One of the hatless young women advised me when to get out. Mercifully, the porter seemed satisfied with the coin that I offered him. I am afraid it was half a crown.

CHAPTER
TWO

(1)

The little Sussex village in which my aunt lived had a dual personality. Half of it, tucked away in the twittens and behind the high stone walls of the larger houses, belonged to a bygone England. The other half, represented by the high street, where an incipient cinema had begun to show its horns, belonged to the England of to-day. My aunt's house, in one of the more withdrawn country lanes, had somehow managed to elude both atmospheres. It was simply her own particular and personal shrine.

A.B. was a pretty old lady with soft white hair and a *penchant* for piety. She and the devoted maid-companion who waited on her divided their time between church-going, gardening, and the worship of a small and extremely undisciplined black-and-tan dog.

The sudden irruption of an elderly niece of almost unprecedented mentality into this quiet household must have been something of a trial. If this was so, A.B. certainly dealt with it in the grand manner. She flung wide her boxes, her cupboards, her wardrobes, her chests-of-drawers, and proceeded to clothe the very-nearly-naked with a generosity which must surely have won her a great reward in the world to come.

★ ★ ★

During these peaceful weeks in Sussex — exteriorly so uneventful — a great many quite important things happened to me within my mind.

At first I felt so exhausted that I could do little more than behave like a vegetable. Some such reaction was, I suppose, inevitable, for the last years before I left the convent had been a time of very great strain. Little by little, however, I felt that life was slowly creeping back to me. I tried to do some constructive thinking, and deal with a few of the problems that were lying, piled up like left luggage, on the doorstep of my mind.

The Sussex lanes were very lovely in the autumn. I started going for long lone country walks among the spendthrift gold and glory of the year-end, giving myself up to the earth-scents and the sky-winds and all the magic of the countryside which is ordained for the healing of the soul.

The first question, of course, was, What was I going to do with such years of life as might remain to me?

I thought about this till my head ached. Finally I shelved it. It seemed to me that until I knew something about the world in which I was going to live, it was clearly impossible to know the kind of life I wanted to lead.

On one thing, however, I was determined. For the first few years, I would change my occupation and surroundings as often as possible. I would experiment with places and people. I would explore different layers of society. In fact, I would try to acquire Experience of Life.

★ ★ ★

Next came the money problem. Canon Law — which is to the Catholic Church what Civil Law is to the State — lays down that the dowry brought by a nun at the time of her religious profession must be returned to her if she should be dispensed from her vows and leave the convent. Unfortunately my dowry was overseas, and, owing to war conditions, untouchable for the time being. By special arrangement, however, the interest would now be paid to me. It was not very much, but with the small — though rather uncertain — income that came to me from other sources, I might just be able to make ends meet. I determined, however, that while the war lasted I would join the ranks of the workers. This, if I were careful, might also enable me to save a little to fall back upon in time of need.

But above and beyond all my own little petty personal problems, there was the giant nightmare of the war. Trying to sort out my thoughts and marshal them into some kind of intelligent order, kept me miserably awake at nights. I have no new ideas about war and, as yet, no logical theories. I don't know enough about its causes. All that I do know is that, with all my mind and heart and soul and strength, I hate and detest it as the most cruel, evil, devilish, but above all *stupid* way of settling difficulties that has ever been known.

It came home to me when one day I met a detachment of the Canadian regiment then quartered in the village. They were marching off to some exercise on the Downs. I have seldom seen a finer set of men. Young, good to look at, magnificently developed, they swung past with a grace and poise that caught and held my eyes till they were out of sight. A month later, what had become of them? Here is the answer: I cut it out of some daily paper and kept it near me. It helped me to say my prayers for the fighting forces with greater intensity before I climbed into my comfortable bed . . .

"War to-day is not what our forefathers understood by battle, but a filthy mechanized business of hatred and destruction on a scale hitherto undreamed of by man . . . Smoke, reek, roar, din, ravaged faces, torn, tormented bodies, mangled limbs . . . gangrened, perhaps, to be sawn off in hospital, leaving a hideous maimed trunk where so much beauty had been. Nervous systems, shattered by noise and shock beyond all hope of ultimate recovery; bombs, shells, machine-guns, spattering broadcast the blood and brains and bones and bowels of the youngest and finest of the race."

Why did all this splendid youth and strength have to be slaughtered in that maelstrom of horror? Whose was the responsibility? What could be done to prevent such idiot frightfulness from happening again? Why, *why* did God permit it? How could a God who was Love and Beauty allow such things?

War and cruelty to animals are two subjects on which I have felt at times that it might be difficult to keep my sanity. Sometimes I wonder whether — in this life — there *is* an answer to these problems or whether it is not futile to speculate about such things. To understand the ways of God would make one his equal if not his master; may it not, perhaps, be arrogant for the creature to try to understand the Creator's mind? How could a snail expect to understand the workings of the human intelligence? And yet the gulf between snail and man is at least measurable, while that between God and man is infinite. "*As the heavens are exalted above the earth, so are My ways exalted above your ways, and My thoughts above your thoughts.*" Had one a deeper sense of God's transcendence, instead of revolting, one would — I suppose — make acts of heroic faith and trust in God's wisdom and love. "*Though he should slay me, yet will I trust in him.*"

I cannot say that these reflections gave me a great deal of consolation but they at least provided me with something to hold on to when the things I read about in the newspapers made me feel physically sick.

I determined that I would cast the widow's mite of my unskilled service into the war effort. Unfortunately, I possessed no qualifications for the kind of work on which most of the women of my age and class were employed. Probably a munition factory would be my fate — illogical as it might appear. It seemed clear that the only way to stop the killing was to speed up the output of weapons and so get the whole bloody, horrible business ended with the utmost possible rapidity. Never had I been faced with so urgent a necessity for doing evil that good might follow. In my opinion, however, the end more than justified the means.

I found the wireless instructive.

A.B. switched it on thrice daily for the war news, which taught me many things; unfortunately, she did not care much for anything else. I could have sat there, listening and learning, from dawn to dusk. One can't, however, indulge these passionate cravings for miscellaneous information in somebody else's house.

I wondered how best to tackle the problem of my self-education. I determined to read a few books by as many as possible of the more representative authors of the period I had missed — 1914 to 1941. It appeared that, after the last war, the predominant form of literature was fiction. So I hunted about among my aunt's book-shelves and in the local library to see what I could find.

The first book I tackled was *As We Are* by E. F. Benson. I chose it because the title-page described it as "A Modern Revue". This, of course, was exactly what I needed. It interested me because, while I was still inside the convent, Uncle Stan — who at the time was Prime Minister — had come to see me and had told me things which had given me a lot to think about. I can still remember his explaining to me, for instance, how, when the 1914 war was ended, the world had run completely mad. This book filled in the details — or at least some of them. As I read it, I felt my eyebrows lifting till I knew they must have disappeared into my Eton crop.

The first words of the opening chapter increased the Rip Van Winkle-ish sensation which was gradually turning into a rather tiresome complex in my make-up.

"Across the chasm which, in 1914, split time in two, making, for the space of a generation at least, a new era, A.B. or Anno Belli, from which to date our chronicles, little glimpses of a world, very distinct, but immensely remote, as if seen through the wrong end of a telescope, occasionally flit across the field of memory."

So that was how the people of to-day looked back upon the world that I lived in — the only world I knew, and to which I belonged with such awful completeness just because no more recent civilization had ever blurred the sharp edges of the only imprint I had ever received! It was grim. As I read the words, a curious cold sensation of isolation swept across me. I felt myself to be a monstrosity — *unique de mon espèce*, as if I had just dropped out of the moon.

The last novel I had read before entering the convent was *Sheaves* by E. F. Benson. It gave an exceedingly faithful picture of the manners and customs of that far-away period before the old world war. The first novel I read on coming out was Miss Helen Ashton's *Mackerel Sky*. I compared them and, for the first time, realized how tremendous a change had taken place in the relations between men and women in the twenty years or so which had elapsed between the publication of these two books.

It was interesting to wander round the libraries and discover what the various authors had been up to while I was away. Mr. Compton Mackenzie, who, if I remember rightly, had just published *Carnival* at the time of my departure, appeared to have been extremely busy. So had Mr. H. G. Wells, whose *Ann Veronica* I had, as a girl, been forbidden to read. Sir Hugh Walpole, too (how I had raved over *Fortitude* in 1913!) had not been wasting his time. And there were rows and rows of new Kiplings and Chestertons and Galsworthys; and some books by a recent arrival, Mr. Charles Morgan, whom I sampled, but found curiously dull.

I began to wonder how I should ever manage to catch up on such an output, especially as I still did not know even the names of the newer authors whose works must be explored.

Put Out More Flags by Evelyn Waugh made me gasp and wonder what the world was coming to. So did *Ordinary Families* by Arnot Robertson. Next, I stumbled upon a book about the atom, by an author whose name I forget, but which informed me that nothing but mutual bumpings, at the rate of eight million bumps a second, prevented the countless billions of atoms of which my chair was composed from rushing to China and back in a second or two. Faintly appalled, I observed that Science, as well as Literature, had been hard at it while I was away . . .

The books of Miss Rachel Ferguson made a profound impression upon me, especially *A Harp in Lowndes Square* and that astonishing piece of virtuosity, *The Brontës Went to Woolworths*. As for Aldous Huxley's *Brave New World*, I can only say that it opened my eyes to a number of things that I had hitherto ignored.

After a fortnight or so of this kind of reading, I found myself wondering whether I should ever acquire the point of view of the people who looked at life like this.

Reading the papers always made me feel particularly idiotic, especially the *Observer* and the *Sunday Times*. The writers of the book reviews and leading articles used *clichés* and allusions which were incomprehensible to me. I had never heard of the Unknown Soldier, Jazz, Isolationism, Lounge lizards, Lease-Lend, *Cavalcade*, Gin-and-It, Vimy Ridge or the Lambeth Walk; neither did the words Nosey Parker, Hollywood, Cocktail, Robot, Woolworth, Strip-tease, Bright Young Thing, convey anything to my mind. Unknown names, too, were always cropping up: Epstein, Schiaparelli, James Agate, Greta Garbo, Picasso, D. H. Lawrence and Dr. Marie Stopes . . .

It was really most disheartening. I decided that the only thing I could do about it was to concentrate desperately upon the present moment, trying, bee or vampire fashion, to suck from it the very last drop of Experience of Life that it could possibly hold.

Unfortunately, there didn't seem to be much experience to be sucked from the surroundings in which at that time I was planted. All my aunt's friends were dear old ladies of over seventy: somehow I felt that they were not quite the ones to teach me the sort of things I needed to know.

(3)

One day I summoned all my courage and took a big green bus to Brighton.

The white road curves like a river between the great humped shoulders of the Downs: on either side stretches country, over which the shadow of something the Sussex folk call "ellynge" still seems to brood.

All my life I have felt far more alive to the past of the places I have visited than to their present: everything that *is* seems to be somehow overshadowed by what it *has* been.

That day, a ghost-grey mist hung over everything. It was a special kind of mist: you felt that there was nothing that it might not conceal. Behind it, all sorts of strange and terrifying things might be happening; I remembered *The Knife and the Naked Chalk*, beloved in childhood; the Beast who waited hungrily for the flocks by the dew-ponds; the Men of the Long Barrows who hunted boar and wolf with leaf-shaped arrow heads and little axes made of flint. I almost fancied I could see them peering back at me out of the mist: men of small stature, half-naked, scarred with wolf-bites, shaggy-haired and with stupid, scared little eyes. Perhaps they were just setting out to explore the great black swamp that was London. I pictured them fording the Thames and beginning to build their causeways over the marshy jungle of the Strand. Didn't it all happen about the time that Abraham arrived in the Land of Canaan? I wished I could leap back four thousand years and talk to them. I doubted whether I should have felt more at sea in their London than I did in the London of to-day.

On the whole, I was not impressed with my visit to Brighton. It looked bomb-scarred and dingy and not at all like the gay and glittering town I remembered more than thirty years ago. The sea-front was a mass of wire entanglements and the streets a jam of tanks, tommies and bare-legged young women with painted lips and canary-coloured hair.

The wind was icy. I grew hungry, but was nervous of going in anywhere alone for lunch. When at last I had gathered sufficient courage to enter a café, I could make neither head nor tail of the dishes listed on the bill. At last, in desperation, I ordered something called "ravioli", which, when it appeared, might have been anything from cats' meat to fried spam. After that, seeing "Ices" incredibly advertised, I ordered one. I imagine it must have been the last in England. I was thrilled. I had not tasted one for twenty-eight years.

In the shops I fared badly. A.B. had replenished my stock of coupons, so I bought some gloves and was eyed despisingly by the blonde who sold them to me because I had no idea what size I wore. I also bought a dress. It was quite the most noncommittal garment I have ever encountered. The shop-assistant assured me that it was equally suitable for morning, afternoon or evening wear. This seemed to me a remarkable achievement and I paid the three guineas which was its price (if it had been thirty, I should hardly have noticed the difference, so vague was I concerning the value of money), feeling that I had done something worth boasting about.

(4)

One of the things I found it hardest to get used to was the smallness of people's houses. Even A.B.'s, which was quite a reasonable size, felt like a mousetrap. I suppose this was because the convent where I had spent most of my life was so large.

Built originally round a small open courtyard, it had grown with the centuries till it lay like a long, grey, sleeping lizard, clutching two other courtyards and a cloister garth between its claws. In winter, the cold cut into you like a knife. The pale light crept in through deep-silled, leaded windows and was frozen immediately into the same wan blue as the white-washed walls. You might have been standing in the heart of an iceberg, so strange it was, so silent, so austere.

Out of the cloister, heavy oak doors led into the rabbit-warren of the kitchen quarters; to the Infirmary; to the Refectory; and to the great damp vaults below.

The Refectory was the oldest part of the building. To the last, I never entered it without an instinctive feeling of reverence. The wide, open space in the middle was paved, like the cloister, with grey and white flagstones,

42

worn irregular by daily contact with generations of heavily-shod feet. The massive, beamed ceiling was ornamented with sacred monograms in low-relief, and delicate mouldings whose sharp outlines had been blurred by the repeated white-washings of centuries. The unglazed paintings on the walls were such as one sees in Continental churches: a Nativity, a Flemish *grisaille* of the Adoration of the Magi, a Marriage of St. Catherine, and, behind the Prioress's table, a great, tragic canvas of the Crucifixion, with weeping child-angels who held chalices beneath the wounds of the tortured Christ. Under the pictures, a dado of plaited rushes hung behind the narrow benches. Long, massive, polished tables, dark with age, stood, like the benches, on a platform of boards raised a couple of inches or so above the level of the floor.

Nothing here had been changed since it was built three hundred years ago. The same thick-paned latticed windows overlooked the same high-walled garden; the same bare, oak tables were set with the same plates of dinted pewter and brown earthen mugs at each one's place. Above all, the same quite indescribable atmosphere of silence, aloofness, and a kind of spiritual intensity hung in the air like some delicate, distilled fragrance from another world.

Further along the cloister, important-looking double doors opened into the Community Room. This, though more homely than the Refectory, had none the less a severe and simple dignity of its own. The light from its long row of — alas, almost invariably closed —

windows poured in upon what was practically the living-room of the nuns. White-washed walls; a bare-boarded floor, scrubbed to an unbelievable degree of spotlessness (the Mother Subprioress could be thoroughly unpleasant to people — especially novices — who came in from the muddy garden without wiping their feet); an ugly, carved Renaissance altar with twisted barley-sugar columns and a display of aspidistras, and a series of narrow oak tables set close together in a long line just under the windows, where sixty nuns or more could have sat comfortably side by side.

Against the walls, a row of heavy rush-bottomed chairs alternated with plain oak cupboards and massive chests, in whose deep, coffin-like drawers the nuns might keep their books and work. Above, the score or so of Prioresses who had ruled the convent looked down from unglazed canvases — stern, ascetic faces, pale, tight-lipped, tranquil, under their mediaeval coifs of fine starched linen and shadowy veils.

Here the nuns sat sewing from nine till eleven in the morning and from half-past one till three; and again from four to five in the afternoon. It was always "out of recreation", which meant that nothing that was not absolutely unavoidable might be said. No wonder that the walls seemed saturated with the silent aspirations, the unspoken joys and sorrows — sometimes agonies — of so many human hearts. For nuns, after all, are only human; and until a kind of mystical death has taken place in the earthly nature, resulting in the triumph of what is spiritual over what is merely natural, suffering cannot be avoided. It has been truly said that suffering is the price of sanctity.

Here, too, the community assembled for recreation. This took place in the evening, after supper. The Prioress sat at the top of the long row of tables with the nuns down either side. The rule of silence no longer held; the walls echoed with laughter and conversation. The Community Room was indeed a kind of sanctuary of the Common Life. A grave room, so large that even when the entire community were assembled it never seemed crowded. Order and decorum produced an impression of space.

Quite at the end of the cloister was the Library. This was the largest room in the convent. What an enchanted kingdom for anyone in need (as I, alas, so often felt myself to be) of an escape. From the floor of dangerously polished parquet to the ancient ceiling-beams, were stacked tier upon tier of books — each in its way a magic casement opening on the foam of — sometimes — perilous seas. Here were Didon's lovely romantic *Life of Christ* and the more modern and realistic study by François Mauriac; Fouard and Le Camus, besides the many-volumed masterpieces of Le Breton, Lagrange and de Grandmaison. There were commentaries on the Scriptures; books of reference (shall I ever forget the day I discovered Adrian Fortescue's racy articles on certain of the Fathers of the Church in the *Catholic Encyclopædia*); lives and writings of the saints and mystics (I detested St. Teresa, but was profoundly attracted by St. John of the Cross); the complete works of the Fathers and Doctors of the

Church, which made marvellous meditation books when prayer was arduous. St. Bernard, for example, in his exposition of the *Canticle of Canticles* soars to heights which, I should imagine, have hardly been surpassed in mystical exegesis; and St. John Chrysostom with his exquisite images and highly realistic descriptions of fourth-century Antioch. There were volumes on biblical topography (H. V. Morton's *In the Steps of the Master* nearly saved my reason once during a period of quite appalling inward strain); Church History — one of the most fascinating subjects I ever embarked upon, especially during the first five highly controversial centuries when the great heresies were raging like dragons in the rapidly disintegrating civilization before the Fall of Rome; spiritual biographies from the Prophets to Teresa Higginson, taking in Joan of Arc and John Knox — from the Catholic point of view — on the way; mystic and ascetic theology; (I was happier with *The Cloud of Unknowing* than with St. Thomas's *Summa Contra Gentilium*); treatises on the virtues, Church music, sacred art (alas, some Victorian-minded religious had seen fit to clothe all the reproductions which she considered in need of it with neat little *perizometas* or flannel petticoats of chinese white. One or two pages in some of the more beautiful collections of pictures had been considered unfit for contemplation and had been stuck together with paste). The Library contained, in fact, everything that could possibly be needed for instruction or enlightenment upon every possible aspect of the spiritual life.

46

Besides the Great Cloister, there were two others, wide, lofty, cool, with their chill atmosphere of perpetual silence; the stern, sombre Chapter House leading through the stuffy Lay Sisters' Chapel (ten minutes of it was enough to send me speeding away in search of oxygen) to the domed Renaissance church with its altar of apricot-coloured marble and the stained-glass windows, where the light poured through two not over-successful compositions — one a symphony of grey and indigo, the other, rust-red and copper-gold.

High up, at the back of the Church and over the Lay Sisters' Chapel, was the long, beautifully proportioned Choir. It had a fine, wrought-iron grille before it, and the double row of dark carven stalls on either side was reflected in a parquet floor, so highly polished as to suggest the sea of glass in the Apocalypse.

Throughout the convent — except in the nuns' cells, which were as small as possible — one was met by the same atmosphere of cold, clean spaciousness. The place breathed silence and consecration. In fact, living there was rather like being perpetually in church.

(5)

Early in January I travelled down to Worcestershire to stay with the Stanley Baldwins at Astley Hall.

I had not been there since the coming-out dance which they gave for me two years before I entered the convent, though Uncle Stan had been to see me several times while I was a nun. I remembered a big, grey, stone house — rather Jacobean in character — with a drive that curved upwards through a park where oak trees drowsed in pools of shadow and tall, wrought-iron gates led into a garden that overlooked what Uncle Stan declared was one of England's loveliest views.

When last I stayed there, the house had been overrun by a flock of cousins; Diana, Lorna, Margot, Oliver — who was at Eton — Windham and Betty, still in the nursery. I remember, too, John and Elsie Kipling, and the tall, extremely good-looking Denis Mackail.

Memories of Uncle Stan, as he was in those days, are many and vivid. Chiefly I remember him standing, pipe in hand, before the fireplace in the library, giving me fatherly advice about how to write a cheque, and the kind of people not to make friends with when one was travelling in Italy.

The library had a fairy-tale frieze of white-sailed ships that lay at anchor in a sea of pure cerulean blue. In the foreground were chalk cliffs, suggesting the coast at Rottingdean, where the family had spent so many happy summers. When first I saw it, Uncle Stan told me of how, when he sat there, reading in the evenings, a sea-breeze sometimes blew through the room and, looking up, he would see the white sails bellying and the waves tossing and then, one by one, the little ships would go sailing by . . .

Once, many years later, when my cousin Windham came to see me in the convent, I asked him whether the white ships still sailed round the library at night.

Apparently they did; and he had the room photographed for me. It was a long time since anything had given me so much pleasure.

Uncle Stan was waiting for me at Worcester station. "Waiting" is the perfect word, for the train was at least an hour late. I thought he looked faintly apprehensive, but, all things considered, this was hardly to be wondered at. I observed with interest that he gave sixpence to the porter who carried my suitcase. This caused me deeply to regret my thrice-repeated largesse of half a crown.

During the drive out to Astley I experienced the kind of thrills that fill British bosoms when, after long sojourns on the Continent, the cliffs of Dover once more appear out of an English mist. I am Worcestershire born and this was my homecoming. Despite my antiquity, something within me began to show signs of wanting to dance and sing.

I must here explain that to me, who still looked upon the briefest taxi-ride as supremely exciting, this nine-mile drive in the large, luxurious Rolls was an adventure of the most breath-taking kind. The countryside sparkled in the frosty sunshine; the upturned Worcestershire soil was sorrel-red. At my side, Uncle Stan pointed out half-forgotten landmarks: Hallow, Grimley, Shrawley . . . the curving Severn . . . and, on the horizon, the lovely well-remembered shapes of the Malverns, with Bredon Hill, Woodbury, and Abberley.

In spite of Aunt Cissie's warm welcome, the excellent lunch to which we immediately sat down was rather an ordeal.

I was slightly alarmed by the display of glass and silver round the centre-piece of toad-coloured orchids on the luncheon table. (In Sussex A.B. had suppressed the stove in the dining-room, owing to the war-time shortage of fuel, and our meals had been served very simply at a little table near the sitting-room fire.) I wondered how on earth I should ever know which of those many knives and forks and spoons I ought to use for what. In the convent, one of each had to serve for everything. You had your own: they were kept in a small leather sheath round which your table-napkin was tightly rolled and pinned when not in use. Between meals they lived in little cupboards under the table at each one's place. It was the custom to use a small piece of bread — Continental fashion — with one's fork. This had to be swallowed after being used to clean one's usually very greasy pewter plate. This made me feel slightly sick until I got used to it. (There are, indeed, very few things that one cannot get used to if one perseveres.)

I determined to seek salvation by keeping my eyes fixed firmly upon Aunt Cissie and doing in all things exactly as she did.

I felt oddly embarrassed, too, by the knowledge that I was being scrutinized by eyes which, however kindly, were none the less alarmingly experienced. What were they thinking about me — strange, freakish creature that I knew myself to be, after my long encagement behind those walls and bars? There I sat, clothed largely in other people's raiment: a hat of my sister's, a coat of my cousin's, a dress of my aunt's. And I was only too painfully conscious that my interior make-up was even odder — a great deal odder and more unprecedented, even, than anyone had any idea. The Rip Van Winkle complex began to steal over me like cold ink into blotting-paper. Between me and these kinsfolk of mine who had lived so thrillingly, so fully, an abyss yawned. Whether or no I should ever be able to bridge it remained to be seen.

Probably no one who has not lived long in a convent will be able to form any idea of the contrast between my first luncheon at Astley and meals as they are served in the Refectory of any large religious house. Of these, the Lenten collation is perhaps the most characteristic.

In Lent, those who fast have their principal meal at midday. After Compline — that is to say, about six p.m. — a second, light meal, called collation, is served. (The amount consumed may not exceed eight ounces for those who fast.)

Nothing could be more other-worldly, monastic, austere, mediaeval, than this meal as I so vividly remember it. The Refectorian, clanging the deep-voiced iron bell that hangs in the cloister; the nuns, genuflecting two and two as they leave the choir; the slow, dignified procession descending the great wide staircase into the purple darkness under the cloister arches, unlighted save for the tiny crimson flame of a lamp that burns before the image of some saint. And the refectory — long, cold, severe and sombre, its windows shuttered and curtained to keep out the icy evening mist; and the guttering candles in their ancient battered candlesticks of burnished copper — two to each table — casting weird, grotesque shadows that leap and shudder over the ceiling and across the walls. It is extraordinarily beautiful; and when the long line of white-garbed nuns files in, each inclining profoundly to the great crucifix that hangs in the gloom above the Prioress's table, it seems as though the stage were being set for some strange, mystic drama, some solemn court ceremony of a bygone age.

When the whole community is assembled in two long rows one down either side, the Prioress gives the signal. The reader steps out of the shadows into the middle of the refectory.

"*Jube Domna benedicere . . .*"

The age-old request for a benediction which the Church sets on the lips of her official lectors breaks the silence; then the blessing is given: "May a tranquil night and a perfect end be vouchsafed to us by the Lord Omnipotent." The quiet white figures incline once more to the crucifix and go noiselessly to their places. A *Pater* and *Ave* for benefactors are then recited in silence: the Prioress touches the small brass bell suspended over the table and the meal begins.

The Refectorian rises from her knees — an aproned figure in a pinned-up habit — bows ceremoniously before the Prioress and goes to the hatch at the far end of the refectory. Here — framed in the opening like a three-quarter-length Holbein portrait — the Cellaress stands, busily wiping the jugs and dishes that a lay-sister brings in from the kitchen quarters before handing them in through the hatch. There is little enough — perhaps a few dishes of boiled potatoes with great jugs of vegetable soup. The Refectorian ladles it out into the little pewter porringers set at everyone's place as she passes by. The rest of the food is already prepared on the tables; loaves of coarse brown bread, butter and cheese, perhaps a dish or two of figs or dates . . .

Against the western wall, the reader in the dark oak pulpit raises a clear voice above the sound of scurrying footsteps and the soft clash of dishes and plates. It may be a passage from the Scriptures or a treatise on the virtues, or the life or writings of a saint or a pious biography: whatever it is, the Rule ordains that it must be listened to attentively. Not to do so is, therefore, a minor breach of Rule. During so gross an occupation as the feeding of the body, it is fitting that the mind should be occupied with spiritual things. That is the central idea lying behind all the elaborate ceremonial of the refectory. Every movement is regulated. Those who receive, as well as those who offer the dishes, must incline to one another with the most profound respect. As Hilaire Belloc epitomizes it, in the refectory — as everywhere in the convent — "the grace of God is in courtesy". Again, no one may raise her eyes. Should she who is served before you help herself to more than her portion from the dish of cherries, or the nun on your left spill soup or make sucking noises with her teeth, you must contain yourself. Silence is absolute. If you want more water or bread or salt, you may only ask for it by the official gestures. Penances are enjoined for any who make a noise or spill things. Even in the choir, the observance of decorum is not more rigorous. The refectory is a cenacle in which the taking of food is transfigured almost into a sacrament.

By the end of lunch I had learned quite a number of useful things of which I made a note as a guide to future behaviour.

To begin with, the old-fashioned habit of sitting up straight and keeping one's hands beneath the table when not engaged in eating had apparently died out. One now leaned back comfortably or rested one's elbows on the table, joining one's hands as a kind of support on which to lean one's chin. Then I noticed that I left my plate a great deal too clean for correct behaviour. (In the convent, one had to eat absolutely everything that was humanly swallowable.) Another thing — one must always remember the presence of servants. A warning glance or two had reached me across the orchids from Uncle Stan.

I went up to my room feeling not only provincial but prehistoric. The Rip Van Winkle complex had got me rather overwhelmingly in its grip.

(6)

At Astley, my education advanced with the greatest rapidity.

I had not been there long before I discovered that I had an irritating habit of opening doors so quietly that nobody knew when I had entered a room. This, of course, made people jump when they turned round and encountered me unexpectedly. One day, Uncle Stan spoke to me about it which made me feel that something must be done. Before a fortnight was ended, I had taught myself to stamp up and down stairs, rattle doorhandles and bang doors in such wise as to make my presence felt by everybody in the vicinity. It was extremely difficult, as I had spent the greater part of my life in trying to be noiseless. However, by now I was growing accustomed to doing everything upside down and inside out.

My cousin, Di Kemp-Welch, who was living with her parents for the duration, opened for me a number of windows into life, through which I gazed with considerable astonishment.

She was as good-looking as anyone needs to be, with a most up-to-date vocabulary, a rollicking sense of humour, and expensive clothes. We had mutually illuminating conversations in the old nursery — now transformed into a sitting-room. Sometimes we listened to the wireless. Di liked "Shipmates Ashore" and the messages to the fighting forces from their families. I learned to appreciate the sallies of Miss Doris Hare and such songs as *A Wing and a Prayer*. Left to myself, I think I might have liked other programmes better, but I certainly learnt a great deal that was of the utmost value to me while I listened to these items and to the comments of my witty and experienced cousin Di.

Margot, Di's younger sister, was married to Maurice Huntington-Whitely and lived at The Old Hill, just over the borderline of the Astley grounds. She was a person of quite extraordinary vitality and although — or was it possibly because? — her conversation was apt to deal with slightly embarrassing topics (as when she described with vivacious detail the latest scientific methods of inseminating the domestic cow), she was excellent company. Her son Hugo, who was just passing from Eton to Dartmouth, took me to my first cinema. We were accompanied by Kiloran Howard (child of Uncle Stan's second daughter, Lorna), who was also home for the holidays.

I cannot forget the solicitude with which they treated me. There was an awful solemnity about it. It was exquisite; it was also rather touching. Few elderly spinsters can have been treated so delightfully as I was by those two representatives of the Younger Generation that afternoon.

The cinema of my girlhood had not been a very enjoyable entertainment. To begin with, it had joggled rather badly and, as the talking film was nowhere near being invented, the dramas were in dumb-show and one had to read long and sometimes rather tiresome captions between almost every scene. The technique, too, was in its crude and rather uninspiring infancy. Hollywood and Technicolor were, of course, as yet unknown.

My astonishment may, therefore, be imagined as the afternoon's programme gradually unfolded itself upon the screen.

The first film was a rollicking farce of the slap-and-tickle variety. Most of the jokes were, needless to say, rather beyond me and even those I managed to

56

grasp, aided by the tactfully whispered explanations of Kiloran and Hugo, were not exactly my cup of tea.

(Yes, it seems incredible, but I had now reached the point when I began to use such expressions as "too, too dreary-making, my dear!"; "believe it or not"; "well and truly"; "your pigeon"; "I have a hunch"; "it's your funeral" — and even worse. *Not* "lousy" or "mucky"; one had to draw the line somewhere; and I drew it there, for aesthetic reasons, though the fluidity of their meanings deprived me of two of the most widely used expressions of the day.)

The next item was a super-gangster thriller in broad American. Its shootings, rescues, kidnappings, and double-crossings left me dazed and bewildered. Kiloran and Hugo translated as much as they thought good for me. I was thankful that it was not a great deal. Finally a *Donald Duck* of the most shattering variety. In all my life I had never dreamed of such lurid colours, undreamed-of situations, or amazing technique. People ought not to be taken to see their first Disney film without suitable preparation. The shock is too overwhelming. I sat there with my tongue cleaving to my dried-up palate, and my eyes popping out of my head.

I was more or less in the condition of a mental stretcher-case when my two young cousins — though I doubt whether they realized it — conducted me home.

One of the things that I most enjoyed at Astley was my daily breakfast *tête-à-tête* with Uncle Stan. (Aunt Cissie and Di appeared later in the morning.)

At that hour the average Englishman is apt to be morose and taciturn. Not so Uncle Stan. He was then at his wittiest and best. I could have listened to him indefinitely, held captive by the interest and fascination of his talk. How I regret the endless opportunities for asking questions which I missed through sheer stupidity! But for more than a year after my exodus from the convent I was in such a condition of daze and bewilderment as to feel temporarily bereft even of such intelligence as I possessed.

It was during these breakfast conversations that I first began to glimpse something of the stupendous changes that had come over the world as I remembered it.

In 1914, Europe had been a tidy chessboard of kings and queens and emperors: a Czar in Russia, a Kaiser in Germany, an Emperor in Austria, a King in Spain. Greece and the Balkans still had crowned sovereigns to rule over them; the Ottoman Empire had a Sultan-Caliph and Persia a Shah. Japan ("those brave little Japs", as we called them enthusiastically in those days) had recently become an Eastern power through waging war successfully on the wicked Russians; and as for China . . . well, one had known vaguely that some terrific upheaval had rent her for a year or two, but as to what it really was all about . . .

Whereas, now . . .

Everything that I had looked upon as static and invincible appeared to have been swept away. Thrones had toppled, dictators had arisen. Massacres, blood-baths, purges, pogroms had followed one another with a ruthlessness and ferocity for which there appeared to be no precedent. Entire sections of society had been "liquidated" (another of those old words with slightly sinister new meanings) because they had stood in the way of one man working out his own idea.

The very map of the world had been remodelled. Entire countries had disappeared. In their places, others with new and fantastic names had been constructed. Even those which remained had changed their outlines and been sliced away in unexpected places or made to bulge where they had never bulged before.

One day Uncle Stan lent me Virginia Cowles's *Looking for Trouble*. This gave me my first "close-up" (another new word that had to be explained to me) of the dictators — of Fascism and Communism and, incidentally, of our present-day selves. I liked none of them. It was my first real glimpse of the sinister power that seemed to be sapping the very foundations of the world that I had known.

CHAPTER
THREE

(1)

ME (lamely concluding a slightly impressionist sketch of my Plans for The Future): So you see, all things considered, I do really believe the best thing would be for me to try for a job in a munition factory.

UNCLE STAN (from his armchair on the window side of the fireplace): . . .

AUNT CISSIE (from a cushioned corner of the sofa): . . .

DI (from the window-seat): . . .

The scene of this devastating outburst of silence was the White Parlour at Astley, where it was customary to foregather in the evening after the nine o'clock news.

All day I had been steeling myself to tackle the perplexing subject of my future; and immediately the news was ended, I had drawn a deep breath and begun. When I paused, it had been to encounter this streamlined silence. It needed no outstanding gift of intuition to perceive that my suggestion had not met with the approval that I had hoped.

The trouble, of course, was that I lacked all qualifications for the jobs which might otherwise have been found for me.

I had, I suppose, received a more or less average education, first by governesses and then at a Continental finishing school for what in those days were called rather pompously *les jeunes filles de la société*. But as there had then been no question of my having to earn my living, I had never bothered about trying to matriculate or provide myself with any of those useful diplomas which unlock the doors of every worth-while post. And, as I was entirely ignorant of shorthand, book-keeping, car driving, cooking, or the care of infants, it was not much use my answering the advertisements which filled long columns in *The Times* or *Daily Telegraph*.

It was true I knew how to typewrite; but the "experienced stenographers" required by heads of firms appeared to be incomplete unless they were experts at shorthand as well. So that was ruled out.

I also knew a little about libraries. Books had always been to me the breath of life. As a nun, I had for some years held the office of Librarian, and had classified, indexed, and catalogued the convent library, which was of quite a reasonable size. The snag here appeared to be that you must possess a diploma from the Association of Librarians — or whatever it calls itself. Without this, no Librarian would look at you.

I might possibly have secured a teaching job without much difficulty. I had taught for a good many years in the school which belonged to the convent[1] and had found it enthralling — but in no way conducive to the contemplative life. But I knew that to do this would mean sequestration in the ultra-feminine atmosphere of a school for girls. I felt that I had had enough of this, and needed mixed company. Men interested me profoundly because I knew nothing about them. I wanted to study their manners and customs; to discover the way their minds worked; to find out the kind of things they did and talked about; to watch the way they behaved.

One thing that I felt I did know something about was the ancient art of illuminating manuscripts. During the whole of my life in the convent I had been employed intermittently in this fascinating work. It was my business to turn out books of devotion, decorated texts, and "holy pictures" by the dozen, to serve as book-marks for the breviaries, missals, diurnals used by my own and other religious communities.

Up among the rafters in one of the garrets was a tiny room which had been given to me as a scriptorium. Here, for many hours a day, I used to work in solitude. Here, too, I was allowed to keep the tools of my trade.

---

[1] Though theirs was in no sense a "teaching order", the nuns did not consider the work of education incompatible with the contemplative life. Their ideal was a high one. A religious who was "sent down to the school" was expected, not only to teach well, but to aim at such close union with God that Christ truly lived in her. Thus, and only thus, could she transmit him to the children. The measure in which she achieved this aim would be the measure of her success.

62

Boxes of hand-made paper, cut into every imaginable size. Sheets of milk-white vellum, used for the more important and elaborate kinds of work. Parchment, carefully pressed between weights, upon which each nun would write and sign her Vows when the time for her Profession arrived. Brushes of every conceivable texture and shape and size. Pencils of almost metallic hardness, used for tracing designs on to vellum, from which not the slightest mark can be erased. Saucers and shells of gold and silver. Agates for burnishing. Cases of gold-leaf. Gum arabic for mixing with powdered gold and paint. Dusted pumice, with which to remove all grease from the surface of vellum and parchment. Bottles of ox-gall and *gouache*. And paints, in little cakes and tubes and pans and bottles; scarlet and emerald and peacock-blue and flame and olive-green — colours that made the stiff pages glow with the brilliance of gems.

Every old monastic house has its *Ceremonials*, which are brought out for the Bishop's use on state occasions such as Clothings, Professions, and Jubilees. These *Ceremonials* are exquisitely-bound volumes whose every page represents weeks of intense application and arduous work. Here, at last, was a subject about which I felt I *did* know something. But who, in these days of battle, murder, and sudden death, wanted illuminated addresses or initial letters from the *Très Riches Heures du Duc de Berri*, or the Book of Kells? Such luxuries belong essentially to times of peace.

★   ★   ★

It was a pity I could not turn my nursing experience to some account. In the convent I had for some time held the office of Apothecary, which meant that it had been my business to look after anybody who might be suffering from cuts, burns, bruises, or what are known in religious communities as *petites misères*. This rather ambiguous term has always struck me as one of the most convenient in the language. Who cannot call up in their imagination some small, unpleasant bodily infirmity which they would greatly prefer to leave unspecified? How infinitely more convenient to state vaguely that one was suffering from a "Little Misery" than from any of those faintly revolting minor ailments which one always prefers to conceal.

I loved nursing. I'd seldom enjoyed myself more than when an influenza microbe decimated the community and I had been allowed, in my official capacity, to distribute a few little comforts and to tuck the sick nuns snugly into properly warmed beds.

But here, as in everything else, my way was blocked by the lack of any official training. I had not so much as a Red Cross diploma to fall back upon.

Finally — and this was far and away my best line of country — there was St. Augustine. (I refer, of course, to the author of the *Confessions*, not the Angles-and-Angels saint.)

For the last ten years before I left the convent I had been a St. Augustine specialist.

It had come about like this.

I was given by my Superiors a piece of literary work to tackle, which can best be described as the construction of a historical background to the life and works of the saint. Anyone who has more than a superficial knowledge of the writings of that enchanting personality will have realized — especially if they have attempted the *City of God* or the two hundred and seventy shorter *Letters* — that it is practically impossible to appreciate them unless one knows a good deal about the times in which their author lived. There is hardly a page that is not packed with allusions — historical, classical, and contemporary. And unless you are aware of what was going on in the minds as well as the lives of his contemporaries, a very large part of what he wrote about will have little meaning for you at all.

So I was set by my Superiors to make a detailed study of the entire Roman Empire during Augustine's life-time. This covered the years between A.D. 354 and 430.

I was given the opportunity of reading every history, biography, and monograph which could in any way throw light upon the period; even articles from French and English books of reference were obtained for me. I studied the lives of the Roman Emperors from Constantine to Honorius. I followed the campaigns of Julian the Apostate from Northern Italy into Gaul. I watched the gradual disintegration of the Empire while the barbarian invasion swept down through Europe across into Northern Africa. The behaviour of Jerome the Dalmatian — his treatment of the noble Roman ladies and the amazing conception of Christian charity revealed by his quarrel with Evagrius, made me wonder how he obtained his place in the Calendar of Saints. I marvelled at the Fathers of the desert — St. Antony of Egypt and St. Simon Stylites on his terrible pillar — pioneers of that movement which spread so swiftly from East to West. The romantic adventures of Galla Placida enthralled me; so did the doings of the Manichees and Donatists. In Britain, too, there were exciting happenings; Rome was withdrawing, and in the dark years that followed, the heroic figures of King Arthur and his fellowship were beginning to take shape in the dim mists of legend and romance.

At the end of ten years or so of fairly intensive study, I had amassed a surprising amount of extraordinarily interesting information. This I sorted out and collated into a highly detailed historical biography, inserting every contemporary happening that I could discover into each year of St. Augustine's life.

And I was up to the eyes in this perfectly enthralling occupation when untoward circumstances — some of them connected with Hitler's earlier incursions into Europe — brought my unfinished labours to an end.

That, for the present, is enough about my accomplishments. They are only mentioned to illustrate the kind of things I had to display in my shop window.

Unfortunately, they were not the sort of wares that anyone wanted to buy.

★   ★   ★

Aunt Cissie thought it might be a good idea for me to become a *masseuse*. In her kindness of heart, I think she had visions of me staying around in country houses with "really nice people" — to whom she could, of course, have introduced me — restoring, by the simple process of massage, the figures of society ladies who had just produced an infant.

But even if I had felt attracted by the notion of massaging duchesses — which, oddly enough, I didn't — there were quite insuperable snags. Di, who knew all about everything — how I envied her her vast and varied experience of life! — assured us that the training required was not only long and arduous, but also extremely expensive. Unless you had an imposing array of letters after your name, you could get nowhere. So that was the end of *that*.

I began to feel very Rip Van Winkle-ish indeed.

(2)

So far as I can remember, the idea originated with my cousin Margot.

Land Girls were at a premium in Worcestershire. Everybody's gardeners had been called up, and the ladies of the countryside were all breaking their backs in a heroic effort to "Dig for Victory" without the assistance of an Outside Man.

Margot herself was the greatly envied employer of half a Land Girl. The other half belonged to Mrs.

Batley, a friend who lived only a few minutes' walk from Astley Hall. This arrangement was not altogether satisfactory, since Mrs. Batley wanted someone to herself. Margot, too, didn't like having only a portion of the Land Girl. It was pointed out to me that if I took a job with Mrs. Batley, the situation would be improved from everybody's point of view. Mrs. Batley would then possess a Land Worker; I should have found a job; and Margot herself would be able to monopolize the whole, and not merely a section, of the Land Girl's services.

To me it appeared obvious that this must be the career for which Providence had intended me. Fortunately I knew something about gardening, having had charge of the grounds for a time while I was still behind the grilles. I therefore fell in with the excellent plan suggested by my cousins and, by six o'clock the following evening, the thing was done.

Margot very kindly undertook all the arrangements.

Though I was beyond the age-limit of the Land Army, I was none the less hired out according to their regulations and rules. This simplified things considerably.

It appeared that my services were to be divided between Mrs. Batley and her friend, Mrs. Cornish, whose house was just across the road. Four days a week I was the henchwoman of Mrs. Batley; the remaining two days were Mrs. Cornish's affair. I was to board with the latter. My pay would be the official Land Army wage — one pound eighteen shillings a week — of which a pound would go to Mrs. Cornish for my keep.

My duties, it appeared, would be many and distinctly various.

Mrs. Batley's vegetable garden was her great preoccupation. She also had a car, which would certainly require cleaning from time to time. And in the depths of an old disused well outside the kitchen, a petrol-driven pump lurked, dreadful as a dragon. It was a bad starter, Margot said. The Land Girl sometimes had no end of a job to get it going on Sundays before she went to church.

Moreover, Mrs. Cornish possessed a cow. On such days as I whisked temporarily into her service from that of Mrs. Batley, it was quite conceivable that she might give orders for this animal to be milked. Margot insisted that I must be prepared for any and every possibility.

It was Adams, the Baldwins' chauffeur — a most prosperous gentleman — who initiated me into the mysteries of how a car should be cleaned. Both he and Aunt Cissie's maid — the inimitable Ridler — took a keen interest in my future, and were very good friends to me later on, as I shall presently relate.

The lesson took place in the stable yard. I wore, for the first time, the outfit which Margot had procured for me (most of it was presented to me by my cousins) — corduroy breeches, a pullover, a sou'-wester and a large pair of Wellington boots. There was also a waterproof of vast dimensions in which the wearer resembled nothing so much as a barrage balloon.

I endeavoured to do what was required of me. But I was curiously unskilful. The life I had led seemed to have made me unfitted for active work of any kind.

I still have the paper on which Adams wrote out for me the classic method: (1) brush, (2) dust, (3) slosh, (4) dry, (5) polish — by which the best results are supposed to be obtained.

Before actually entering into bondage, I went from Astley to spend a fortnight with relations who had a country house not far from Hereford.

My recollections of that visit are chiefly of my agitated journey (try as I would, I could not overcome my alarm at having to change so often at stations which had no names); of the war news, which grew daily more depressing and humiliating; of the excellence of the Herefordshire cider; and of being taught to milk a cow.

I have never liked cows. The two I frequented were obstructionist and disobliging. They made not the slightest attempt to co-operate. One of them had a nasty way of squinting round at me while the milking was in progress, giving short, sharp, slightly hysterical shudders all over her body if I so much as brushed her side. The other was more difficult to deal with, for she turned off her taps at the main immediately I sat down to the pail.

Ten minutes or so of this rhythmic squeezing usually made my wrist muscles ache so agonizingly that I was obliged to leave off. The cowman — a kindly, weather-beaten creature with eyes the colour of a kingfisher — would stand by, sympathetically criticizing my technique. The pain in my wrists, he assured me, would continue until my muscles hardened. So I just had to set my teeth and return to the assault.

Even in February, Hereford was exquisite. I went for long country walks in deep lanes, under low skies of watchet-blue and mother-o'-pearl. Hereford city itself gave me an odd impression: its romantic Saxon and Norman background seemed a curious setting for the crowds of soldiers — British, Indian, Canadian — and the swarms of war-workers from neighbouring factories who thronged its streets.

On the whole — apart, of course, from the lessons in milking — I can't see that my stay there did much to enlarge my Experience of Life. Like most dwellers in the country, my aunt and uncle were reduced by the petrol shortage to something not unlike the condition of people marooned upon a lonely isle.

(3)

Whenever possible, I make a point of avoiding very tiny women.

I have observed tendencies in them which alarm me. They interfere. They are inclined to bully. Most of them — probably to compensate for what they lack in stature — seem to be endowed with an overwhelming sense of their own superiority. Also, they are inclined to talk too much — and a great deal too noisily — for their size.

Mrs. Batley, though diminutive, was fortunately free from these failings. She did not flaunt her very remarkable efficiency; she was rather quiet, and I never heard her compare herself other than unfavourably with anyone else. It was quite by chance that I discovered that she held the office of church-warden and counted the offertory after the Sunday collection had been made in church. After that, my admiration for her gifts became positively slavish. (As a child, I myself had so detested arithmetic that I had refused to learn it, and have been paying the penalty of those who can only do addition on their fingers ever since.)

Everything about her was neat, precise, and methodical. The house and garden had to be just so and no otherwise. Had she a fault — though God forfend that I should suggest it! — it might have been a tendency to exact from the unforgiving minute just over sixty seconds' worth of distance run. That, however, was merely the outcome of her thoroughness.

The only time I ever saw her angry — and then she really flamed with indignation — was when I once neglected to shake the earth sufficiently from a tuft of freshly uprooted grass.

"An *egregious* way of weeding!" she wrathfully exclaimed. "There ought not to be a *particle* of soil left on the roots!"

She bent and shook the grass-tuft as an angry terrier shakes a rat.

Land work, unless you are built on a rather particular pattern, is not specially interesting. I will not, therefore, trouble you with details of celery-lifting or the culture of the artichoke. Actually, I knew very little about vegetable-growing, having only had charge of the flower-garden when I was a nun. And there is a vast difference between the aesthetic sensations induced by the culture of roses and delphiniums and the utilitarian angle from which one observes the development of turnips and brussels sprouts.

Fortunately, Mrs. Batley — have I not said that she was efficient? — had learnt a surprising amount on her own since the war began. Her method was to study the publications of the Ministry of Agriculture, to ask questions, to make experiments, and to use her common sense. The results were phenomenal.

My working-day began at half-past six. When I had "done" my room, I breakfasted in the kitchen with Mrs. Cornish's maid. I then went forth into the marvellous cold stillness of the winter dawn.

Astley Town — which was the curious name of the lovely black-and-white timbered farm-house where Mrs. Batley lived — stood in a hollow with flower-beds set in a lawn in front of it, and a steep vegetable-garden on the slope behind. There were orchards, and a little wood, and a big ploughed field, and the curve of the road all round it; deep in the country, it was about as characteristic a corner of Worcestershire as you could find.

Sometimes, when I arrived in the early morning, the whole place would be shrouded in delicate veils of ghost-coloured mist. It was like walking down into the heart of a dream in which the house slept, dim and unreal — a phantom house, charged with quiet little rather uninteresting memories of bygone days. It did

73

not strike me as being a particularly happy house. It was too cold. Its atmosphere was reticent; it kept itself to itself. I did what I could to be friendly, but it was no use. It didn't like me. I felt this keenly. It is extraordinarily humiliating to be snubbed persistently by a house.

I used to begin by cleaning the row of shoes that were waiting for me in the scullery. After that, a scuttleful of yesterday's ashes had to be carried out and shaken through a sieve on to the ash-heap near the barn. If there happened to be a wind, you were smothered in powdery grey dust; if it rained, the dust merely thickened into a curiously adhesive species of mud. Sometimes there was coal to be brought in from the outside dump as well.

Usually I was then met by kind Sarah, who lived with Mrs. Batley, and who told me what vegetables were needed for the day.

Nobody who has not actually fingered one can have any idea of the degree of iciness to which a brussels sprout can attain if it really makes up its mind; nor of the rapidity with which this iciness can be communicated to the hands of anyone who attempts to sever it from the parent stalk at half-past eight on a cold and frosty morning in the early days of March. By the time I had gathered a basketful of the things, my fingers were blue and stiff. I could have yelled with pain.

So, to warm myself up, I used to repair to the woodshed.

Chopping wood is one of the most heating occupations I know. It is also quite amusing — if the

74

wood is of the kind that allows itself to be chopped. The splinters fly merrily to the four corners of the woodshed: the severed pieces leap up and hit you on the ankles or crack you savagely across the nose. The very block skids wildly off beneath the blows of the hatchet, so that quite as much time is spent in gathering up the fragments as in actually doing the job.

Usually, after three-quarters of an hour of this, I was too exhausted to continue. It was about this time that Mrs. Batley generally appeared.

The moment Mrs. Batley became visible on the horizon, everything in the garden immediately began to hum.

I can't imagine how she did it. I suppose she just happened to be that sort of person. For, no matter how vigorously you might have been working, one glimpse of that small silhouette, even in the distance, galvanized you into an even more terrific output of activity.

Never shall I forget the hectic energy with which I staggered up and down that garden path with a barrow full of ashes to be used for road repairs; or my endless to-ings and fro-ings from the bean-bed to the toolshed, struggling to carry four dangerously wobbling *cloches* with but a single pair of hands; or my panda-like ascent to the loft above the woodshed for a sack of hop-manure that burst all over me as I descended with it hoisted on my back; or my leaps and prancings on the summit of the compost heap, with Mrs. Batley at my elbow to remind me that On No Account Must the Contours of the Corners Be Destroyed; or — seared into my memory for all eternity — the long hours spent in the frightful and back-breaking occupation of digging the rich, moist, chocolate-coloured, and incredibly heavy Worcestershire soil . . .

"I do *hope* that digging isn't going to be too much for you!" Mrs. Batley would sometimes say when, on the stroke of one, I straightened out my long back, scraped the clods of earth from my boots with the edge of my spade and turned my crimson and shining nose towards where my long-yearned-for lunch was awaiting me at Mrs. Cornish's.

Naturally (I was usually half-way up the lane by this time) I only laughed and assured her — over my shoulder — that, on the contrary, I rather liked it.

What else could one do? There was a war on. And anyhow, what was the use of taking a job as a land-worker if you hadn't sufficient strength in your miserable body to use a spade?

(4)

I should here like to pause for a moment, in order to introduce you to Mrs. Cornish. After meeting her, you will, in all probability, be annoyed with me for not having done so before.

There is a fairy-tale by George Macdonald — is it *The Princess and the Goblins?* — about a king's daughter who, in her father's palace, found a room at the top of a secret stair. In this room dwelt a lady with snow-white hair and eyes that were younger than the springtime. White pigeons flew in to her from the windows and nestled on her shoulders; and in a deep furnace-pool were flame-waves, like petals in the heart of an enchanted rose.

Well, the moment I set eyes on Mrs. Cornish, I knew immediately that the pigeons and the roses could not be far away.

As it happened, I was perfectly right. She was what I believe is called a Nature Mystic. She knew all the ways and secrets of the hills and trees and fields and shrubs and flowers. Blackbirds perched on her fingers. Larks flew to her out of the sky. She knew, I think, all that there was to be known about dogs and horses. I could never make up my mind whether there was more in her of St. Francis of Assisi or of Pan. She had read widely, thought deeply, lived intensely: as a result, her mind was a storehouse filled with lovely and unexpected things. To me, perhaps the most surprising thing about her was her deep and absorbing passion for Jersey cows.

The first time she took me into her charming garden — like her house, every inch of it had been planned and designed by herself — she pointed out to me a large gap in the hedge. She had actually caused a piece of it to be removed in order that she might enjoy an uninterrupted view of the daily doings of her favourite cow. To her, stock-breeding held very much the place that politics do to a Prime Minister. I doubt whether there was anything she didn't know about it. If there was, it would have gone comfortably on to the back of the proverbial — and now extinct — threepenny bit.

★ ★ ★

Mrs. Cornish was responsible for a good deal more of my education than she will ever realize. In the evenings, I often sat with her in her bedroom. She was a great sufferer, and obliged to spend a large part of her time in bed. One would have to be at least as clever as she was to give any idea of the charm and interest of her conversation. Tired as I generally was, I much preferred listening to her to retiring to the rest for which my body craved.

She loved reading. She introduced me to Agatha Christie and Mr. Fortune; she also read aloud to me Norah Waln's exquisite *House of Exile* and lent me the works of her kinsman, Siegfried Sassoon. From her, too, I first heard of Peter Scott and learned to appreciate his marvellous paintings of water-fowl in flight.

It still puzzles me how anyone who had lived so much *dans le monde* could still remain so untouched by it. She was utterly incapable of any of those unpleasant things one associates with "worldliness" — small meannesses, snobbishness, love of this world's goods, an unkind tongue. Everything about her was not only noble but beautiful. And I will conclude this slightly alarming catalogue of virtues by mentioning that her sense of humour was as keen and ironic as it was irrepressible.

I tear myself with difficulty from the delightful task of contemplating Mrs. Cornish. I am not at all sure that she was not the best chapter in my Book of Exodus.

Once, for five days, it froze so hard that it was impossible to do anything in the garden.

That week, Mrs. Batley used me as her Inside Woman instead of her Outside Man.

I swept floors. I brushed and dusted furniture. I cleaned windows. I polished brass. I took up carpets and laid them down again. And I was just beginning to recover from the general state of invertebracy engendered by these activities when the snow came.

There are two angles from which snow can be regarded.

One is the angle of people like Francis Thompson and Walter de la Mare, who sit and look at it, and then write poetry. The other is the angle of people like myself, who have to sweep.

Nobody, unless they had actually tried it, could imagine from its exquisitely feathery appearance what heavy stuff snow is to shift — especially after the first three-quarters of an hour. After clearing the courtyard, the drive and a path or two in the garden, I used to have bets with myself as to whether my arms would drop off before my back broke, or the other way round.

When at last the thaw set in, I could have shouted for joy.

Of course, it was not always quite so exhausting.

Now and again there were days that one loved: blue, gusty afternoons when the wind-sprites chased each other among the tree-tops and there was only quiet raking and weeding to be done. Or mild, still mornings of mother-o'-pearl and silver, spent in the comparatively effortless occupation of preparing the soil. I used to love forking-in the tobacco-coloured hop-manure and scattering a rich top-dressing of soft grey wood-ash and velvety soot.

But to me there will always be something unsatisfying about looking after other people's gardens. Rather like being nursery governess to someone else's children instead of taking care of your own.

(5)

We will now return to my *horarium*.

The lunch hour was always rather a scurry. One rushed in, removed the more outstanding traces of one's morning's work from one's person and then joined Mrs. Cornish in the dining-room. As always, her conversation was entrancing. I seldom, however, felt capable of assimilating what she said. My only longing was to devour my dinner with the utmost rapidity and fling myself in an attitude of slightly abandoned relaxation on my bed.

I still wonder what my hostess — or, to be more exact, my mistress — must have thought of me at meal-times.

I suppose the long hours in the open air were largely responsible: anyhow, the ferocity of my appetite reached such a pitch that I myself became alarmed. It still puzzles me how such an ethereal being as Mrs. Cornish survived the ordeal of watching, three times daily, such a display of ravening wolfish-ness. It must have been only too evident that I could and would easily have swallowed not only the dining-room table but the contents of kitchen and pantry, with herself and the cook thrown in.

To my last hour I shall maintain that Mrs. Cornish deserved a decoration for the quasi-miraculous way in which she always provided me — despite the difficulties of war conditions — with enough to eat.

In common, I fear, with a number of other elderly persons, the last thing I felt inclined to do immediately after lunch was to start working again.

Especially when it rained.

One then had to buckle oneself firmly into one's barrage-balloon, cram on a sou'-wester and get on with the job as best one could.

I remember one almost unbearably frightful afternoon when a species of deluge was emptying itself with unusual *élan* from the skies.

It was my business to bed out several rows of adolescent onions in what had become an almost completely liquid stretch of bog. As fast as I planted them, the swirling rain washed away the soil from their roots and the things collapsed, like Victorian ladies with the vapours, into the mud.

Half-blinded with the rain I struggled on, my back bent into the shape of a hairpin, while the wind perseveringly destroyed my handiwork as fast as it was done.

At last, after about a couple of hours' ferocious battling with the situation, I emerged victorious.

Three rows of subdued-looking onions stood before me, all erect as grenadiers. I eyed them with the same emotions as those with which Alexander must have viewed his battlefields.

At half-past five my working-day was over.

To say that I was by then dead to the world would be an understatement. Tea, however, restored me sufficiently to prepare the food for Mrs. Cornish's fowls. This, when she herself was not well enough to do so, I generally took out to them.

The way lay through an exquisite tiny coppice of silver birches. I still remember with delight the lace-like tracery of their delicate sepia branches against the twilight sky.

After supper we sat together, I fighting miserably against the ogre of sleep until it completely overwhelmed me; she talking, always so delightfully, of birds, dogs, her grandchildren, books, flowers and the well-beloved cows.

(6)

The most unpleasant day in the week was Saturday morning.

I had to sweep the cobbled courtyard with a stable-brush; dig out the detestable tuftlets of grass that clung so tenaciously between the clefts; clean the foot-scrapers and shake the dust from the heavy outside doormats by beating them vigorously against the wall.

It was work which, in the convent, would have been described as "extremely against nature".

Which is exactly what it was.

Saturday afternoons were free. I usually spent them in answering letters and in washing and mending my clothes.

Sunday — so far as I was concerned — was hardly a day of rest.

One rose early, because the nearest church was over at Stourport, which meant a three-mile walk each way.

Try as I would, I could never bring myself to do anything but dislike this tiny chapel-of-ease.

It was cold. It was hideous. It was airless. And it was crammed to bursting point with Welsh and Irish factory hands.

Mass could only begin when the priest had finished hearing confessions, which went on indefinitely. During Mass, those members of the congregation who were not engaged in unrestrained bouts of coughing, sneezing or making almost unbelievable noises with — or without — the aid of a pocket-handkerchief, sang, unaccompanied, the more flowery and unctuous of Father Faber's hymns.

The only possible way to prevent oneself from flying from these horrible surroundings before one's obligations had been fulfilled was to stamp heavily upon one's feelings whenever they attempted to raise their heads.

One just had to seize one's soul firmly by the scruff of its neck and lash it mercilessly into those stratospheric regions of faith which completely transcend the world of sense; to remind oneself, over and over again, that the cold, the discordant voices, the stale odour of unwashed persons, didn't matter one bit. What *did* matter was that there, just before one, on that shabby and hideous little altar, the most stupendous Event in the world was taking place. The Sacrifice *of* Christ was being offered *by* Christ to the Almighty and Supreme Creator, for the purpose of bringing all the graces of the Redemption to the souls of men. Surely one could put up with a little discomfort to be present at such an Act?

After all, it was faith that mattered, not feeling. And didn't St. Thomas Aquinas define faith as "an act of the *intellect* which assents to a divine truth by the influence of the *will*"? No mention of feelings at all. They simply didn't count; which, considering what my feelings would have said if I had allowed them to express themselves, was just as well.

Later, Mrs. Batley very kindly arranged with Sir Sydney Lea, a neighbour of hers, to drive me part of the way back with two of his own Irish servants. I remember being much impressed by his amusing conversation, cerulean corduroys and Quartier Latin tie.

One Sunday the servants waited for me after Mass to say that there wouldn't be any car that day as the master was away. So we all walked home together. They treated me quite as one of themselves and I can only hope that my conversation entertained them half as much as theirs did me.

Now and again I was invited up to Astley. It was only a few minutes' walk along the lane, and the park seemed always to be full of snowdrops. I wish I could find something new and beautiful to say about them but they have been done to death by the younger authors of to-day. Perhaps their exquisite virginal aloofness has a special appeal for the corrupt and rotten civilization in which we live.

On these occasions I generally paid a visit to my friends Ridler, Aunt Cissie's maid, and Adams, the chauffeur.

One of the first things I discovered when I started to earn my living was that the best people from whom to ask advice upon the problems that beset one were those who, like oneself, were obliged to work.

Ridler and Adams showed great interest both in my future career and present welfare and always did everything they could to help me when I consulted them.

It was from them that I learned all about Insurance Cards and Hospital Schemes and Approved Societies. In fact, I really don't know what I should have done if it had not been for their advice.

I shall never forget being driven into Stourport by Adams on the important occasion when I made what perhaps might be described as my *début* at the local Labour Exchange. Talk about being presented! I don't know when I ever felt so proud of anything in my life.

All the same, it would have felt a little odd to drive up to the place where you were about to be registered as an agricultural labourer in a magnificent Rolls Royce, complete with coronet, cockatrice, Garter and all that, emblazoned on the doors. So I and the Astley car parted company at the corner, and I trudged up the remainder of the dingy little street on foot.

I detest Labour Exchanges.

They generate an atmosphere of bleakness, bureaucracy, and belligerence which it would be hard to beat. On this occasion, the belligerence emanated from the young man behind the counter, who received every statement I made with an incredulity which he made not the slightest attempt to conceal.

Nevertheless, when at last I succeeded in extracting from him the coveted card which established me definitely as one of the world's war-workers (for such was the light in which I perhaps rather optimistically viewed my job) I was, to put it mildly, exceedingly content. Had I guessed what lay before me, it might have been otherwise.

This episode, however, belongs to the earlier stages of my career as a Land Worker. I cannot imagine how it pushed its way in here.

(7)

The end came — as ends sometimes have a way of coming — rather unexpectedly.

One evening, as I was dragging myself home along the lane after a more than usually exhausting day, I felt my knees suddenly beginning to wobble, while the surrounding landscape gave rather alarming indications of being about to disappear from sight.

86

Feeling quite unable to proceed, I sat down, rather unhappily, in the hedgerow and awaited developments.

Presently a farm labourer appeared in the distance. As he drew near, I called out,

"Hi! Can you help me, please?"

I thought he looked just a little shocked, and concluded that he had judged me to be slightly drunk.

He approached. When I had explained the situation, his disapproval melted into a solicitude that was really touching. He then extended a pair of immense, earth-blackened hands and hauled me to my feet.

Unfortunately, I still found progress impossible. My knees, like those of the man in the psalms, had turned to water. I therefore stood still and continued to cling.

The labourer — he was elderly and enormous — looked down at me very much as he might have done at a sick calf or a newly-born foal.

"If you wouldn't 'ave no objection to my catchin' 'old of you . . ." he suggested, apologetically.

I assured him that, far from objecting, I was only too thankful for his aid.

Upon which he twined a brawny arm completely round my person, thus relieving me entirely from the burden of my own weight.

And in this romantic, if slightly misleading, attitude we proceeded down the lane.

It was perhaps fortunate that Mrs. Cornish's cook — who disliked me — was out of the kitchen when my escort finally deposited me at the back door.

That night, after long meditation upon the subject in my bath (how astonishing is the power of a really boiling bath to restore temporarily exhausted vitality), I determined that henceforth my humble contribution to the war effort would be made in some other capacity than that of substitute for anybody's Outside Man.

CHAPTER
FOUR

(1)

So, early in April, feeling a little pensive because my cousin Margot insisted that by giving up my job I was letting Mrs. Batley down, I went to London.

The aunt and uncle with whom I had spent my first night after leaving the convent had invited me to stay with them. They were struggling to restore some kind of order to their partially blitzed house, and it had been intimated that my assistance would be acceptable.

Naturally I was anxious to do anything I could to help. Indeed, the prospect of handling grand pianos or carrying billiard-tables up and down stairs held no terrors for me. Anything would have been child's play after the output of physical effort demanded by my brief adventure in Worcestershire.

I determined, however, that, before undertaking further activities, I would insist upon twenty-four uninterrupted hours of brutish slumber. After that, they could do with me what they pleased.

Unfortunately, this delightful project was never realized.

The moment I set foot in Portland Place, I was told that my services would be required for other purposes.

★　★　★

At this point, my cousin Desdemona steps into the story.

There is not a great deal to be said about her, for the simple reason that, after whisking unexpectedly into my life for the briefest of periods, she as suddenly whisked out again. And — so far, at least, as I am concerned — she has not been heard of since. I only mention her now because, in her person, I came up against two scraps of Experience of Life which were new to me. One was a "modern marriage", which had not worked according to plan: the other, that peculiar new religion known as Anthroposophy.

I do not feel in any way competent to hold forth about modern marriages. I know little about them. But even the few months that I had spent in the world had made me realize that the angle from which most people now looked at marriage had altered considerably since I was a girl. As a Catholic, my views on the subject are naturally those of my Church. I am not now, however, speaking of Catholics. And I was astounded when someone whom I knew intimately told me of how when she and her husband married, they arranged beforehand that, if it "didn't work out", they would divorce.

Another story that made me open my eyes was that of a husband and wife who agreed to divorce simply from boredom. Both subsequently remarried, the four persons involved remaining on most friendly and intimate terms — even going so far as to stay for long periods together in one another's homes.

On the whole, the impression I received was that in marriage — as in so many other states of life to-day —

society seemed far more eager than it had been in the past to discover and seize upon easy ways of escape from difficulties and responsibilities.

It appeared that my cousin — a leisurely and decorative blonde with a small son who made one think of a portrait by de Laszlo — was at that moment in the throes of house-moving. Since her husband was henceforward to be excluded from the *ménage* and she had as yet engaged no servants, it seemed likely that she might be glad of aid.

"So we think, Monica," said my aunt, readjusting her lap to the requirements of the plump treacle-coloured cat whose slumbers had been disturbed by my arrival, "that it would be a good plan if you were to go down and stay with Desdemona, and do anything you could to help."

Looking back, I shall always remember that visit to my cousin as the supreme revelation of my incompetence. It is humiliating to confess it, but I was not of the slightest use to her. I had no idea how to light a fire. (My experiments with the kitchen stove are best left unrecorded.) I knew nothing about cooking, not even how long it takes to boil an egg. When I went out to buy groceries, everything had to be carefully set down in writing, because the names, quantities and prices of things conveyed nothing to me. I knew how to make a bed, and I could dust. And there my accomplishments ended.

The only way in which, perhaps, I may have been of service to my cousin was that I provided her with something of which she appeared to be sorely in need

— a Listening Ear. And, as I listened, certain things became clear to me.

One of them was that the complications which had invaded her life appeared to be due, either directly or indirectly, to the outlook induced by the teaching of Mr. Rudolf Steiner.

What I feel about Mr. Steiner coincides very closely with what St. Augustine felt — and said, with some vehemence, in his *Confessions* and elsewhere — about a certain Manichee called Faustus. Their doctrines had much in common, though that of Mr. Steiner struck me as the more fantastic of the two. Though his name had been unknown to me, I had not been long in the house before I knew all about him. In her deep-voiced, rather fascinating drawl, Desdemona explained to me with what amazing thoroughness the prophet of Anthroposophy had gone about his work. While we unpacked trunks, set up beds, cooked meals, or wandered among the delicate spring greenery of the Surrey lanes, I was shown how profoundly each aspect of life had been explored and dealt with before being woven into the vast and complicated tapestry of Steinerism. Folk-lore, Theosophy, High Anglicanism, Natural Science, pseudo-Mysticism, all seemed to have a place in it. And, permeating everything was a strange, and — to me — slightly sinister occultism, intended, so far as I could gather, to develop those supernormal faculties which, Mr. Steiner declared, were latent in every human soul.

Like all devout Anthroposophists, my cousin brought up her child on the lines laid down by the Master for those in whose temperaments fire and air — as opposed to earth and water — predominated. And, at night, when she had sung him to sleep with *lieder*, whose Teutonic origin simply refused to be camouflaged, the lovely creature would sit on the hearthrug and discourse to me of reincarnation, of the purifying effects of vegetarianism, of the spiritual interpretation of Grimm's fairy tales, of the marvellous properties of herbs and minerals and of the strange influence of the stars . . .

Even at table there was no escaping Mr. Steiner. Our *menus* were rigidly Anthroposophical; and each meal was prefaced and concluded with a mystical incantation in lieu of grace.

On the whole, I was faintly relieved when my uncle and aunt drove down and bore me back with them to London.

I liked my cousin Desdemona and found her enchanting to look at. But Mr. Rudolf Steiner — *nein*!

J'en avais assez . . . pour la vie.

(2)

So there I was, back in London again, with forty-six pounds, nine shillings and fourpence in the bank and not the remotest idea what was going to happen next.

I was not left wondering for long.

★   ★   ★

Another cousin — this one was called Joyce — wrote to me that she had just heard of a job — in fact, of two jobs — which might suit me. If I would ring her, we could discuss their possibilities. This was exciting.

Unfortunately, before I could communicate with her, it was necessary to perform what would have been called in the convent an Act of Self-Conquest; for, among the objects in modern life with which I most disliked dealing, the telephone held at that time the first place. Incredible as it may sound, I doubt whether I had used one half a dozen times before entering the convent. Dialling made me so nervous that I invariably forgot the number before I had finished and had to begin all over again. As for the dreadful little red boxes in the street where one stuffed pennies into slots and did things with levers — or whatever they were — marked A and B, I would as soon have entered a den of lions.

Of the jobs into either of which my cousin now proposed to waft me, I chose the second. (The first was in Portugal. It sounded delightful, but somehow I didn't feel that my Experience of Life — the phrase was becoming an obsession — was as yet quite sufficient to justify the risk of such a plunge.) The second was that of blue-print designer to an aircraft factory; and, though it would have to be preceded by a short course in a drawing-office, a job — provided that one passed a test at the end of it — was always guaranteed. Two friends of Joyce had in this way obtained excellent positions.

She said, "I'm told it's frr-rrightfully interesting and not particularly difficult. And, as you can already draw and are accurate . . ."

Finally it was agreed that I should present myself at the drawing-office as soon as might be.

By this time I was feeling altogether brave and reckless. So, after a bout of furniture-shifting with my aunt, I thought I would fare forth and try to establish contact between myself and the London streets.

It was the first time that I had been out alone on foot in London. I blush to say that my principal reaction was one of fear. Fear at the complete unfamiliarity of everything. Fear of the crowds. Of not knowing the way to anywhere. Of the noise. Of the hurry. And a fear, which amounted almost to terror, of crossing the street.

This so hampered me that I felt something must immediately be done about it. It began to look rather as though another Act of Self-Conquest might have to be performed . . .

I therefore propelled myself by sheer will-power into the midst of the traffic and began an epic progress down Regent Street which, if I live till doomsday, I shall not forget. Between the Polytechnic and Piccadilly Circus, I zigzagged madly backwards and forwards across the street at least a dozen times. It was drastic; but it ended my traffic-shyness. To-day London holds no more intrepid street-crosser than I.

Which only shows, as my Novice Mistress used to say to me, what very unpleasant things you can force yourself to do if only you make up your mind.

Soon after this, I started work at the drawing-office.

It was run by a stout little Irishman who had been an instructor in the Air Force, with an efficient young woman — who looked as if she had just stepped forth from the pages of *Vogue* — as his partner and secretary. The office itself was a big L-shaped room with a sort of hutch at the back of it, where the Principal interviewed prospective pupils and gave tea-parties to the friends who always seemed to be drifting out and in.

Besides myself, there were about fifteen other students, mostly young married women and girls in their 'teens. They struck me as an unusually empty-headed collection. Indeed, anything more completely vapid than their conversation — which was unceasing — it would have been hard to find.

To me, however, even their inanity was interesting. As types, they were completely new to me. I studied their free and easy behaviour, their curiously small vocabularies, their *clichés*, their comments on books and films, their coiffures, their love-affairs — which gave me a lot to ponder over — their cosmetics and their rather attractive clothes.

It was quite an education — of a sort.

For myself, I lay low and spoke as little as possible. I knew that everything about me was odd and peculiar. I couldn't talk their jargon and felt that not only my clothes, but also the way I wore them were somehow wrong.

★ ★ ★

The work was interesting. Provided you could draw a little, had a smattering of geometry and were perfectly accurate, you could hardly fail to succeed.

As soon as you had learnt to use the compass, protractor, set-squares, springbow and the rest, you were given machine diagrams to copy. I don't know what else to call them. To this day I have no idea what half of them represented. Meanwhile, the Principal, a plump little partridge with a twinkling eye, would stroll around, bending over the desks and tables to explain the mysteries of dimensioning, of screws, lugs, plates, struts, ball-bearings and castle-nuts — all very technical.

When these were mastered, you would be given your first "rough".

A "rough" was the very sketchiest of sketches, supplied, presumably, by the inventor, consisting of a scrawl or two, a few curves, and some measurements. From this you were expected to produce a detailed diagram of the entire machine, in all its parts and from every point of view. A tracing was then made, from which blue-prints were taken off for distribution to the workshops.

I used to do a good deal of drawing at home in the evenings. One day I discovered the excellent Marylebone Public Library and, with books borrowed from the section of Engineering Draughtsmanship, taught myself quite a reasonable amount of geometry.

Every now and then a pupil would be sent for by the Principal, either to be dispatched to some engineering firm in the provinces or interviewed for a post in one of the Ministries.

In London, "The Norwegians" — which was, I believe, a Scandinavian Ministry — appeared to be the Mecca of everyone's dreams. They paid well. The work was pleasant. The employees consisted almost entirely of charming Norwegian young men.

The Ministry of Works and Buildings was less sought after. Rumour had it that most of the lesser intelligences got landed there . . .

And just now and again, one of the Principal's special favourites (it was astonishing how well some of these fluffy little creatures could draw) would be presented with a plum in the guise of a job as head designer in the office of some really important aircraft firm.

Those, of course, were the jobs that everyone coveted. The only snag was that the work, which had to be microscopically accurate, was extremely trying to the eyes. More than once I rather wondered whether I had been wise in attempting it. However, as I had almost finished my course when the fiercer kind of headaches began to bother me, I decided to give it a trial.

(4)

In between times, I did what I could to continue my education.

Once a week I went to the Public Library and, beginning with February 1941, worked through a year of the *Illustrated London News*. This seemed to me as good a way as any other of catching up on contemporary history.

I also prowled about London, studying the street and buildings, the clothes-shops (in the vain hope of getting modern fashions into my head), but, above all, the crowds. I saw a great many films, among them *Mrs. Miniver*, which struck me as too American in atmosphere to be convincing, and *In Which We Serve* — my first introduction to Noel Coward.

I also read every book that I could lay hands on, and received in consequence a number of — probably salutary — shocks.

As yet, I could not bring myself to meet people who had known me in the convent. And, as my aunt's friends all seemed to be out of London, I lived a rather solitary life.

One day, my cousin Windham, who was in the Air Force, walked into the drawing office.

He said, "Did you remember? You're lunching with me today."

Outside there was a taxi waiting. (I still greatly enjoyed going about in taxis.) We drove to a restaurant in Sloane Street. No one had taken me out to lunch before, so I was much excited. I hoped there would be no pitfalls. The first time of anything was always a little agitating.

I thought the restaurant marvellous. But when my cousin proceeded to feed me on whitebait and *pêche Melba*, my delight knew no bounds. It was far and away the most wonderful food I had tasted for nearly thirty years.

He asked me whether I would like a cocktail.

I had to explain, with some embarrassment, that — though I had met with them in books — I was a little uncertain as to the nature of the things. So he ordered me a Dry Martini, which I much enjoyed.

As I sipped my first cocktail, I watched my cousin mixing his own drink. He called it "shandygaff". To this day, I have no idea of what it was composed. He mixed it himself, while a waiter stood by, handing him the bottles. This method of procedure was new to me, and filled me with awe.

When the coffee was brought, I flung my bonnet over the windmill and accepted a cigarette.

Altogether, it was a great experience.

Now and again, I saw a bachelor uncle, who, though kind, made no attempt to conceal his disapproval of me. What exactly it was that he disapproved of, he never revealed. I just had a general impression that everything about me was wrong. However, he possessed an unusually beautiful radiogram. For its sake I occasionally darkened his doors.

He was determined to educate me and would play me "modern" music and then question me about my reactions. As a rule, my unique reaction was to stick my fingers into my ears. Prokovieff's *Pas d'Acier* was, naturally, utterly beyond me; so was Stravinsky, whose *Sacre du Printemps*, instead of evoking — as my uncle insisted that it ought to do — "sub-racial-memories below the surface of normal consciousness", struck me as a Gargantuan nightmare. Ravel's *Histoires Naturelles* suggested Whipsnade; Scriabin's *Poème de l'Extase* baffled me; while *The Swan of Tuonela* — as did everything by Sibelius — plunged me into an abyss of gloom. Altogether, there seemed to be something completely lacking in me where the music of the past two generations was concerned.

When I became a nun, I knew that music would be one of the things that it would cost me most to leave behind.

So, just before I entered, I was taken to see *Parsifal* at Covent Garden, as a kind of solemn Last Farewell. It was the first time that it had been performed in England and it completely overwhelmed me. I came away almost in tears. I thought that from henceforward I should only hear Plain-chant for the rest of my life.

In the Order to which I belonged, Plain-chant held an extremely important place.

The Order existed chiefly for the purpose of carrying out the Church's Liturgy. This meant that the nuns were especially dedicated to the recitation of the Divine Office in choir.

The eight "Hours" of Matins, Lauds, Prime, Terce, Sext, None, Vespers and Compline were, so to speak, a radiation from the central Sacrifice of the Mass, five or six hours daily being spent thus in the official praise of God. Besides this, there were other devotions — Benediction, hymns, litanies, visits to the Blessed Sacrament, the conclusion of the long Latin Grace after meals, and the hours allotted by the Rule to mental prayer.

On Sundays and feast-days it was considerably longer. In fact, the higher the festival, the longer and louder we sang.

It will, therefore, be easily understood that on the conventual horizon Plain-chant loomed large indeed.

When first I entered, I so disliked everything connected with Plain-chant that, during Vespers, which were sung in full, and at the conventual Mass on Sundays, it was all I could do not to run out of the choir.

Every afternoon the Choir Mistress came to the Noviceship to teach the younger nuns the antiphons which it was their special duty to sing. To me, her voice was always faintly suggestive of the poultry-yard, though she undoubtedly possessed an artist's soul.

Plain-chant, she would tell us, was as different from "the other kind of music" as water is from wine. Indeed, it had something of the clear simplicity of water. Pure melody, it belonged to an age when harmony was still unknown; that was why it should always be sung unaccompanied.

Here, however, you came up against a difficulty.

Plain-chant was essentially for men's voices; and a choir of nuns, unless instrumentally accompanied, had an uncomfortable tendency to sound like a choir of cats. That, of course, was because only a small proportion of the nuns were really *singers*. The rest (here the Choir Mistress would eye those of the novices who were more or less tone-deaf) merely made well-intentioned noises, which explained why — in the majority of convents — an anachronism known as the organ had found its way in.

The Choir Mistress was, naturally, distressed at my lack of appreciation.

"Ah, but you do not *understand!*" she would exclaim. (She pronounced it "ondairstahnd", for she was Belgian.) "*Vous cherchez dans le Plain-chant* what you have seek in Wagner, Tchaikovsky, Chopin," (these, I had confided to her, with some diffidence, were my favourite composers) "*mais . . .* Plain-chant is not like *that. Ça appartient essentiellement* to the realm of the spirit. *Le Plain-chant, c'est la musique de la priere. Attendez, ma petite,* when you yourself have become a little more spiritual, you will see how it is."

Being at the time only a postulant, I made no attempt to argue, though I disagreed with her. As the years went on, however, I realized that what she had said was true.

Plain-chant — partly, perhaps, because everything sensuous has been expelled from it — is, for most people, an acquired taste. If the "other kind of music" suggests the splendour and colour of a sunset, Plain-chant has the austerity and purity of dawn.

Unfortunately, inside, as well as outside religious houses, the exponents of Plain-chant are sometimes inclined to be fanatical.

Some hold that the sense of the words should entirely dominate the music; others, that the sound is at least as important as the sense.

103

The Choir Mistress, highly strung and much tried by the idiosyncrasies of a Chantress who favoured the latter school of thought, would sometimes quote — not without malice — St. Aelred of Rievaulx in support of her own point of view. "Making noises like horses ... or the dying ... waving hands like mountebanks, preferring sound to sense" — already in the twelfth century this saint had described with some irritation the mannerisms of certain of his brethren in choir.

Now and again the opposing parties would become belligerent.

Indeed, upon no other subject except perhaps politics and religion have I known people be so thoroughly obstinate and intolerant. I have known chantress and organist reach a complete deadlock over the phrasing of an Easter Gradual. Indeed, it was only too evident that either of those ladies would sooner go to the scaffold than moderate an iota of her opinion. This delicate situation was handled with admirable tact by the Superior, who, if I remember rightly, declared that henceforward the singing was to be interpreted according to the teaching of the monks of Solesmes — namely, "sung with half-voice throughout, and an ever-increasing *pianissimo*".

It so happened that this thrice-blessed *pianissimo* was what first opened my eyes to the possibilities that Plain-chant held.

The shortest route from Portland Place to the drawing-office took me three times a day through the old cemetery off Paddington Street.

It had been laid out as a rather lugubrious "pleasure ground", though what pleasure the depressed-looking persons who haunted it could find in gazing at the ancient tombstones, it would be hard to say. My own affection for the place was inspired partly by the fact that two Stuarts, descended from Charles II, whom I adored, were buried there; and partly because it was the nearest approach to a garden in that much-blitzed and always rather squalid corner of Marylebone.

I suppose that in everyone's life there are certain moments which have been stamped so sharply on the memory that they can never be quite effaced. Well, once, in that graveyard, such a moment came to me.

During the week-end, my thoughts had been making little worrying excursions into the future. What, for instance, were one's plans for after the war? A career was clearly impossible, for, being as one was, what success could one hope for? As for all the agreeable things that might have happened had one been but a few years younger — well, it was now definitely too late.

Whereupon, unpleasantly nostalgic sensations began to make themselves felt in the regions of my heart. There was something demoralizing in the knowledge that one simply hadn't a notion what one was going to do with the remainder of one's life.

I set out on Monday morning feeling profoundly depressed. I kept telling myself that this soul-sapping vagueness must cease. I must lash myself out of this indifference about the future and begin immediately to make plans. Especially plans concerning how and where I could — with as much decency and unobtrusiveness as possible — retire to spend my rapidly-approaching old age.

But it was all to no purpose. Not the vestige of an idea was to be extracted from my brain. I had no idea what I wanted. The future remained enveloped in an impenetrable haze.

At this point I arrived at the cemetery.

Now, the week-end had been warm. In a single night, the graveyard had been transformed into a garden. Magic was abroad and everything had taken on the translucent quality of stained glass. Trees and flowers were incandescent, the light shining not down upon, but forth from their leaves and petals. Tall irises, magnificent in purple and velvet, smouldered against a blaze of golden privet; laburnum blossom, the yellow of clouded amber, dripped pale fire from green-gold branches overhead. Everywhere was a plenitude of light and colour, almost too dazzling to be looked upon. And in the air hung the adorable, faint smell of spring.

For a moment I stood there, surrendering myself to the enchantment. Then, suddenly, and for no apparent reason, things began to happen.

First of all, the miasma of depression lifted. It was as if some sea-borne wind had rushed in and whirled it away.

Next, in the wake of this sweeping and garnishing came, not a still small voice, but something that was like a burst of song.

And it took possession of me, so that I found myself suddenly and inexplicably filled with a longing so violent and overwhelming as to be almost unbearable. And I knew — beyond all possibility of doubting — that what I really *did* want, fiercely and dreadfully and more than anything else in the world, was a home of my own with perhaps a scrap of garden in the offing, in which and with which I could do exactly what I pleased.

And then — just for an instant (and not with the eyes of the body, mark you, but with what St. Augustine speaks of so often as the "eyes of the soul") — *I saw it*.

It was crouching, as you might say, on a little nest of cloud, in a kind of rift in my inner consciousness, and *looking at me*. And I knew immediately that it was the palace of my heart's desire.

The smallest imaginable mouse-trap of a cottage; with a frill of garden round it; and a cliff behind. And in the foreground rocks and sand and the sea; and at the gate of the garden a cat was sitting. I am nearly sure it was a Siamese.

Then, gently and softly, as they had opened only an instant before, the gates swung to.

(6)

To anyone who has persevered as far as this rhapsodic interlude, it will be obvious that, after such an experience, nothing could ever be quite the same again. One had been drifting, vaguely, and with no apparent end in view: and then, in a single blazing instant, everything in one had suddenly found itself fixed in this tremendous Act of Wanting upon that Vision in the clouds.

It changed everything. Life took on a new meaning.

Instead of walking abstractedly past rows of houses, one examined them thoughtfully. Always, one felt, there might be something to be gleaned: a door-knocker; an idea for window-curtains; more often, some detail to be avoided. One gazed into shop windows. One studied baths and basins. One meditated upon the mysteries of coal-holes and kitchenettes.

Obviously, it would be a long time before the dream could materialize. Certainly not until after the war. But, in the meantime, one could at least learn some of the endless things about houses and domesticity of which one was so calamitously ignorant. And one could lay aside every possible penny "against the day".

Now, I am fully aware that this sudden and quite overwhelming desire for a small country cottage may seem rather extraordinary. The fact is, however, that — although it appeared to me in the form of a cottage — it stood, in reality, for a great deal more than that. The cottage — and its surroundings — were the

108

outward and visible sign of an inward and psychological fact, which was that, by it, and through it, but — best of all — in it, I was at last, quite simply, going to be ME.

But to understand just what that idea meant to me, we must return to the convent.

Looking back, it now seems to me that what was hardest on human nature in religious life was the absolute subjection, day by day, hour by hour, minute by minute, of one's free will to the exigencies of the Rule.

It would not be too much to say that in those few words are contained all the agonies of what is called "a life of perfection".

From the moment of awakening, till the hour when at last you are permitted to fall asleep, the Rule holds you in its grip.[1]

Nothing, except the degree of obedience to what is commanded, is left to individual choice. Not only what you do, but when, and even how, you do it is meticulously prescribed.

The five years spent in the Noviceship are all too short in which to master the vast amount of

---

[1] In convents, the Rule is looked upon as the expression of the Will of God for the religious. A French Carmelite, Sœur Elisabeth de la Trinité, described the Rule as "*la forme en laquelle Dieu me veut sainte*". Each act of fidelity to Rule is thus seen as an act of conformity to the Will of God, an opportunity for "satisfying the Beloved" — down to the most apparently trivial details. It is, of course, when this point of view is forgotten or ignored that the Rule becomes arduous.

information that has to be acquired. The Rule itself — the endless, intricate ceremonial of choir and refectory; the complicated observances of Holy Week; the *horarium*, varying as it does for the countless feasts and seasons of the liturgy; the slow and arduous acquisition of what is called "religious behaviour"; the observance of silence, including absolute noiselessness in one's movements, especially in the opening and shutting of doors; the avoidance of anything "worldly" in one's speech or actions, such as slang, exaggerated language, a loud voice, the habit of excusing oneself when corrected; dealings with the rest of the religious; or, indeed, any departure from the customs of the house.

Each moment of the day is provided for. One prays, reads, eats, walks in the garden, at the appointed hour; no religious is allowed to follow her own inclinations in the disposal of her time.

When the cloister bell rings as the signal for a change of occupation, all must abandon whatever they are doing with the utmost promptitude. Should you be writing, no matter how ardently genius may burn, the Rule exacts that you should break off in the middle, not only of a sentence, but of a word. To "disobey the first sound of the bell" and continue — even for an instant — an occupation which, the moment the bell sounds, has ceased to be "of Rule", is to commit a fault.

Neither are you left free as to the manner in which you do things. Everything is ordained, down to the very way you sit or move or hold your hands.

Even when you sweep or dust, it must be done exactly in the particular fashion that was taught to you

110

in the Noviceship. Should an enterprising novice attempt to try out some "new and better" way of doing things, she would be corrected at once. One soon realizes that, in Religious Life, what one does seems comparatively unimportant; what matters is that it should be done at the time and in the manner that the Rule ordains.

So conservative are the old religious orders that, for a thing to have been done *in principio* is quite sufficient reason for it to continue thus — even when there has ceased to be any reason for it — *in saecula saeculorum, Amen*.

No better illustration of this could be given than the case of the choir-mantles.

From time immemorial, long, heavy cloaks lined with rough serge were worn in winter by the nuns, while reciting the Divine Office in an entirely unwarmed choir. (And even then they would often come out with their toes and fingers blue with cold.) After the 1914 war, central heating was installed in the damp and icy church — chiefly for the sake of the priest and congregation, who found mediaeval austerities very little to their taste. The radiators were enormous, which quite often made the choir extremely hot. Yet the heavy, serge-lined mantles continued to be worn. At the same time, even when the snow lay on the ground, or the wind blew cold and glassy as an iceberg, the mantles might not be worn out of doors. Spiritual Reading had to be performed as one walked up and down in a blast that suggested a lunge from the weapon of a horribly expert swordsman. One walked about in house and garden, winter and summer, wearing identically the same clothes.

I remember once asking the Mistress of Novices why it was that we were made to wear mantles in choir when we were too hot and no mantles in the garden when we were too cold.

She said:

"All these things are a part of the life of penance and mortification which we embraced when we made our Vows. If you feel the cold too much when you walk in the garden, you had better wear a shawl."

This solution to the problem did not appeal to me at all.

So deeply did the Rule cut into one's liberty that even the mind was subject, at certain times, to the most rigorous discipline. Though one was always taught to be on one's guard against "vain, perverse and even wandering thoughts", there were occasions when even more than that was required.

Half an hour before the last bell which summoned the nuns to the Divine Office, the cloister bell rang solemnly to remind them that "Strict Silence" had begun and that, from now onwards, until that particular "Hour" of the Divine Office should be ended, to occupy the mind with anything but spiritual thoughts would be a fault against the Rule.

In fact, wherever there might otherwise have been a chance of escaping down one of those lush green lanes of individual choice which are so dear to human nature, the Rule invariably stepped in — an Angel with a flaming sword — and barred the way. For the Rule, even in its smallest and apparently most insignificant details was, to the religious, the Will of God. And so, in all things and at all times, her own individual will was voluntarily sacrificed.

There was another point.

By the Vow of Poverty, none of the religious might possess anything whatsoever of their own.

In the Order to which I belonged, the nuns, like the early Christians, had "everything in common". There was no such thing as mine and thine; everything was always spoken of as "ours" — "*our* knife and fork", "*our* breviary", "*our* choirmantle" . . . even "*our* brush and comb". In the world outside, people express themselves through their surroundings. By their books and clothes and furniture, even by the houses they live in, one can generally tell, more or less, the kind of people that they are. In Religious Life, however, nothing of this sort is possible. There is no scope whatsoever for the expression of individual taste. Everything one has is, to begin with, exactly like that used by everybody else; and, since it is only lent to one, nothing of one's own personality is to be found in it. The enjoyment of seeing one's own ideas and tastes mirrored in everything around one, because one has chosen it and arranged it exactly as one likes, is unknown.

Indeed, everything in the convent combines to prevent, as much as possible, the external exercise or expression of anything personal at all.

It will, therefore, be apparent that such phrases as "my very own", or "exactly as I please", held for me a peculiar and urgent fascination. The idea of possessing

113

— actually possessing, as my own — a place (no matter how small and simple) in which I could put furniture that *I* had chosen, curtains whose colours *I* had decided upon, books and pictures that I actually *wanted* and *liked*, was almost too wonderful to be realized. And the thought of a garden of my own, with potential roses and delphiniums . . . and the knowledge that I should be able to cook my own meals, weed my own garden, say my prayers, read (and, perhaps, write) books, and get up and go to bed exactly when and where and how I pleased, was — well — so intoxicating that I hardly dared let my mind dwell upon it for too long at a time.

It is a very wonderful experience indeed when, at fifty years old, you suddenly discover that for the first time in your life you are really free to be *yourself*.

(7)

I am still doubtful whether my second job was a comedy or a tragedy. Perhaps it would be best to describe it simply as a flop.

One May morning, when I was nearing the completion of my drawing course, the Principal summoned me into the hutch at the back of the office.

Here I found a sulky-looking young man with a fat back to his neck and a marked disinclination to look one straight in the eyes. This was Mr. Percy Hambledon, representative of a firm in the Midlands.

114

They specialized in aircraft repairs and wanted a lady designer for one of their factories. It was suggested that I might like to consider the job.

Mr. Hambledon struck me as what this generation would call a really nasty piece of work. I knew, however, that fastidiousness would get me nowhere; so, being anxious to start on war work as soon as possible, I composed myself to hear what he had to say.

Mr. Hambledon told me that the job was a "composite affair", for, besides sketching the damage on aircraft that came in for repairs and preparing diagrams for the factory, I should be required to operate what he called "the photostat" — a comparatively new and somewhat complicated process of photography. This last would necessitate my undergoing a short course of training before actually taking up the job. About this, Mr. Hambledon promised that he would "let me know".

He then handed me an official form of really staggering dimensions. It was the first of its kind that I had encountered and it filled me with considerable awe. Such precautionary probings and pryings into the most intimate concerns of prospective employees must surely indicate a post of quite supreme importance. The long hours, compulsory overtime, and low wages — one pound fifteen shillings a week, including war bonus — in no way daunted me. I even remember a vague thrill of satisfaction at the thought of various uncomfortablenesses which would allow me, though even in so small a measure, to experience something at least analagous to what was being endured by some of those who were actually fighting the war.

In the end, I signed the form; and the unpleasing Mr. Hambledon promised to ring me up later about the photostat.

I then went forth, feeling — if possible — even grander and more important than when I had made my début at the Stourport Labour Exchange.

About a fortnight later, a trunk call from my new employer directed me to report to South Africa House. There, I was told, I should receive instructions about the photostat.

As I cautiously lowered myself from the bus into Trafalgar Square, I wondered inconsequently how long it would be before I really felt myself to be a part of this odd, exciting, noisy, scurrying world. Everything in it seemed to be the antithesis of all that had made up the greater part of my life. The expressions of the passers-by — unhappy, hard, coarse, bestial, or just vacant — what a contrast they were to the serene, spiritual faces which had hitherto surrounded me! For nuns should — and almost invariably *do* — look serene, as they are not only holy but happy. If they fail to do this, there is something wrong.

I asked the way of what appeared to be a policeman. How different was this quite unpadded and slightly disdainful young man from the huge and rubicund bobby of my youth. And why, instead of the traditional helmet, was he wearing a peaked cap like that of an army officer? His voice and speech when he directed

116

me were unmistakably those of a gentleman. It was all very bewildering.

I tried to assume a suitable air of self-possession as I entered South Africa House, though I could hardly have felt more nervous if its portals had been those of the Kremlin.

In the hall, an omnipotent-looking official, whose uniform suggested that he must be at least a field-marshal, took charge of me. By him I was wafted in lifts (a new and exciting experience), conducted down corridors, and finally led into the presence of a Personage with the most unsmiling eyes I have ever seen. I remember them even now: they were long-distance eyes, which never once during the interview that followed condescended to focus upon me.

I told him my business; and when he had asked me a few questions, he did some telephoning. Finally, with his eyes still contemplating an invisible horizon, he told me that there must be some mistake, because nobody at South Africa House had ever heard of either Mr. Hambledon or his photostat.

And the strange thing is that, both at Africa House in Kingsway — whither I was subsequently directed — and at the Ministries of Air, Supply and Information, to which it was there suggested that I should apply, I received the same answer. None of them had ever been in communication with Mr. Hambledon.

What is even more odd is that to this day the mystery remains unsolved. Whether there ever was a photostat, or whether Mr. Hambledon was merely the kind of lunatic who amuses himself by directing gullible

117

persons to imaginary courses of instruction in the manipulation of non-existent machines, I shall never know. Probably, if I had followed the matter up, interesting discoveries might have resulted.

But I anticipate.

(8)

Somewhere about two o'clock, I found myself in the neighbourhood of Victoria. I was feeling so cross and tired I could have cried.

I saw a place with "Empire Restaurant" over the door. So, with hunger gnawing at my vitals, I went in.

It was crowded with what looked like shop-girls, office clerks, weary middle-aged women, and youth of both sexes in uniform. As I had never heard of the cafeteria system, I just sat down at one of the little tables and waited for someone to come and attend to me.

Nobody came. So far as I could see, there was nobody to come. I looked about and observed a long queue of people with trays in their hands, apparently serving themselves at a kind of counter behind a bar. To them I joined myself, a little nervously, and presently secured a cup of coffee and some rather unappetizing food. With this, I proudly returned to my table.

And here, for the next fifteen minutes, I sat and meditated upon the experiences of the last few hours.

★　★　★

Never had I dreamed of anything like these great Ministries — the power-houses, I supposed, of our Government — into which I had just been permitted a glimpse. Several of them were not even in existence in 1914 when I retired from the world. And even those that were must have been far less vast and complicated than they are to-day.

I was particularly impressed by the gloom of Africa House in Kingsway and the sheer immensity of the Ministry of Information. There was something faintly terrifying in the thought of those gigantic buildings, honeycombed with endless passages, along which men and women scuttled like ants; and the tiny cell-like offices where millions spent their lives clicking away on typewriters or dealing with official forms. But the power and intricacies of our titanic government machine left me without enthusiasm. Some instinct within me even rebelled at the thought of a civilization that had such a system at its nerve-centres. And I began to ask myself frightening and paralysing questions — questions that had no answers, or, if they had, I certainly hadn't a notion what they were.

How different was the government of empires from that of convents!

About the more modern congregations I am confessedly ignorant; but the old mediaeval monastic houses were ruled on highly efficient lines.

The communities — which might number anything from a dozen to close on a hundred members — were divided into Choir Nuns and Lay Sisters.

The Choir Nuns — each of whom had brought a dowry — spent their time chiefly in prayer, manual work and the recitation of the Divine Office in choir. The Lay Sisters, who were drawn originally from the peasant class, gave — instead of dowries — their services for the heavier work of the house.

The Superior — known as the Reverend Mother Prioress — was elected triennially by the votes of the Choir Nuns. (Lay Sisters were not allowed a vote.) Her position was less that of mistress than of mother to the Community. The extreme respect shown to her was based upon the idea that in the monastery she held the place of Christ. The nuns, until they had been for a certain number of years in the Community, always knelt when she spoke to them. When she passed, they had to rise and bow to her as she went by. For anything that was in any way an exception to the Rule, her leave had to be asked. Her will was supreme.

She herself was expected to be in all things a model of perfection — a point which, surprisingly, seemed in no way to daunt those members of the community (and they exist in every convent) who felt themselves to be peculiarly fitted by Providence for the office of Prioress.

From among themselves the Choir Nuns also elected perhaps sixteen or seventeen who represented them, much as an M.P. represents his constituency. These Sisters were consulted when important decisions had to be taken by the Prioress; they would be asked to vote, for instance, when there was a question of a novice being allowed to take her Vows.

To these few fell also the choosing of a much smaller and even more carefully selected body. This was the Council: a kind of Privy Cabinet who assisted the Prioress in the administration of the monastery.

The actual work of the house was divided up among the heads of the various departments. These were known as the "Officers". The more important were elected triennially; the rest were nominated — usually once a year — by the Prioress.

Each nun had her business laid down for her, even to the minutest details. Thus and thus was each thing to be done, and no otherwise. Short work was made of enterprising novices who came forward with bright ideas for new and better ways of doing things. Moreover, every least object employed by a nun in her "Office" was entered in an inventory and an exact account had to be rendered when another Sister succeeded her.

First in rank among the Officers was the *Subprioress*, whose chief business was to safeguard the observance and internal discipline of the monastery. She also replaced the Prioress when the latter was unable to preside and, like her, was treated with the greatest reverence by the community. As she was liable to severe criticism if ever she failed to be kind, humble, wise, patient and a living example of religious observance at all times, her Office was hardly one to be coveted.

The *Procuratrix* ordered and gave out the provisions, had charge of the Lay Sisters, and looked after the general upkeep of the house. A Martha-job, if ever there was one, and fatiguing — but apparently a swift highroad to holiness.

The *Cellaress* did a certain amount to help the Procuratrix and had besides quite a number of odd little jobs of her own. One of these was to wash the eggs served to the community; another, to read aloud the life of some saint to the Lay Sisters as they sat over their sewing in the afternoon. She also presided at the hatch between the refectory and kitchen-quarters at meal-times, and gave out any special dish that had to be served to anyone who was ill.

The *Refectorian's* work was to keep the refectory in order, lay the tables, and, with the assistance of the weekly server, to wait upon the community at dinner and supper every day. She had to keep the great oak tables clean and polished, set the salt, lay a plate and porringer at each one's place, and wash the water-jugs in the lavatory outside.

And on Maundy Thursday, when the Prioress served in the refectory and washed the feet of the twelve eldest nuns (in memory of Christ, who on the eve of his Passion washed the feet of his disciples), the whole room had to be scoured, polished and adorned with flowers and draperies.

An *Under-Refectorian* helped the Refectorian to set the mugs and porringers. It was also her task to remove with a moist and malodorous dish-rag all stains from the Refectory floor.

The Office of Refectorian was not particularly sought after. The daily serving could be intensely tiring and it was not easy to keep oneself free from a faint aroma of grease. There was, too, a most unattractive duty attached to it — that of mending the vast sheet-like table-napkins which custom ordained that, when the Prioress gave the signal, each nun should affix to her bosom with a pin. These had to be darned *before* the Lay Sisters washed them. And it was an occupation which — to put it mildly — could be very unpleasant indeed.

The *Sacristan* had one of the most important and arduous Offices in the monastery. Two other nuns — usually chosen from among the strongest in the community — were allowed her as helps. One of them was always responsible for the bell-ringing in choir and cloister which called the nuns to various duties during the day. She had also to start the "peal" rung in the choir for five minutes or so before each part of the Divine Office. On high festivals, the *Under-Sacristan's* life was a perfect nightmare of bell-ringing; for, besides the peals for Mass, Office, Strict Silence and Spiritual Reading which enlivened the morning, she had also to ring in the cloister at 2p.m. for the Lesser Silence; at 3 o'clock in choir and cloister for Strict Silence; again there at 3.15 "because such was the custom"; at 3.25 in the cloister, summoning the nuns to Vespers, and again in the choir at 3.30 to "start the peal". And with Compline, a whole programme of evening ringing began. As it was a considerable distance from choir to cloister, the Under-Sacristan seldom put on weight for lack of exercise. Should she be late to ring, or forget altogether, the earth shook and trembled, for the entire community would be seriously inconvenienced.

Between them, the Sacristans were responsible for keeping the church, choir and sacristy in a state of spotless perfection. The High Altar and the Altar of Our Lady had always to be immaculate; there were the huge brass and silver candlesticks to be polished, flowers cut and continually rearranged. Twice daily the massive sanctuary lamp needed replenishing; new candles had to be unpacked and set up in place of others that were scraped and laid away in the long shelves behind a curtain in the outer Sacristy. Vestments were prepared for the two daily Masses and for Benediction; while bells, censers, crucifixes, incense-boats, lanterns, cruets and holy water-stoups were constantly in need of a refill or a rub.

The Head Sacristan had the key of the safe in which the sacred vessels were kept. Amongst them was an exquisite jewelled ciborium of pure gold and a beaten silver chalice that might have belonged to the shrine of some mediaeval saint. I remember, too, a great gem-encrusted monstrance — magnificent but hideous — which literally blazed with brilliants when the Host was lifted up at Benediction on the greater feasts.

The Church linen and vestments were kept in a small, ancient room called the Custry. Here were long chests with deep drawers full of cottas and albs, each one folded according to custom, in the tiniest possible accordion pleats and then bound tightly — like a della Robbia bambino — with strappings of linen or tape. The snowy gossamer lawn out of which most of them were fashioned was lace-edged — priceless, historic lace, inducing sharp intakes of breath and wide eye-openings when shown to connoisseurs. And what masses of it. Cream, foam-colour, ivory, linen-white, ghost-grey or palest oyster — all the faint, indescribable quarter-tones between white and white that exist only in lace. Each piece had its pedigree. Most of it was well over a yard in depth.

On wide, sliding shelves, inside deep cupboards, vestments were laid full-length between dust-sheets and damp-proof paper to prevent the gold and silver embroidery from tarnishing. To describe such a magnificent collection in these pages is impossible, but I cannot resist the temptation to mention two or three which, if I ever attempt to burgle the convent, I shall certainly carry away with me in my bag.

There was a set — complete with cope, chasuble and dalmatics — of stiff, sprigged Jacobean silk. It dated from the time of James II, and was as much a masterpiece as any of the ancient church-pictures in the refectory. Despite the passage of centuries, neither the lovely old-fashioned gold "galloon", nor the enchanting colours in which the silk was woven, were tarnished or faded. Old rose, pale green and pinkish lilac made a delicate background to embroidery worked in heavy ropes of twisted gold. The linings were mulberry-colour, shot with a curious green, like shadowed cypress. When you lifted the chasuble, the faintest possible fragrance — suggesting lavender, pot-pourri and ancient incense — exhaled from its folds. To me it was a living link with a historic past. It evoked awareness of all kinds of long-forgotten happenings, about which nobody would otherwise have known.

There was another complete set of cloth-of-gold, enormously heavy, and only used once a year at Midnight Mass — perhaps because the embossed angels on the magnificent material suggested a vision of the first *Gloria in excelsis Deo* seen through Melozzo da Forli's eyes. It was lined with stiff, poppy-coloured satin and produced the effect of a fanfare of golden trumpets under a sunset sky.

Another set, presented to the convent when Queen Anne was reigning, was of many-coloured tapestry, thick as a carpet, an unusual medley of curious reds, dull greens, deep purples and mysterious blues. There was white in it, too, and a brownish gold that somehow suggested Byzantine mosaic. This, too, was used only once a year, for the Ceremonies of Holy Saturday. To me, it always seemed like a harmony of the colour and magic of spring.

The more modern vestments, especially the new Gothic chasubles used for the greater festivals of Our Lady, were perhaps faintly reminiscent of evening gowns. But, after all, why not? I remember especially one of silver *peau d'ange* with a lining of palest hyacinth. Its chief glory was a medallion of Fra Angelico's *Coronation of the Virgin*, perhaps unequalled as an example of the technical skill to which the embroiderer's needle can attain. I have never seen anything lovelier of its kind than the way in which the delicate rainbow-hued draperies were treated. They might have been dipped in the heart of an opal. The whole thing was like a key-hole glimpse of heaven's glory, seen through a veil of iridescent mist.

Finally, there were the splendid copes worn for Vespers at Easter and Pentecost. Cloth-of-silver with a stupendous hood and jewelled orphreys; and one of embossed brocade whose magnificent lining suggested firelight glowing dimly behind claret-coloured glass.

Even to handle such vestments gave one emotions that were at once sensuous and aesthetic. The rich hues, exquisite textures, faint, subtle perfumes, were somehow a little intoxicating after so much that was bleak and austere.

The *Vestiarians*, charged with the making, mending and distribution of the habit, were usually about six in number — two head officers and four underlings. Their lives could hardly have been a greater contrast to those of the sacristans. For about five hours daily they sat and sewed in silence in a hot stuffy room whose windows were nearly always tightly shut.

And when, on a green and golden April morning, the blackbirds fluted among the lilac bushes and called them out into the sun-drenched garden to smell the fragrance of spring, the vestiarians had to remember that the Rule — which was the Will of God for them — forbade the lifting of their noses from their work, unless it should be absolutely necessary. The fact that the outer garments worn by the religious had, like the table-napkins, to be mended before being sent to the laundry, certainly did not make the temptation to join the blackbirds easier to resist.

When, every six weeks or so, there was a great "wash" of some part of the habit, the vestiarians had to ensure that each garment was properly dealt with before being put carefully away. This was a tremendous business. At about eight o'clock in the morning, every member of the community who was able to stand on two legs was expected to scurry along to the long low-raftered garrets under the monastery roof.

Here the Lay Sisters had prepared great baskets of wet linen or woollen garments which the nuns had to shake, lay out on the long wooden tables, slap and flatten by way of ironing, fold across, and finally hang up to dry on the long wire lines that stretched across the garret from end to end.

This business usually took from one to three hours, according to the quantity of the garments and the numbers of those who had come to help. With the exception of the vestiarians, it was not obligatory to show up for "Garrets"; not to do so, however, was looked upon as shirking and, sooner or later, one would be sure to hear about it from the Superior.

Talking was generally allowed till the bell in the cloister rang for work; after that, silence reigned. In summer, "Garrets" was a pleasantly cool occupation, but in winter — when the snow was sometimes lying on the roof a few feet above one's head — the cold was frightful. Quite often, the wet linen was frozen stiff in the baskets and one's hands became so numbed that they refused to work. Later on in the morning, when the circulation was restored to them, the pain in one's blue and chilblained fingers was quite agonizing.

The *Infirmarian*, with a Lay Sister as her handmaid, ruled over the infirmary, which had a special wing to itself. Here the *grandes malades*, with the very old nuns, and anyone who might be recovering from an operation, were looked after with extraordinary kindness and care.

Any infirmarian who carried out all the detailed instructions laid down for her in the Rule and Constitutions could hardly fail to make of the infirmary a place of happiness and peace. The idea, of course, behind all this charity was the one set forth in St. Matthew, xxv. 40, "*Mihi fecistis* . . . I was sick, and you visited Me . . . What you did unto *them*, you did to Me."

In the convent infirmary, the sick were looked upon quite simply as being Christ. The rest followed automatically.

The minor ailments of the community were, as has been said before, attended to by the *Apothecary*. Should you need her services, you knocked at the door of the dark little stone-floored chamber where she plied her trade. Within, the white-washed walls were hung with rows of pots, pans and tiny long-handled pipkins of polished copper and brass. An immense, sinister-looking cupboard contained remedies for every emergency: bottles of elder-syrup for coughs in the winter; orange-flower water for insomnia; large, round, gelatinous pills containing black, fishy-smelling liquid to be taken as a "help" to fasting during the forty days of Lent; bark — another unpopular but efficacious remedy for weakness; "tilly-tea" — brewed from the flowers of the *tilleul* or lime-tree — sovereign cure for colds . . . and more modern remedies, tubes, boxes, bottles, packets of them; and a small, ancient bookshelf containing endless little old wives' recipes and instructions for the care and healing of the sick.

Here was to be found the short, simple, but absolutely infallible *Remedy for Rheumatism*, which produced its astounding results in under fifteen days. Here was *Dr. Ralalife's Recipe for a Consumption*, consisting of crabs' claws finely powdered, asses' milk, and crabs' eyes. And here — in *Mr. Jenison's Receipts, Both Galenicall and Chimicall Who First Teach Us to Make Our Drugs in the Year* 1702 — is the account of the virtue contained in *Lady Carrington's Cerecloth*, which "cured ye King's evil or any other sore by washing your sore with milk or butter and beere" and "applying this cerecloth till it's cured".

When I myself was given the office of Apothecary, I wrote to one of my aunts, lamenting my ignorance of even the most elementary medical knowledge. She immediately sent me a large and excellent *Encyclopaedia of Nursing*. This — though I should have found it quite invaluable — was immediately taken away from me. The reason given was that it contained a great deal which it was quite unnecessary for me to know.

The most responsible office was undoubtedly that of *Mistress of Novices*. To train young and chosen souls in the way of perfection was undoubtedly an exacting occupation; and in some ways the Novice Mistress ruled over her small domain rather like a queen. Canon Law obliged the novices to be separated as much as possible from the community during the earlier stages of their religious life. Until they had made their Vows, the young nuns had their own table in the Refectory, their own living-room (known as the "Noviceship"), their dormitory, their garden, and a special cloister where they walked up and down for spiritual reading on rainy days. Conversation with the community nuns was prohibited, and — except upon special occasions — they seldom saw the Superior. As a result, the Novice Mistress soon became everything to them — guide, philosopher and friend, as well as mother and confidante.

The position was one of great trust and great importance. It was accompanied by privileges, not the least of which was much intimate converse with the Prioress, to whom everything concerning the novices had to be made known. Small wonder that she who held this office had sometimes to pay a price for it at the hands of certain members of the community.

The *Organist, Choir Mistress, Chantress* and *Succentress* were responsible for the music.

The *Librarian* kept the books in order and watched, argus-eyed, lest any Sister should so far forget herself as to take out a volume without marking it down on the shelf-catalogue.

The *Portress* and her relief opened the *guichet* to visitors, dispensed bread, soup and alms to the poor, and flew backwards and forwards between the Great Door and the Prioress' chamber for "leaves" and directions whenever the door-bell rang.

★ ★ ★

One more office — that of the *Prioress' Chaplain* — must be mentioned. The title is misleading, since it suggests that nuns sometimes encroach upon the territory of the priesthood. Actually, the office was simply that of a kind of lady-in-waiting to the Superior. Chaucer's Prioress, it may be remembered, was attended by one:

> "Another Nonne also with her hadde she
> That was hire chappeleine, and Preestes thre."

She prepared and marked the places in the Prioress' Plain-chant books and breviary; arranged hours for her interviews with members of the community; accompanied her at the annual visitation of the cells and on Maundy Thursday, when she served in the refectory and washed the feet of the community.

Three times a day she gave round letters to the nuns, after they had been previously examined by the Prioress. This obliged her to be constantly in and out of the Superior's room, so that she had many opportunities of slipping in a suggestion or tactfully sowing the seeds of an idea. This could make her a valuable friend — or, possibly, a dangerous enemy.

Perhaps the most tiresome of her jobs was the adornment of a number of the "little altars" — wooden brackets on which were set a statue or picture of a saint. These lurked in every corner of the monastery. Practically every nun had charge of one. This meant that a vase or two of flowers, with perhaps a few candles or a lamp on "occasions", had to be crammed on to the bracket, and the whole affair dusted carefully every day. When the saint's festival came round, the nun was expected to do something spectacular in the way of decoration. So, on the eve, she would spend such free moments as she possessed in decking out the altar and its immediate surroundings with ferns, foliage, flowers and a forest of elegant candlesticks mounted on wooden stands.

(The idea was, I believe, that the larger and more elaborate the "dress", the more fervour it betokened in the dresser. A meagre "dress", suggesting that only a short time had been spent upon it, was thus a sure sign of tepidity.)

A carpet, with a cushion supporting a book, was then spread before it; so that when the community assembled at the appointed hour, the Prioress could recite the prayer or litany in honour of the saint.

To me, this business of "dressing" the little altars always seemed rather a waste of time. Time was so scarce, and there were so many things one longed to do in it . . .

The actual mode of government was simple.

It was based upon faith — which has been defined as a super-natural faculty of discerning the divine through, and in, the human.

Those who embrace the Religious Life believe that it contains three special channels by which the Will of God comes to them. These are, (1) the Rule, which outlines the spirit and observances of the Order; (2) the

Constitutions and Customs, which fill in details; and (3) the commands of the Superior.

By faith, each Religious sees God in the Superior. "Never", says St. John of the Cross, "look upon your Superior, be he who he may, otherwise than if you were looking upon God, for he stands in his place. If you reflect upon the character, ways . . . or habits of your Superior, you will change your obedience from divine into human . . . and obedience influenced by human considerations is almost worthless in the eyes of God."

As a result, the more complete the submission of one's will to that of the Superior (sin always, of course, excepted), the more perfectly one's will is united to the Will of God.

I once consulted the famous Dominican, Father Bede Jarrett, about this matter of submission.

He was a man of deep humour, profound learning, and wide experience. I told him about an order which had just been given to me by a Superior and which had struck me as being neither wise nor just.

"I can submit my *will* sufficiently to do the thing I've been told to do," I explained to him, "but as for forcing my *mind* . . ."

He looked at me with those intent yet curiously brooding eyes that were so unforgettable.

He said: "I once took that same problem to my Novice Master. He told me to re-read *The Charge of the Light Brigade*. The idea, you see, is, that you do what you're told, no matter how certain you feel that someone has blundered. To ride fearlessly into the jaws

134

of death without reasoning why adds splendour to your obedience."

"Even," I persisted, "if you feel convinced that what you've been told to do is sheerest lunacy?"

He smiled.

"Ah, but don't you see? — that's just where the heroism comes in."

This point of view impressed me. Of course, it fits in perfectly with another basic principle of the Christian life — that one is not made or unmade by the things that happen to one, but by one's reactions to the circumstances of one's life.

That, as the Dominican assured me, is all that God cares about.

But there was another theory which helped to influence the decisions of those in authority. This I found harder to assimilate. It was the theory of *la grâce d'état*. In practice, it really meant that if a nun were appointed to an office, that nun — provided that she prayed sufficiently for God's grace and did what lay in her to make the thing a success — was certain not to fail. "*I can do all things*," one was reminded by one's Novice Mistress, "*in him who strengtheneth me*" — a heartening belief when the day for the annual Change of Office came round and a kind of General Post took place in the community.

I have seen a young and quite inexperienced little under-vestiarian summoned on such an occasion to the Superior's room. She came forth in a terrified daze, unable to realize that she had just been appointed Mistress of Novices. Another, who knew nothing of medicine and had never nursed anyone, appeared equally stunned when informed that henceforward she would hold the office of Infirmarian.

I myself felt the need of all the support which *la grâce d'état* could provide for me at an extremely early stage of my career. After barely six months in the convent, I was told suddenly that in a fortnight's time I should have to go down to the school and give classes in English, Geography and History.

I was panic-stricken.

My own school-days had been delightful, but the classes were dull and I had never bothered about studying. My time had been spent in devouring Malory's *Morte d'Arthur*, the works of Kipling and the plays of Oscar Wilde, whose epigrams dazzled my adolescent mind. As a result, the *lacunae* in my education were such that it would have been hard to find anyone less fitted for the instruction of youth.

This I tried nervously to explain to the Prioress.

She assured me, however, that, in the spiritual order, one was never justified in saying that anything at all "could not be done".

"If you put everything you've got into it, and trust God," she insisted, kindly but firmly, "*He* will do the thing for you. Remember St. Peter walking on the waves." And an eminent Jesuit, to whom I confided my apprehension next time I went to Confession, advised me to imitate the apostles when Christ told them to feed five thousand people with five barley loaves and a few cold fish.

After that, of course, there was nothing more to be said.

(9)

That evening, I wrote a faintly acid note to Mr. Hambledon, asking for an explanation.

Unfortunately, according to the maddening habit of letters, it just crossed one from him to me. In it, he said that some changes had just been made at the airfield and asked if I could possibly take up my work there in a couple of days' time. There was no mention whatsoever of the photostat.

It was, I suppose — all things considered — rather unwise of me. But, after I had thought it over for a little, I wired to Mr. Hambledon that I would come.

CHAPTER
FIVE

(1)

I greatly enjoyed the journey from St. Pancras to —
perhaps we had better call it Shuffleborough.

This was largely because of the panorama to be seen
from the carriage windows. I suppose I had been shut
away for so long that I had forgotten what mustard
fields looked like; but they seemed to me one of the
loveliest things I had seen since I came out. Sheet upon
sheet of blazing yellow, half-way between sulphur and
celandine, with hot golden sunshine pouring down upon
them out of a dazzling June sky. It thrilled me like music.

I had a book, too, called *High Rising* by Angela
Thirkell. This caused me to utter such yelps of delighted
laughter that the gaggle of stolid-looking A.T.S. girls
sitting opposite kept looking across to see what it was
all about.

As had been arranged, I was met at the station by the
Welfare Officer. By the way she shook hands, I could
tell at once that something was wrong.

"It's just too bad!" she kept lamenting. "I really hardly
know how to give you the message . . . it's just too bad!"

This was alarming. Had the aerodrome perhaps been
destroyed by enemy action? Or had Mr. Hambledon
committed suicide?

138

"Look," I said at last, "do let me know what has happened. I promise you I won't collapse."

Mr. Hambledon, it appeared, had sent for her that morning and given instructions for me to be told on my arrival that the job had fallen through and that I had better return to London by the next convenient train.

I gazed at her, dumbfounded. What on earth was I going to do?

I thought it over for a moment. Then, breathing forth fire and brimstone against Mr. Hambledon, I determined that I would beard him myself and discover what lay behind this extraordinary affair.

So the Welfare Officer and I packed ourselves and the two suitcases which contained all my earthly possessions into a taxi, and away we drove along the hot white dusty road to the aerodrome.

The Welfare Officer, whose soft pale face made me think of a magnolia, assured me that she had no inkling as to what the cause of Mr. Hambledon's behaviour could be.

"But then, of course," she concluded, "at *that* place you do always feel that *anything* might be done to you." And she proceeded to relate tales about what *had* been done to her since she worked there. None of them in any way increased my esteem for Mr. Hambledon.

The aerodrome, when at last we arrived there, did not impress me. A huddle of lizard-coloured huts clustered round about the entrance; further on, two enormous corrugated sheds stretched half-way down the cropped turf of the landing-ground. I followed the Welfare Officer into one of them. A girl was working on

139

some stiff, sour-smelling canvas at a kind of sewing-machine. Further on, a group of tousled, pasty-faced mechanics tinkered at the smashed fuselage of a war-scarred plane. They stared as we passed, but took no further notice of us. Beyond this shed, a hut stood in a hot pool of sunshine. Men and girls in boiler-suits and overalls were pouring in through the open door.

"The canteen," said the Welfare Officer. "I'll leave you with the manageress while I look for Mr. Hambledon." And she disappeared in the direction of some office-like buildings over the way.

A kindly woman in a check apron pulled me behind the counter. She set a very thick cup of fierce-looking tea before me. While I drank it, I took stock of those whom Providence had so nearly ordained should be my fellow-workers.

Most of them were smoking. The girls, who for no apparent reason shrieked and giggled incessantly, struck me as rather a brazen-looking crowd. Two or three had a frightened, hang-dog air which was rather sinister. The men lounged about on the benches, shouting to one another and indulging in rough horse-play with the girls. Their language was new to me. Most of their swear-words I had not heard before. All of them stared at me as though I had dropped from another planet.

Presently the Welfare Officer returned and said that, if I would go across and wait on the airfield, Mr. Hambledon would come to me.

So I went.

I may as well confess at once that Mr. Hambledon was too much for me. True, I allowed myself the luxury of telling him quite a lot — though, alas, not all — of what I thought about him; but against his particular technique I really hadn't a chance. It was like banging a balloon. Never have I met anyone who so skilfully bounced and slithered away from every question put to him. Especially about the photostat. His replies simply had no bearing at all upon the situation. The only explanation he attempted to offer was that "the job had fallen through". And he repeated that I had better go back to London as soon as possible.

After about half an hour's unsuccessful manoeuvring to get him cornered, it struck me that it would be as well if the first move towards concluding the interview came from me. I therefore, in the grand manner, and with an air of ineffable hauteur, dismissed him from my presence, as though he were a refractory kitchen-boy. This took him so by surprise that he withdrew, with no more than a mumble, from the scene of combat. I remember observing that his ears were claret-coloured as he slouched away.

Outside, while I was shaking the dust of the aerodrome from my feet, I saw the Welfare Officer waiting for me. I told her the result of the conversation. This in no way appeared to surprise her.

She said, "I do wish I could help you. I've been thinking up a little plan while you and Mr. Hambledon were talking. I wonder what you'll say to it?"

141

Still smarting a little from the sense of injustice induced by my recent contact with that gentleman, I looked down at her. I felt suddenly and strangely comforted, for the eyes that looked back at me from behind the horn-rimmed spectacles were among the kindest I have ever seen.

(2)

At this point the chronicle becomes suddenly and violently saturated with the atmosphere of the *Acts of the Apostles*.

This was due in the first place to the behaviour of the Welfare Officer, whose name, it appeared, was Olwen Price. She insisted that, instead of returning to London, I should go back, then and there, to Shuffleborough, and spend the night with her at the flat which she shared with her school-teacher friend. This friend, she assured me, was One In A Thousand; and, if I cared to discuss with her what she called "the possibilities of my position", she thought I might find help in her advice.

I accepted this extraordinarily kind invitation. It would have been almost impossible to refuse. Upon which, the atmosphere to which I have alluded began to make itself felt.

The *Acts of the Apostles* has always seemed to me one of the greatest thrillers of all time. The chapters, however, which now concern us are those which describe how the earliest Christians lived. They had "but one heart and one soul"; they "dwelt together in gladness and simplicity of heart"; "all their possessions were in common" and they "distributed to everyone according as he had need". An idyllic picture, of which every detail was faithfully reproduced in the household across whose threshold I now stepped.

I hope that I shall not be misunderstood if I say here that I am not what is usually described as "pious". But I fall down flat in the dust with admiration when I come across people who take the Sermon on the Mount literally and practise it, point by point, in their daily lives. And that was what Olwen and her friend quite obviously did.

The flat was small and light and beige-coloured, with a style of furniture that was new to me. Everything was as plain and pale as possible, and shaped, so far as might be, like a box. I was regarding it with interest when a door opened and a young woman in a blue dress came in. One had the impression that a light sea-wave was about to break on the shore . . .

"Meet Wendy Nicholls!" said Olwen dramatically.

I jumped a little — I hope not too noticeably — for I had never before heard this form of introduction. It struck me as peculiar . . .

I find it a little difficult to write about Olwen and Wendy. This is because I do not know how to reproduce the unique atmosphere in which they lived. To relate merely what they said and did would be dull. To the non-religious it might even sound funny; whereas it was actually all rather beautiful. Like Helen

Waddell's *Desert Fathers*, their every action seemed to show forth a standard of values that just turned the world upside down. They were clean-hearted, like the nicest kind of children; they were absolutely honest; and I never heard either of them offend in the smallest degree against charity.

We had a supper-ish kind of meal in their little kitchen, where they lavished upon me everything that their tiny war-time larder contained. Afterwards, we sat in armchairs and made ourselves known to one another. Their outlook on life was unusual. I feel, however, that to analyse it would need a more competent pen than mine. All I can say is that their warm-hearted human sympathy and kindness was unforgettable; and that it impressed me more and more as we talked ourselves far into that hot summer night.

They urged me to stay down there with them for at least a day or two. They were sure they could find me a job. Then began a great ringing up of their friends; and, before I knew where I was, an interview had been arranged for me with the works manager of an electrical engineering firm who had a large factory just outside Shuffleborough. Just what the prospective job would be, I did not find out; but "Jack", Wendy assured me, would do anything he could for me. ("Jack" and Wendy, I gathered, were kindred spirits where the things of the soul were concerned.) Finally, when sleep laid its hand rather heavily upon us, these surprising women knelt down like two children at their mother's knee and started to say their prayers. *Out loud.*

144

It seems incredible, but they really did it. And though I was curiously embarrassed, to them it was the most natural thing in the world. They talked to God exactly as if they saw him there before them, and knew for a fact that he cared tremendously about their smallest concerns. Wendy even thanked him politely for having guided me to their flat and requested that she and Olwen might be instrumental in finding the right kind of work for me.

I quite realize that the idea of such proceedings will give rise to sensations of nausea in the stomach of a certain kind of person. For my own part, I found it most touching. And when, dizzy with sleep, they got up from their knees and said good-night to me, it was with such good and kind and happy faces that I could have hugged the pair of them.

(3)

We had breakfast at an early hour because they both had to be at their jobs by nine o'clock. Wendy then presented me with a latch-key; and they departed, leaving me alone for the day.

Such trust was embarrassing. I might have devoured their provisions, ransacked their papers, burgled the flat. This idea, however, did not apparently occur to them.

My interview was for eleven o'clock; so I spent the hour before it in exploring Shuffleborough.

It struck me as rather a platitudinous kind of place. Everything — church, cinema, post office, town hall — was all exactly what one would have expected in a new, ugly, industrial and aggressively communist community. It was only remarkable for the numbers of curiously bulgy-looking women who thronged its streets. This last detail puzzled me. I remember remarking on it to Olwen in the evening. She explained, smiling, that Shuffleborough had been a refuge for prospective mothers since the beginning of the war.

I felt a fool.

The interview at the electrical works was interesting.

"Jack", kind, courteous, and obviously overworked, did all that he could to help me. During our conversation I got many sidelights upon the inner workings of a vast, impersonal company — such as that by which he was employed. His own job appeared to be that of a kind of liaison officer between capital and labour. Like Wendy and Olwen, the *Acts of the Apostles* was obviously his spiritual home.

The post he offered me was that of supervisor in a part of the factory where the girls and women worked. I was taken over the buildings for whose inmates I should be responsible.

The inside of a factory is too familiar to need description: to me, however, everything was new and astonishing. The great sheds with their avenues of machines running from end to end of the building . . . The girls, manipulating mysterious gadgets that buzzed

146

or clicked or clanged with torturing monotony . . . The foul air, poisoned with the smell of oil and dust and stale humanity . . . The perpetual glare from the unshaded bulbs suspended from among the shadowy girders in the blacked-out roof-lights . . . Worst of all, the frightful, deafening whirr and roar of the machines. Here, with a vengeance, was Milton's "horrible discord" and "the dire noise of madding wheels . . ." As I glanced at the pretty, painted, bored-looking girls in their oil-stained boiler-suits, I suddenly understood *why* they behaved so outrageously when they escaped from the factory in the evening. Nothing that I had been told surprised me. After a day like that, in such a place — no! I could not blame them for wanting to kick up their heels.

I'm afraid I was not as sorry as I might have been that I failed to secure the job. An essential qualification appeared to be the possession of a certificate for having completed a course of Red Cross training. This, of course, I did not possess.

So that was the end of that.

On my way back, I plucked up courage and presented myself at the Labour Exchange. A bleak-looking woman in spectacles offered me a job in the Post Office. She pointed out that a pension was attached to it and seemed astonished when I murmured that I feared it wasn't quite my cup of tea . . .

That evening — I rather think it was by way of cheering me up — Olwen and Wendy escorted me to a Function.

They said it was a Meeting of Professional and Business Women for a Discussion on Vansittartism. As I had never met any Business Women and had no idea what Vansittartism was, I set out in some trepidation. To my surprise, however, I enjoyed it. The Business Women, as might have been expected, talked sense, and I came away with much new subject-matter upon which to reflect.

My recollections of the next day or two are a little hazy.

I remember Wendy appearing at breakfast with a pencil and paper and reading aloud something which, she explained, she had received as Guidance during her Quiet Time. It was about my affairs — I forget exactly what — but it caused me to set aside for a while the wire saying, "Come home at once", with which my uncle and aunt in London had replied to my account of Mr. Hambledon's defection. It seemed to me that to go on trying my luck in Shuffleborough for a day or two could do no harm to anyone; and Wendy's Guidance certainly seemed to point that way. Anyhow, another interview was arranged for me, this time with a doctor who wanted to start a *crèche* where working mothers could leave their babies for the day.

Unfortunately, the doctor only had the scheme on paper and said it would be months before anything came of it.

So that, too, fell through.

★ ★ ★

Next day I had an inspiration.

I called at the presbytery of the Catholic Church and asked the priest who admitted me whether he knew of any job in Shuffleborough for which I could apply.

He was sorry, he said, when I told him my story; but he knew of absolutely nothing. Couldn't the people I was staying with do something for me?

I told him of all that Olwen and Wendy had already achieved; but it was only when I mentioned Guidance and Quiet Times that he showed any interest.

He said, "Why, it sounds to me as though you had wandered into a nest of Buchmanites!"

As I had never heard the word before, I looked blank. So he started explaining to me all about Buchmanism and something called the Oxford Group Movement.

I found it most interesting.

Walking back through the unlovely streets, I meditated upon what he had said to me. Buchmanism, according to him, was undoubtedly a heresy; even I could not help seeing, as a Catholic, where the danger-signals lay.

And yet — and yet —!

There simply was no denying that Wendy and Olwen had got hold of *something*. To me it seemed like an inner spirit that shone through all they said and did, making it potent for good. Whether this was due to Buchmanism or merely to their own impassioned efforts after the perfection of Honesty, Purity and Charity, I cannot say. All I know is that, as I let myself

149

into the flat, I was uncomfortably aware that they were far better women than I was ever likely to be.

(4)

Shuffleborough and I having apparently no particular use for one another, it seemed advisable to return to London and hunt for another job of war-work there.

There were a great many soldiers travelling.

I wished I knew what their various pips and badges signified. That was another disadvantage of having been "out of things" for so long. One was completely ignorant of a thousand details that other people knew instinctively.

Some of the soldiers had wives and babies with them. Those babies fascinated me. I had not seen one of the fat pink things at close quarters for nearly thirty years. Their clothes filled me with admiration. How infinitely more practical were their brief and scanty garments — in most cases, simply one that pulled up and one down — than the system of mummification prevalent in my youth. Faint sensations of melancholy, however, began to possess me when I reflected that even if one of these intriguing creatures were given over to my charge, I shouldn't have the remotest idea how to handle it. I had been shut away from all that side of life for too many years.

I turned my eyes resolutely away from soldiers and babies and began to meditate.

150

There was no doubt about it. I had certainly missed a good many of the best things in life. And among them were the joys of free intercourse with other minds. How I regretted it!

Looking back even upon those few days at Shuffleborough, I was surprised at the richness of experience with which they had provided me.

I believe it is Strindberg who says that personalities do not develop out of themselves. Instead, they absorb something from each soul with which they come in contact, as a bee collects honey from a million flowers. I myself was astonished at the way in which my vitality had been increased and quickened by this contact with other minds since I had left the convent. Doors and windows had been flung open through which new and undreamed-of ideas rushed in and stimulated me.

In contemplative convents, this intercourse with other personalities is not encouraged. The idea is that you have come there to dwell alone with God: *solus ad solum*. If you have unnecessary dealings with other people, you will find that, sooner or later, human passions begin to show their horns. And that, of course, is death to contemplation.

Solitude of spirit being essential to union with God, it is safeguarded by the rule of silence.

Nuns who keep this rule faithfully find they hardly ever have an opportunity to exchange a word with one another except at evening recreation, when the conversation is "general". And even then, the "contacts" are extremely limited. For a nun may never change her place in the community; for better or worse, her life must be lived out between the two who made their Vows before and after her. In choir, in the refectory, at recreation, at all the community gatherings, she can never escape from them or they from her.

Besides the rule of silence, solitude of spirit is safeguarded by another, which — though unwritten — is rigorously instilled into the novices from the dawn of their religious life. This is the rule prohibiting what are known as "particular friendships". Against these, most spiritual writers — especially if they are French — are inclined to fulminate.

It is important to differentiate between "spiritual" and "particular" friendships. The first, rare as they are beneficent, run on the lines of those between St. Clare and St. Francis of Assisi, or St. Jeanne de Chantal and St. Francis de Sales. The others are when two nuns, possibly not quite as "fervent" as they might be, get together because they find in one another's company some solace for the extreme loneliness of religious life. This is definitely a slipping down from high perfection, and can become a great source of annoyance and irritation to the rest of the community.

French ecclesiastics use alarming adjectives in describing "particular friendships". Perhaps that is why some Superiors are so obsessed by the fear of such happenings in their communities that all conversations which are not "general" are so strongly discouraged as to be practically banned.

★　★　★

The result of all this is, of course, to throw one back more and more upon oneself. Everything that would normally be learnt from other people — new words, new ideas, new ways of looking at things — is ruled out. So that a large part of one's being never really develops. One remains rather like a child, with the same outlook and vocabulary as when one first "went in".

(5)

London was like an oven.

Moreover, a pall of gloom hung over everything, for Tobruk had just fallen and was on everybody's lips.

At Portland Place the aunt and uncle were most kind and sympathetic. I believe that the uncle had even made quite a little rumpus at the drawing-office on the subject of Mr. Hambledon. My other uncle, too, was indignant, and helped me to compose a letter to the firm, complaining of my treatment and demanding the refund of my expenses. No answer was vouchsafed. A second letter was ignored in like manner. After that (rather feebly, I'm afraid) I let things drop. Actually, I was assured that if I went to law — as I longed to do — it would probably run me in for a good deal more money than I was likely to get from Mr. Hambledon.

That evening I was rung up, to my great surprise, by a friend of my school-days called Gay. Though she declared, when I entered the convent, that she had no use for nuns, she still remembered me; and, having heard from a mutual friend about my exodus, asked me to come and have tea with her in a couple of days' time. I accepted with delight.

It now remained to find another war job as soon as possible. What should I attempt?

Unfortunately, I was now rather handicapped by my eyesight. Already at the drawing-office it had given me a good deal of trouble. Now I was told that it would be most unwise to attempt a job that involved any kind of eye-strain.

This was a blow. I hoped, however, that if I could manage some other kind of work till I recovered, I might go back later to the job for which I had been trained.

So, next morning I set out for the nearest Labour Exchange. It was crowded, and the heat was quite overwhelming. I waited for over forty minutes in a queue composed chiefly of foreigners and immense, steaming Jewesses. Here, when eventually I reached the counter, I was told that I had come to the wrong Exchange. The one that dealt with the district named on my identity card was, it appeared, a considerable distance away . . .

As I went out, my eye fell on a poster in the doorway, announcing that the Citizens' Advice Bureau in Baker Street was at the service of anybody who had a problem to be solved.

It was the first time I had heard of such a place, but I liked the sound of it. I was a Citizen; I needed Advice;

and it seemed that the State ran a Bureau expressly to provide it. To Baker Street, then, I would go.

Several worried-looking persons were waiting for their turns when I arrived, so I took my place on the last of a row of chairs. Presently, a dark, rather distinguished-looking woman beckoned me to one of the little tables. We sat down and she began to question me.

I should like to put on record that, although since my exodus I have been interviewed by literally dozens of persons in Ministries, Public Institutions, Labour Exchanges and various other branches of the C.A.B., not one of them dealt with me so efficiently as did the Dark Lady in the bureau at 128 Baker Street. Her name was Miss Dunn. It deserves to be remembered. If ever these pages should meet her eye, I can only hope that they may prove to her how much her tact, wisdom, and kindness were appreciated by at least one harassed citizen.

Miss Dunn was an education enthusiast. Her view was that no war job could be more important than that of training Youth to cope with the problems that peace would bring.

"If you *can* teach," she insisted, "you ought to. School-teachers are badly needed. You shouldn't have over-much difficulty in finding a post."

"But I'm so dreadfully tired of nothing but girls and women," I objected feebly.

Miss Dunn looked at me as though she had no use for anyone who could be tired of anything while the war was on.

She said, "I'll give you some addresses." This made me feel a little ashamed of myself. I said no more.

The well-known agency in Sackville Street to which Miss Dunn had directed me was one of the most devitalizing places I have ever been in. The hall and staircase were depressingly dark and stuffy, and by the time the two tight-lipped female clerks in the outer office had dealt with me, I felt as if my appearance and mentality must have become at least as bleak and desiccated as their own.

The interview which followed was extremely ageing. The elderly lady who conducted it was the perfect school-marm. I sat there, quaking inwardly, while she bombarded me with questions concerning my qualifications as an instructor of Youth.

To my surprise, she was rather encouraging. Quite a number of schools, it appeared, were in need of an English mistress. She gave me a list of addresses and a bundle of green forms (I eyed forms with suspicion since the *affaire* Hambledon), upon which my application must be made.

"And I hope," said this formidable person, extending a claw-like hand to signify that the interview was ended, "that you may be successful in securing a suitable post. *Good* morning!"

And, as I stumbled down the dark staircase into the heatwave that was transforming Regent Street into an inferno, I tried to hope so too.

During lunch, the telephone tinkled excitedly. My cousin Joyce had just received my letter, telling her about the Shuffleborough fiasco, and — with characteristic kindness — had been casting about to find me another job.

She now told me that all sorts of good things were apparently to be had for the asking, *chez* the Americans. They were still pouring into London in fantastic numbers. A large Red Cross Club had been opened near the branch of the War Office where she was working, and Young America could be observed from her office windows, washing behind its ears every morning from 10a.m. Most entertaining. Meanwhile, there was a certain Miss Mainwaring, "quite frrrrrightfully charming", who was rather a potentate at the U.S.A. Headquarters in Grosvenor Square. Joyce knew her. If I cared to ring up — mentioning Joyce's name — she was sure I should get an interview. And then — who knew that something marvellous might not be the result?

By now, I had quite ceased to feel shy about attacking unknown persons on the telephone. So I got on to Miss Mainwaring without more ado. Astonishingly, she suggested that I should "come round right away". Her tone was encouraging. I therefore set out immediately for Grosvenor Square.

As might have been expected, the U.S.A. Headquarters were large and luxurious. I felt slightly nervous of passing through the hall; such numbers of huge square-shouldered Yankee Apollos were standing about.

157

Their smartly-cut, two-coloured khaki uniforms looked odd to me, but they held themselves nobly and were obviously sons of a taller race than ours.

I walked twice round the hall in order to admire them. Some just stood around, looking important. Others swaggered about as if the earth were theirs. I had the impression that they were all terribly, terribly young and sure of themselves and were just longing to show old London the way things ought to be done.

Miss Mainwaring sat in her office like a very attractive spider in an extremely complicated web. She appeared to be much interested in my story. But, though she was charming to me, it soon became evident that the very last place in which I ought to seek employment was an institution run by Americans. They were, it appeared, the most inveterate hustlers in the universe. Unless you possessed to-morrow's knowledge about everything, had all the up-to-the-minute answers and a good hard-boiled outlook (whatever that might mean) on things in general, you simply hadn't a chance.

"With them, it's Get On or Get off, every time," she explained, eyeing me nevertheless very kindly. "And I very much doubt whether you'd be able to cope with the situations that would inevitably arise."

Several telephone calls came through while I was with her. Considerably awed, I observed the really breath-taking efficiency with which she solved each problem as it arose. After the fourth of these, during which she had straightened out an incomprehensible mix-up with a skill that would have done credit to a

158

Cabinet Minister, I knew that my doom was sealed. Never, in any capacity whatsoever, should I dare to attempt a job in a place where so much clear-headed *sang-froid* and sureness of touch was required.

Before I left, however, she suggested that I should call at a place called Sardinia Street and see a certain Miss Burby, who would — she felt sure — be able to help me in my search for the right kind of job.

More telephoning followed; after which Miss Mainwaring told me that an interview had been arranged for me at Sardinia Street the following day.

I threaded my way out among the Adonises in the vestibule. They were pleasant to look upon — large, hairy, deep-voiced, muscular, smelling of khaki, leather and tobacco . . . as great a contrast to the beings by whom I had always been surrounded as a herd of buffaloes to a flock of canaries in a cage.

For there really *are* points of similarity between hen-canaries and some enclosed religious. They are both so neat, so almost identical in appearance, so perfectly content to continue hopping about from perch to perch behind their bars. Sometimes, in the very early days of my religious life, I remember feeling almost smothered by the rarefied atmosphere of undiluted femininity. I used to long madly for a whiff of cigarette smoke, the hint of a pipe in the offing, the rough, male smell of tweed. I would sooner have died than reveal these shameful thoughts to my Novice Mistress. Instead, I turned my mind deliberately to other matters; with the result that, in course of time, the memory of such things died peacefully away.

The hen-canary, however, is far from being the model upon which the contemplative nun is intended to form herself. This I tried to make clear in the sometimes rather heated arguments which I've had at various times with friends who did not see eye to eye with me on the subject of nuns.

Usually we started off at a gallop with some man — it was usually a man who said this sort of thing — insisting that nuns were selfish because they refused to fulfil the function for which they had obviously been created by Providence. "Which, of course," I would retort, "is not the case. Religious life is not founded on a series of negations. A vow of chastity is a positive thing."

"Do explain yourself," they would ask, rather crossly.

So I would try to explain to them how this particular vow, far from being a backwater was in reality a channel.

I said: "The solemn promise to God by which you renounce human love, marriage, children, the satisfactions of the human heart, is only meant to clear the decks for action. Nuns and monks make that vow in order that their souls may be perfectly free."

"Free for what?" they would all ask, faintly irritated.

And I would reply, "Well, union with God, if you know what *that* means. Which you obviously don't, or you wouldn't talk in the way you do about people who are willing to pay the price demanded for it."

Then they would smile a little patronizingly, and say, "Oh, now she's off on mysticism. That's not playing the game."

160

"Why not get back to where we started," somebody would suggest, pacifically. "Wasn't it the question of why nuns are usually so hyperfeminine?"

"Only some of them are," I would insist. "The really generous ones, who've renounced self so completely that God takes the place of everything they've given up for him, aren't spinsterish and diminished at all. They're the world's greatest lovers. Look at St. Catherine of Siena and St. John of the Cross."

At this point, everyone usually started talking together, interrupting, contradicting and flatly disagreeing; so that, in the end, nobody was at all convinced by anybody else's argument.

The point, however, which through thick and thin I always stuck to was, that if nuns *did* become fussy and spinsterish and ultra-feminine, it was their own fault. The nearness to God, which invariably results when religious life is lived fully and generously, induces a width of outlook, a depth of character, an enrichment of the entire personality, which can be arrived at by no other means.

All the same, as I trudged back along Wigmore Street in the heat-wave, I determined that I would *not* apply for employment in a girls' school.

The glimpse of Young America in the vestibule at the Grosvenor Square Headquarters had put other ideas into my head.

161

(6)

At the Ministry of Labour and National Service in Sardinia Street — which was the address to which Miss Mainwaring had directed me — I was treated with the utmost kindness. Miss Burby — the wise and experienced interviewer who put me through my paces — declared, after careful consideration, that a post in a library was obviously the thing for me. The best war-work for people who had not much experience of the kind of jobs that most women of my age were doing, was that of filling-up the empty places left by the men and women who had been called up. Library staffs were among those which were the most depleted. Applications for under-librarians were constantly being received; so in all probability she would soon be able to send me particulars of just such a post, with a salary of, probably, about £250 a year.

And since I was so keen to make a war effort, why not take a temporary job while I was waiting? If I cared to try again for *crèche* work (I had thought of that, hadn't I, when I was in Shuffleborough?) there was an excellent opportunity at a place near the People's Palace in the Mile End Road . . . She would ring them up immediately, and prepare the ground for me. And in less than five minutes an interview — yes, another interview, believe it or not — had been arranged for me the following day.

Admirable Miss Burby. Had she, I wonder, any inkling of the acute inferiority complex with which I had come into her presence? Contact with all these experienced, highly efficient persons, each of whom had achieved a certain degree of eminence in her profession, was rapidly reducing me to a nervous wreck. Every interview left me a little more conscious of my freakishness and peculiarity; to camouflage it successfully was at times quite beyond my powers . . . Shall I ever forget the awful moment when one of my interviewers — exasperated, no doubt, by my non-committal answers — looked me coldly in the eye and said, "Well, Miss Baldwin, perhaps you could tell me something in life about which you *have* had a *little* experience?"

And now, here were all my heart-sinkings about girls' schools and exclusively feminine society swept away as by a miracle; an opulent future in congenial surroundings seemed assured to me.

I could have clasped Miss Burby to my heart.

I had never been up — or should one perhaps say down? — the Mile End Road before, and I can't say that I found the view I glimpsed through the bus windows particularly romantic. Many of the names above the shops were Jewish; and the further one went, the more dingy and squalid everything became.

I got off at the People's Palace. (It struck me that during the past twenty-eight years the People seemed to have come into their own in more ways than one.) There I looked about me, using my eyes and nose. In a way, it was almost more depressing than an out-and-out slum . . .

I will say no more of my adventures in the Mile End Road than that ten minutes' conversation with the alarmingly competent horn-rimmed lady who "saw" me (her brogue was of the kind that left deep stains behind it) caused me to walk gloomily back to the bus-stop, feeling that there must be something radically wrong with my technique.

(7)

I shall always remember the first time I had tea with my friends Gay and Barbara. It was my first "close-up" of two women of my own age and class, either of whose lives — had Providence arranged things otherwise — might easily have been my own.

They were sisters-in-law, and were running Gay's house in South Audley Street as a war-home for such of their relatives as might need one when on leave.

In the old days, when I'd stayed there as a girl, the door had always been answered by a butler. Now, Gay opened it herself. She wore a ravishing apron made of two bandanna handkerchiefs, and explained, as I followed her up the slightly blitz-scarred staircase, that she and Barbara did most of the work themselves, as servants were simply not to be had these days.

I hadn't seen Barbara since our school-days. Now she was lying back langorously upon what I supposed was the modern equivalent of a sofa. I noticed with interest that she wore a full-length garment of a pattern

164

that was new to me. Tactful questioning revealed the fact that it was known as a "housecoat". This information I filed carefully in the pigeon-hole of my Experience of Life, which I'd labelled "Clothes".

Gay said, "Barbara works in a canteen all night and sleeps all day. She only got up this afternoon because she wants to ask you intimate questions about nuns. Darling, do have some tea and tell us all about how you escaped!"

Then they began to talk. And while they did so, I studied them carefully.

They interested me extraordinarily, because, quite apart from their own personalities, which I found delightful, I saw in them both uncanny glimpses of Myself-as-I-Might-Have-Been.

Or — should I?

Supposing that my life had been run on lines similar to theirs, should I have evolved into that kind of type? For types they undoubtedly were.

I observed their sleek, exquisitely burnished hair, which suggested that both of them had only just stepped forth from the hands of a *coiffeur*. Their admirable clothes — sufficiently shabby to be patriotic, yet — one felt — so indubitably right. Their hands — work-roughened, but beautifully shaped and manicured. Their make-up — almost unnoticeable yet just sufficient to enhance the fading tones of middle-age. Above all, their amazing poise and self-possession. Here was something which not even the most adverse circumstances (one knew it instinctively) would ever destroy.

As for their actual conversation, it was to me almost like a foreign language. Unfamiliar *clichés*. Amusing — and sometimes rather startling — comparisons. Lots of slang — American and otherwise. And, in Barbara's case, much apt and occasionally irreverent quotations from the classics — mostly Shakespeare and Dr. Johnson. (This, it seemed, was an idiosyncrasy peculiar to her family.) On the whole, I think their most breath-taking effects were achieved by the curious choice of adjectives and adverbs. I sat spell-bound. It was like nothing I had ever listened to before.

Perhaps what startled me most was the constant recurrence of words which not even a man would have used before girls when I left school.

"Lousy", for instance, and "mucky"; "guts", "blasted", "bloody" and "what-the-hell".

Both of them were alarmingly competent. They seemed to have met everyone, read everything, been everywhere. And besides those endless social activities with which their pre-war years appeared to have been glutted, they had run houses, families (and heaven alone knew what that might not imply), knew how to drive, dance, ride, swim, fence, play tennis and hockey, ski, row, sail, cook, garden and make clothes. Gay played the piano; Barbara the saw. All this I gathered in an hour or so of casual conversation. Probably there

166

were no end of other things that they could do as well . . .

I began to feel dizzy and bemused, and said so. Like the Queen of Sheba before Solomon, I just felt there was no more spirit left in me.

They only laughed, however, and said cheerfully that they were quite ordinary people. Nearly everyone who had knocked about the world between the wars and who possessed a fairly go-ahead husband had learnt these things automatically as the years went by. One just sort of took them in one's stride.

I sat and stared at them. By now I was feeling completely sub-human. There really seemed nothing left for me to do except disintegrate. What chance could I ever hope for, anywhere, or at anything, if such standards as those of Gay and Barbara were looked upon as average?

After tea, they stuck long slim cigarette-holders into their beautifully lipsticked mouths and began talking about their husbands. (Gay's was a rather important scientist; Barbara's something weighty at the Admiralty.) To these they referred by faintly opprobrious nicknames, using tones that suggested affectionate mothers discussing the slightly absurd behaviour of small boys in the nursery.

Over their daughters, both ladies tended to sigh a little. But neither made any attempt to conceal the fact that upon their sons they doted unashamedly.

As for their grandchildren . . .

★   ★   ★

167

But at this point a thought darted suddenly into my mind which both startled and staggered me.

If I had married and had children, I, too, in all probability, should at that moment be a grandmother.

And yet, here I was, wandering round on the face of the earth with the outlook and mind of a pre-1914 school-girl. I, a Potential Grandparent.

It was fantastic.

How in the world was I to cope with the problem of Being My Age?

In some ways, the convent had certainly tended to keep one static with regard to mental development. Nothing, of course, could be more enviable than a truly child-like spirit; but I've seen more than one young nun in her early twenties relapse into a kind of second childhood after a couple of years or so in the Noviceship. It depends very largely upon whoever happens to be Novice Mistress. I remember one, who so inculcated this spirit of child-like simplicity that her novices continued to rejuvenate till their mental outlook was almost that of eight-year-olds.

Gay and Barbara were not specially helpful when I asked them for suggestions as to how I could most swiftly and successfully acquire the mentality of a Grandparent. They hooted with laughter. Gay assured me that only Experience of Life could help me. Barbara thought that twelve months more of trial and error might add perhaps a decade to my age. Gay said that, provided I went in for fairly riotous living, I might — by the time I was sixty — be somewhere about thirty-five.

Then Barbara said, "Look, shall I be quite *quite* frank with you?"

I said: "Please!"

So then, between slow puffs of cigarette smoke, she was very, very frank with me indeed.

She said that the impression I gave was not that of young-mindedness, but of a really appalling immaturity. Because I'd never used them to live with, whole chunks of my personality had become completely atrophied. She told me that I reminded her of a piano, half of whose keys had gone dumb for want of use. And I ought, absolutely, to do something about it. The best thing would be to start living as hard as I possibly could, with all the bits of myself which had hitherto been ignored. Only thus could I hope for the restoration of balance in my personality.

Gay said, "You ought to go to all sorts and kinds of places and meet crowds of different people. Especially men."

The idea of my teaching in a girls' school was turned down as being too absurd even for consideration.

"My God, what a notion!" said Barbara. "Why, the one thing you ought to avoid at all costs, for the rest of your life, is herds of women! Look here — why not come here and stay with us for a while?"

Unfortunately, this attractive idea was found at the moment to be impracticable, owing to an influx of family expected on leave that very evening. Later on,

169

however, they made me promise that I would hand myself over to the two of them for special treatment.

Gay thought that two months of their society, in which I should meet their friends and share their lives as much as possible, would do more to equip me with Experience of Life than any other plan which could at the moment be devised.

"Though of course, my sweet," said Barbara, as we finally parted on the doorstep, "what would really do you good would be six months on a battleship."

(8)

The next few days were depressing.

London was like an oven.

It made me long madly for the country. The scorched eternal pavements and imprisoning rows of houses were a nightmare. I craved for the feeling of grass beneath my feet, the smell of new-mown lawns, the song of birds in a garden after rain. I began to feel that unless I got away soon from the suffocating London atmosphere, I might start doing all sorts of peculiar things.

What was worse, Gay and Barbara had rather upset me.

They had so utterly destroyed me in my own opinion that I simply hadn't the face to apply anywhere for a job till I had acquired more of that essential yet curiously elusive commodity, Experience of Life.

★ ★ ★

It was difficult to decide what to do next. So, for a day or two, I sat and brooded, much oppressed by claustrophobia and the heat. Then, once more — this time in the form of a letter from Miki — Providence intervened.

I had known Miki as a fuzzy-haired scrap in her early teens. When I left the convent, she had sent me a delightful invitation to come north one day and see the home, husband and family with which she had provided herself in the interim. And now here was another letter, asking urgently for news of me and wondering how long it would be before we met again.

Here, obviously, was the solution of my difficulties.

To judge from her letters, Miki had grown up into a young woman of the most lively and up-to-date type. I felt sure she would be able to teach me all sorts of things I didn't know. In return, I felt that just possibly I might be of some use to her; for, like everyone else one heard of, she appeared to be struggling with shortage of staff in her efforts to run her home.

I wrote to her.

Her reply was instantaneous: a trunk call, followed by one of the warmest, most welcoming letters I've ever received.

Four days later, I shook the dust of London from my feet at Euston station and went roaring up to Scotland by the night express.

CHAPTER
SIX

(1)

Being war-time, there were no sleeping or restaurant cars on the train in which I travelled up to Stirling. So, for a matter of six hours or so, I had to sit bolt upright in my corner.

I felt as excited as a school-child about the adventure that lay before me. A journey to Samarkand or El Dorado could hardly have held more potential thrills.

As usual, I was passionately interested in my fellow-travellers: three huge Commandos, a red-haired sailor with a lovely girl-companion, and a husky-voiced young woman with a husband in Air Force blue, whose head, arm and leg were swathed in cotton-wool and bandages. Amongst their heaped hand-luggage they had a tame brown rabbit in a basket. Half-way through the journey they took it out and handed it leaves of limp-looking lettuce to nibble. It was an enchanting rabbit. When it lifted its split top lip to show long supercilious teeth, it looked like a disdainful elderly spinster. The wounded airman held it close in the crook of his unbandaged arm and appeared to derive much solace from its company.

★ ★ ★

That rabbit rather disturbed my peace of mind.

As children, my sister and I had kept every kind of pet: dogs, cats, pigeons, owls, canaries, bantams, rabbits, guinea pigs, silkworms, pet lambs, white mice, goats, hedgehogs, donkeys, and a distinguished family of tortoises.

We had adored them all. And in the convent I had missed them desperately. Now, watching the rabbit, I felt the old animal-longing beginning to creep over me. It was nearly thirty years since I'd possessed a beast of my own. Probably I shouldn't be able to have one till the war was over. But the moment that Cottage-in-the-Clouds materialized . . .

Before all things, I felt that I required a cat.

Exquisite, runcible creatures, detached, aloof, entirely uncoercible — their strange, secret lives quite impenetrable by any human personality — how I longed for one. The cat in my Vision had been a Siamese — ivory and sepia colour, with huge, pale, sapphire eyes and a slim, kinked tail. I took a long look into the future and saw the lovely, decorative creature frisking alluringly among my rose-bushes . . .

This, naturally, led to dreams about my garden, till, presently, I fell asleep.

I was awakened by an alarming sensation of nausea.

Obviously, a certain quantity of oxygen must have been shut in with us several hours before, when the guard had gone round at black-out time to see that windows and doors were hermetically sealed.

Since then, however, eight persons and a rabbit had been breathing it more or less energetically in and out of their lungs.

It now appeared to have reached exhaustion point.

Another two minutes — and, unless something drastic could be done about it, I knew that I should faint.

Now, absurd as it will surely sound to persons who from their cradles have been accustomed to deal with the things, I must here confess that one of the minor nightmares of my post-conventual life has been connected with windows and doors. When, for instance, I try to enter a bank or a post office, my unpractised instinct invariably guides me to pull when it ought to be push. Or *vice versa*. And it is the same with windows. Whenever, in car or taxi, I turn a handle to lower the window, the door flies open. As for buses and railway carriages, no matter how perseveringly I turn, twist, pull, push or press the gadget intended to control their windows, I have never yet encountered one upon which my efforts produced the slightest effect. And I find it humiliating.

This occasion was the solitary exception. Perhaps the saints of Paradise, whom I so desperately invoked as I fumbled with the blind, had something to do with it. Anyhow, the window suddenly yielded to treatment and, lowering itself obligingly a couple of inches, admitted a shaft of cold night air which cut into the fetid atmosphere like a blade. I inserted my nose into the space between blind and window, and drew a long, life-giving breath. By the mercy of Heaven, I was saved.

174

It is a curious thing, but, as I look back on it to-day, I believe that this trivial incident did almost more to impress me with the sense of my new and bewildering freedom than anything else had so far done.

I had actually dared to open a window, in a place containing several other people, and the universe had NOT rocked to its foundations and then come toppling down about my ears.

It seemed almost too wonderful to be believed.

The reason, of course, is that in convents, windows are such a subject of contention that it is practically impossible to touch one without getting your fingers burned.

Two parties exist in every religious community: the Fresh Air Fiends, who want the windows open, and the Fug Fiends, who want them shut. The odd thing is that, though the first are nearly always in the majority, it is the second who get their way.

It puzzled me when I came up from the Noviceship to the community. Why, since the lovers of fresh air were so numerous, didn't one of them just rise up and fling the windows wide?

The answer is that, in convents, things simply don't happen that way.

I remember one of the older nuns explaining this to me after I had suggested that certain measures should be taken in connexion with window-opening. They were excellent measures, inspired by the most elementary rules of hygiene. And I was much surprised by the lack of enthusiasm with which they were always met. It was then that a certain nun, wise, elderly, and enormously kind-hearted, threw up her eyes to heaven at the crude inexperience revealed by my remarks, and said to me:

"*Ah, mon enfant, croyez-moi:* if it were 'umanlee posseeble for those windows to be flung orpen, flung orpen they would be. *Mais — ça ne vaut pas la peine.*"

I did not believe her. I experimented with the windows. And — I regretted it.

For, unfortunately, even in convents, one sometimes finds people who will stop at nothing — absolutely *nothing* — to get their own way.

Most people appear to think that by the very fact of entering a convent, one ought at once to be transformed, automatically, into a saint. The idea of a nun committing even the smallest imperfection profoundly shocks them.

This is unreasonable. Nuns and monks — although examples of extraordinary holiness are sometimes found among them quite early in their religious life — would be the first to tell you that they are, generally speaking, a considerable distance from sanctity. They have — and carry with them into the convent — human faults and weaknesses, just like the rest of mankind. Many of those can only be corrected after long years of self-discipline and prayer.

Moreover, it sometimes happens that, *after* the period of trial known as the noviceship is passed, a nun will develop some *idée fixe* or eccentricity of character. When this happens, the nun in question can become a positive menace to the community.

In such a case, two courses of action are open to the Superior. The first is to enforce conformity to the accepted standard of life by commanding it "under Holy Obedience", warning the nun that a refusal to obey will result in expulsion from the community. This method, though drastic, has the advantage of ridding the convent of undesirable members. Of its disadvantages nothing need here be said. They are, I think, too obvious to need cataloguing.

The second course of action is entirely "supernatural". Should the Superior decide upon it, the community must just resign themselves to shoulder the cross which Divine Providence has laid upon them, and simply envisage the "difficult member" as a means of acquiring merit.

I once heard a distinguished Jesuit preach a sermon upon how to use disagreeable persons in the community as a means of acquiring an ever-increasing degree of sanctifying grace.

The old nun from whom I have quoted before had — in her long years of community life — made the most of many opportunities. A window-shutting fixation on the part of a certain "difficult member" had deprived her for years of the fresh air that she not only loved, but which was essential to her health. It also, now and again, made virtue arduous among the weaker members of the community.

One day the old nun said to me:

"Ah, *chère petite*, you do not onnerstan'." (It was true; I did not. Perhaps I never shall.) "You t'ink *cette personne-là* is a gret orbstacle to *la perfection de la communauté*. An' eet ees not so. She ees a cross, yes — *mais*, what is a cross? *C'est une petite gâterie de Notre-Seigneur*."

As for "*cette personne-là*", she insisted that, far from thinking her the curse of the community, she had come to look upon her as its greatest asset. For — *voyez-vous* — did she not provide her religious sisters with almost hourly opportunities of practising virtue, with the excellent result that most of them were rapidly attaining to a standard of holiness which they might never otherwise have reached? *Enfin*, if *le bon Dieu* had not presented such a person to the community, it would be their duty — *mais oui*, absolutely their duty! — to "go out into the 'ighwez an' 'edges an' *chercher, chercher, CHERCHER*, onteel won wass found!"

All of which only goes to show that, in convents, your success or failure in the matter of acquiring virtue depends entirely upon your point of view.

(3)

I reached Stirling at daybreak.

Having been told to change there, I climbed out, dragged my two suitcases from the van (the solitary

178

porter was too busy to attend to me) and sat down on a bench to wait for the next train.

The bench was hard and the air extremely chilly. I had an hour before me. To pass the time, I began to say by heart the Office of Prime.

> Jam lucis orto sidere
> Deum precemur supplices . . .

The sun had just risen. The sky, drained hitherto of every vestige of colour, was dappled with little pink and golden clouds. It made one think of the floor of heaven, as painted by Fra Angelico. And, far below, on the shadowy earth, where the world still appeared to be sleeping, the walls and roofs of Stirling clung huddled together against the steep sides of the hill.

Oddly enough, however, it was neither the flaming sky nor the dim grey city that seized upon my imagination, dragging it forcibly away from the words of the morning hymn upon which I'd only just started. It was the abyss that yawned between.

That abyss had already begun to bother me when, as a child at school, I had been given the *Letters of St. Catherine of Siena* to read. She saw it as the abyss of infinity between God and his creation. To her, Christ was always the *Pontifex* — the "Bridge-maker" — between the Creator and the creature who had become separated from him by sin. Thinking on these things (when I ought, I suppose, to have been studying arithmetic and *grammaire française*), it always seemed to me that there could never be too many of those who

179

made it the business of their lives to bridge that gulf by prayer. That, I believe, was largely why, when I entered a convent, I chose an Order the *raison d'être* of whose members was to "stand in the breach" and play the part of "bridge-makers" between God and man.

For this is the work of those whom the Church officially dedicates to the recitation of the Divine Office in choir.

Among the various questions which are so often hurled at me in connexion with convents, one of those which most constantly recurs is, "What really *is* this thing you call the Divine Office?"

Well, this seems as good a place as any other in which to try to answer that question. It is not easy, since it involves the statement of one or two Catholic dogmas. And this bores — or alarms — a certain type of person. To ignore the basic idea, however, is to miss the point.

Catholics believe that God, being what he is — infinite and completely "other" from all else in existence — created man *principally* in order to be adored by him. The other purposes of man's life are only secondary. The right order is: God first, man next.

Here, a difficulty arises.

The abyss which, since the Fall of man, yawns between creature and Creator, is infinite. How then can man's "nothingness" formulate an act of worship which is in any sense worthy of God who is All?

The answer, of course, is that it can't.

180

So — we find ourselves up against an apparently insoluble problem. God, when he created man, knew — obviously — that this "nothingness" of the creature would make his adoration of the Infinite entirely valueless. Why, then, did God create him?

Catholic theology replies that, when God made the world, he foresaw the Incarnation. He, the Infinite, would join himself to that which he had made, thus endowing it with a value which, like himself, would be divine. In this way — since the value of a divine action is infinite — the worship offered by those who are truly incorporated with God-made-Man would acquire the value of him into whose Mystical Body they would thus be drawn.

Which is exactly what happens in the Holy Sacrifice of the Mass. Christ, in the Mass, as on the Cross, becomes "That with which we can at last incorporate ourselves and thus regain our true existence — that of Sons of God".[1]

He lifts up the hearts and souls of those who assist at Mass and holds them within the white-hot circle of his own divine and infinitely holy Heart. Thus the adoration of Christ and his Christians mount up *together* to the Father, and the creature's worship — valueless in itself — is transformed and 'en-Christ-ed' by that ineffable union and embrace.

Now, the Catholic Church — being Christ-on-Earth and, therefore, speaking with divine authority — has

---

[1] See *The Faith of the Catholic Church*, pp. 115–16, by C. C. Martindale, S.J.

drawn up a public, official worship of God, called the Liturgy,[1] which is more important and more powerful than anyone's private prayer. This is because, being the Church's official prayer, it has an absolute value, independent of the person who prays.

A Catholic who uses liturgical prayer — provided always that he is in a state of grace — prays *officially*, as a member of the Mystical Body of Christ. Through this membership, he can offer to God *a worship adequate to the Infinite*. He can adore God *divinely*, through, with, and in, Jesus Christ.

The Divine Office is that part of the Liturgy contained in the Breviary. Originally, it appears to have actually formed a part of the Mass. The early Christians, meeting secretly at nightfall in the shadowy catacombs for the *synaxis* or Breaking of Bread, prefaced the ceremony by psalms, litanies, invocations, canticles, readings, homilies and hymns. Then, gradually, as time went on, these elements evolved slowly into the Night Office of Matins and Lauds. The Little Hours of the day,[2] Prime, Terce, Sext, None, Vespers and Compline, were added later.

The Mass is the heart of the Liturgy. The Office is a radiation from this divine centre, a kind of *cortège* which should never be separated in thought from the

---

[1] "Liturgical Prayer" is that found in the Missal, Breviary, Ritual, Pontifical and Diurnal.

[2] These, besides being in the Breviary, are also found in a smaller book called a Diurnal or *Horae Diurnae*.

182

Holy Sacrifice, whence it derives all its meaning and value.

I have written rather a lot about this — the theological — aspect of the Divine Office, because, unless one grasps it, it is difficult to understand how monks and nuns can feel justified in looking upon it as the object of their lives. The Church sets so much store upon it that all her priests are bound — under pain of mortal sin — to the daily recitation of the Divine Office. And large numbers of religious orders of both men and women, have — as the official reason for their existence — the solemn recitation in choir of this, the *Opus Dei*.

(4)

Looking back, I am not sure that being trained for the service of the choir wasn't one of the most terrifying experiences of my early religious life.

I was so overwhelmed by the atmosphere of solemnity and decorum which pervaded the building that, for the first few months, I hardly ever dared to raise my eyes. This may sound incredible, but it is none the less a fact.

The Mistress of Novices began by explaining the construction and inner spirit of the Divine Office.

Matins, we were taught, was the Great Night Office of the Church. Its three nocturns were like a three-act drama in honour of the feast which was being celebrated. It was our privilege to recite it at an hour when God was almost forgotten by a world chiefly absorbed in pleasure, sin or sleep — at least in this half of the globe. As for the little devil of fatigue who creeps about in every choir when the inmates are more or less exhausted by a day of fasting or heavy labour, novices who listened to him would certainly incur heavy responsibilities. For the souls of sinners, or those struggling against temptation, would thus be deprived of the grace which faithful prayer would otherwise have obtained for them. Therefore — no matter whether your back ached, your voice failed, or your heavy eyelids dropped with weariness — into that great symphony of praise, thanksgiving and supplication must your whole energy be poured. Only thus could you be certain that your part in it was at least as worthy of God as your human powers could make it.

Lauds — the exquisite Office of daybreak — followed immediately on Matins. Its hymns and antiphons were full of symbolism. The rising sun was hailed as the figure of Christ triumphant and glorified. The whole Office was ablaze with the light and splendour of dawn. Now and again one felt an almost ecstatic note in the psalms which the Church had chosen: they were songs of such pure praise as might well have been uttered by lips already half in heaven.

Prime was longer than Lauds and more prosaic. It was the Church's morning prayer and asked for special blessings on the work of the day. The Martyrology was read; the "senses, words and actions" of those present were commended to God; the dead were prayed for. And in the hymn, *The star of morn to night succeeds*

(*Jam lucis orto sidere*), as well as in that ancient and beautiful responsory which asks that "the Splendour of the Lord Our God may be upon us", the "light motif" appears again. In the convent, Prime was usually said at half-past five in the morning. I remember being taught to recite it as a morning prayer for those who forget to pray.

In the early days of the Church, *Terce* was at nine o'clock. This was the "third hour" of the Romans, when the Holy Spirit descended upon the Apostles at Pentecost. In the convent, it followed immediately after Prime. This "Hour" is in a special manner consecrated to the Holy Spirit, "Who," says St. Augustine, "when He has been given to man, sets him ablaze with the love of God and of his neighbour and is Himself Love".[1]

Sext (formerly at the "sixth hour" of the Romans, but now usually recited at 11.30 a.m.) was somehow exactly right for that prosaic hour. In the ancient hymn with which it opens, the notion of *heat* predominates rather curiously. God, evoked as the Author of the morning's splendour and the fiery midday heat, is implored to "quench the flames of strife" and to cool that *calorem noxium* which might imperil peace of soul or body's health. Such a prayer might well have risen from the lips of the early monks as they gasped to God from the furnace of their desert monasteries. It would almost seem — if one may judge from hints such as those in the liturgy — that the midday devil —

[1] St. Augustine, *De Trinitate*, Book xv, ch. xvii, para. 31.

daemonio meridiano — prowled during the lunch-hour then, even as he does to day.

Though *None* often followed immediately after Sext, it should, strictly speaking, have been said at the "ninth hour", i.e. at three o'clock in the afternoon. This was the hour of Christ's death on the cross, which None is intended to commemorate. The hymn asks for the grace of a "good death" — *sed praemium mortis sacrae perennis instet gloria.* In both chapters and responsories the Passion-motif is emphasized.

Vespers was the evening service of the Church, just as Lauds was her daybreak prayer. And whether or no you were liturgically minded, there was no denying the beauty of this, the most solemn as well as the most popular of the Day Hours. In the fourth century, Vespers was celebrated at nightfall by the light of lamps and candles. The Novice Mistress taught us to see in the clouds of fragrant incense a symbol of the prayer then rising from our hearts to God. The lights on the altar were a figure of Christ, the True Light; a memorial, too, of the *sacrificium vespertinum* of the Jewish Temple in ancient days. On High Feasts, the singing was accompanied by the organ and the *Magnificat* was chanted — with immense solemnity — in parts. The plain-chant settings of the antiphons and hymns were often of extraordinary beauty.

Somehow or other, in spite of its importance, Vespers never really appealed to me. I always felt that something about it seemed vaguely "wrong". I think this was because its poetry and symbolism are inspired by, and belong so essentially to, the approach of

186

nightfall. It harmonizes quite exquisitely with the faintly romantic, exalted soul-mood of that hour. It would be difficult to enjoy, let us say, a *bal masqué* at eleven o'clock in the morning. To me, Vespers was robbed of half its loveliness and meaning by being celebrated at the appalling hour of half-past three in the afternoon.

The name *Compline* is derived from the Latin *completorium*, because this Office completes and closes the Little Hours of the day. It is brief, simple, intimate — a perfect form of night prayers, a preparation for death no less than for the hours of sleep, closing as it does on a note of loving submission, lit with hope: *In manus tuas, Domine, commendo spiritum meum. Redemisti nos, Domine, Deus veritatis.*

Initiation into the mysteries of the service of the choir usually began with the alarming ordeal of what was known as the "Little Week". As soon as a postulant had learned to walk and sit and stand "religiously", to "make her bows" with arms crossed and the palms of the hands pressed flat against the knees, to recite the monotone and "take the note" from the chantress, she would be led to the choir and taught by the Mistress of Novices how to conduct herself during the next seven days.

She learnt how to ring the bell in the middle of the choir at the *Sanctus* and at the Elevation at the various Masses — which was considerably more complicated than it sounds. Both bell and rope were so heavy that one could easily have been swung off one's feet into the stratosphere above the stalls. And I shall always remember the day when a too-energetic novice dragged the bell-rope from its moorings overhead and sent it whirling and crashing down the whole length of the choir like a gigantic rock-python with a dozen or so of enormous lessonary-books and antiphonarians in its wake.

Another of the "Little Week" duties was to "join" in the middle of the choir with one's opposite number, and there — after performing the prescribed bows and genuflections — to sing or say certain versicles, a good many of which had very peculiar tunes. There were antiphons to be given out, bells tolled, candles lighted and extinguished and — most alarming of all — the Martyrology to be read at Prime.

This duty — owing to the complicated system of announcing the date, and the outlandish and unpronounceable names of so many holy persons therein catalogued — was an ordeal much dreaded by the novices. Were you careless — or unfortunate — enough to stumble, a sharp "Ahem!" from the Mistress' stall would proclaim the fact to the rest of the community. Were you sharp enough, you might still succeed in righting yourself. Often, however, fright paralysed you, and an appalling silence filled the choir. Then, rising slowly from her stall, the Mistress of Novices, book in hand, would advance like a white wraith and point out to you in a terrifying whisper where you had erred . . .

After that, public penance had to be performed in the middle of the choir, and again — probably — during dinner in the refectory.

After a time — a very long time in some cases — one grew accustomed to the keeping of one's "Little Week". Usually, the acute nervousness which often paralysed one's early efforts, arose from the consciousness that each time one performed a "duty", one was examined by the critical eyes of the entire community. And every novice was aware that the least negligence or forgetfulness on her part (and heaven knows there was much to be remembered) would go against her when the day came for the great decision as to whether or no she should be permitted to make her Vows.

The "Great Week" was even more complicated. One had to lead the choir by beginning each part of the Office with the *Deus in adjutorium meum intende*, uttered on the exact note given by the chantress. There were prayers to be recited, blessings given, Grace conducted in the refectory — in fact, the "hebdomadarian" (such was the official title of the "Great Week" keeper in the *Ceremonial*) was continually in evidence. To a nun who was easily distracted, or who had a noticeable difficulty with Latin, it could be a torment both to herself and to the community. The only time I remember this happening, however, was the occasion of so many acts of humility on the part of the one and such forbearance on the other, that it could only have resulted in the general benefit of all concerned.

Usually, the keeping of one's "Great Week" was looked upon as what this generation would call the "high spot" of one's religious life. Nuns would count the weeks eagerly until their turn as "hebdomadarian" came round again. Indeed, it was a solemn and sometimes an almost rapturous experience to stand in one's stall in the official capacity of mediator, offering to God the needs of the people, drawing down upon the people the grace of God. Surely, this was as near approximation to the priestly office as it was possible for nuns to achieve.

(5)

Oddly enough, I find very little to say about the months I spent in Argyll. I think it must be because my impressions of the *place* were so tremendous, that the *people*, somehow or other, were crowded out. Anyhow, when I look back on my visit to Duror of Appin, I see Miki, her two small sons, and the Laird, her husband, rather as though they were ghosts . . . What really stands out, sharp and clear as though I had only left there yesterday, is the astounding beauty of the place.

Now, there can be no doubt that Scotland — if you happen to be that kind of person — does something to you. But I find that "something" quite impossible to translate into words. All I know is that this *je ne sais quoi* which it possesses gives it the same relationship to other places as poetry bears to prose. Mendelssohn, foreigner though he was, sensed this and tried — not unsuccessfully, I think — to express something of it in his *Hebrides* Overture.

★   ★   ★

From the first moment when I set foot in Duror of Appin (Cuil Bay, where my friends lived, lies on the eastern coast of Loch Linnhe), I was as one in a dream. Enchantment held me. I was bound so fast with beauty that I could not escape. Never had I dreamed of such forms of cloud and skyline; such colour; such effects of light and shadow; such wine-strong, salt-sweet air. In vain did Miki — most accomplished of housewives — endeavour to form me to domesticity. Together we mended socks, wound wool, weeded the strawberry bed, bathed babies, baked bannocks, boiled haggises and stirred saucepans of marmalade and jam. I listened to all she had to tell me about subjects upon which she was something of an authority: cakes, crooners and food-values; film-stars, husbands and the management of the home. Attentively, I lent ear to a vast amount of detailed information, obstetric and otherwise, of which I had hitherto been ignorant. But it was all to no purpose. Try as I would, I could not shake off the spell which had been cast over me. Nothing — absolutely *nothing* — seemed to *matter*, except the thrilling loveliness that pressed upon me from every side.

Sometimes it was the scarred hillsides with their dark, haunted-looking woods and Tyrian embroideries of ling and heather. Or the moors that ran down to the loch edge, slashed and laced with grey and indigo or embossed with emerald and red. Or the massive summits of Ben Cruachan, stained with sunset hues of copper-rose and dusky violet. Or Ben Vair's three savage peaks, brooding eternally behind thin wrappings of white mist. Or the Shuna Isle, dim and lustrous as an opal, floating on the rippled quicksilver of Loch Linnhe. Or, perhaps, the clouds lifting suddenly to show sharp rain falling like long pointed spears of silver on the unearthly, desolate beauty of the lonely cones of Glencoe.

I drank it all in, like strong wine. And it intoxicated me, with the result, I'm afraid, that I was not an altogether satisfactory kind of guest.

There are just a few details which I shall allow myself the luxury of recording.

One is, that if you take the path from Achadh nan Sgiath (the grey-roofed house where Miki and her husband lived) into Duror of Appin at eight o'clock on a summer morning, you will see much that it is not easy to forget.

The thick white mist that rises inch by inch from the sides of Lismore and the hills across the water. The sea, delphinium blue, with strips of indigo. Huge black-cap gulls swooping on mighty wings above lace-edged waves that break delicately on the firm biscuit-coloured shore.

Bracken, up to your eye-level, sparkling with dew and giving forth the subtle earthy odour that wakens so many subconscious memories. Foxgloves, shoulder-high, with their furry clover-coloured bells. A blaze of broom-bushes, fragrant yellow fire against the dark background of their slender foliage. Ox-eye daisies, tall and luxuriant enough to glorify a garden. Wild rose trees, bending beneath the burden of their own pale loveliness, petalled with snow and carmine, gold-anthered, with blood-red thorns.

After Duror, Ardsheal. And, presently, the road by the sea, with Ben Vair, Creag Ghorm, and Sgurr Dhonuill (their very names are like an incantation) looming on the right. To the left, Loch Leven, a sheet of shimmering sapphire washed with gold.

Ballachulish, outpost of Glencoe, with its rushing burn and the little fishermen's church clinging limpet-wise to the steep hillside; and at last, the Glen of Weeping, dark, haunted, and sunk for ever in the deepest melancholy.

Above the loch, gaunt, cone-shaped peaks rise starkly from the water. Their steep sides, gashed with precipices, frown over gloomy tarns unlightened by the sun. Over them broods an eternal solitude. In their more desolate moods, the grim crags have almost the lonely horror of the mountains of the moon.

(6)

During the three months which I spent at Duror, the thought of my Cottage-in-the-Clouds was seldom absent from my mind.

On the Laird's estate were a wooden bungalow and a tiny shepherd's cottage. Miki assured me that either of these would be the very thing for me. I used to gaze upon them reflectively from the boat as we towed back driftwood for the fires from a neighbouring bay. It seemed to me that I could have been extremely happy in either. And yet, recalling the house which had been shown to me in the Vision, I knew that something about them was not exactly right.

193

What was more, the war showed not the slightest sign of abating. And I felt that I couldn't, in conscience, settle down till I had tried, however ineffectually, to Do My Bit.

Now and again a thrill reached me from Sardinia Street in the guise of a neat little honey-coloured form which told me of various librarianships available to persons possessing the qualifications necessary for such a job.

There were Club Libraries, Reference Libraries, Medical Libraries, Engineering Libraries, even Film Libraries. Unfortunately, in every case the snag was identical. It was always emphatically stated that previous experience was a *sine qua non*. Twice, wondering whether I might not be able to bluff my way to success, I took my courage in both hands and sent in an application. In each case I was informed that the post had just been filled.

After eight weeks or so of this kind of thing, I decided that as what I required did not appear to be forthcoming from Sardinia Street, I had better try to find a job for myself.

I therefore began once more to study the *Situations Vacant* columns of the *Daily Telegraph*.

And then, one day, suddenly, I found what I wanted.

It was an advertisement for an assistant matron at a hostel for munition workers in the North of England. And I answered it because it expressly stated that no previous experience was necessary.

* ★ ★

After that, all sorts of things began to happen with the utmost possible rapidity.

There were letters; then telegrams; finally, a couple of long-distance calls. And — before the week was out — I found myself, always accompanied by my small stock of worldly possessions packed tightly into the two faithful suitcases, steaming slowly out of Duror station. Miki and her family stood on the platform, waving me a long farewell.

CHAPTER
SEVEN

(1)

The journey south was rather an ageing experience.

Most people, of course, would have accepted it simply as just one more brief series of war-time unpleasantnesses. To me, however, unused to any kind of travelling, ignorant of how to deal with even the most elementary problems and never before having put my nose outside in the black-out, it had a nightmarish quality which I shall not easily forget.

It was, however, educative. On emerging, I felt that my Experience of Life had been considerably enlarged.

I spent the first half-hour meditating upon what I had learnt from my stay at Duror.

From Miki I had certainly picked up an abundance of miscellaneous information. But there was more to it than that. The whole thing had been a deep and wonderful spiritual experience. There was something about those glens and lochs that simply forced one down on to the knees of one's soul.

More than fifteen hundred years ago, St. Augustine cried to God in his *Confessions*, "Our soul rises up to Thee, helped upwards by the things that Thou hast made . . . passing beyond them unto Thee who hast wonderfully made them".

Well, that was how I felt about it. The beauty upon which I had looked had done something to me. As a result, I longed for solitude. I wanted to surrender myself to the *mouvement d'âame* induced by the vision of so much loveliness.

These pious reflections were interrupted by the train's arrival at Connel Ferry. During this — the first of the many changes which were to enliven my journey — I realized just what a fool I'd been to agree to my employer's suggestion that I should travel by night.

For it was by now quite dark. And there was not a porter to be seen. So that I had to forage for myself in the luggage van and drag my heavy suitcases as best I could across the pitch-dark platform to the waiting train on the other side. Remembering the throngs of obsequious persons in bottle-green corduroy who, in my childhood, used to struggle with one another for the privilege of attending to one's luggage, I reflected mournfully how very much the world had changed.

I feel a little ashamed of the part I played in the next episode of that frightful journey. It taught me, however, an important lesson. This was that the world to-day consists of two classes of people: the Pushers and the Pushed. That is to say, when other people get in your way, if you yourself don't do the pushing, you'll soon find out that they will not hesitate to elbow you out of theirs.

I discovered this in Glasgow.

Here, after much to-ing and fro-ing in the abysmal darkness of the blackout, I found myself at the far end of a taxi queue. I wanted to get across to the Central Station. The queue was long, the rain enthusiastic. To distract my thoughts from the chilly sense of desolation which was beginning to assail me, I examined, by the dim light of a street-lamp, the behaviour of my fellow-strugglers in the queue.

I noticed especially a fat man who seemed to be making his way along with astonishing rapidity. His tactics were simple. Whenever a taxi approached, he simply shoved whoever happened to be in front of him into the gutter and took their place. He was a large man and the tired-looking women who were his victims seemed too weary to retaliate. Very soon, heavy breathing behind me proclaimed that he was close on my heels.

Another taxi drew up at the kerb. The queue heaved. For the first time I experienced what war-time pushing could really mean. The fat man squared his shoulders, gave a mighty shove that knocked my torch out of my hand and sent me and my suitcases flying after it into the gutter. By the time I had collected myself and my belongings (the torch had vanished for ever into the darkness) the taxi had driven away. The fat man stood, triumphant, at the head of the queue.

I took stock of the situation.

I had, I reflected, missed that taxi simply because twenty-eight years of intensive training in charity, courtesy and humility had caused me to stand back instinctively when other people manifested an urgent desire to get past. For a crowd in a convent consists, with very few exceptions, of people who are more concerned that others shall have the first places than themselves. One is taught from the outset that community life would be impossible unless the intercourse of life with life were safeguarded by some definite code. Hence the courtesy towards one another which forms so important a feature of religious life. *"Honour in one another God, whose living temples you are made,"* wrote St. Augustine to the nuns of his sister's community in fourth-century Africa. And superiors were never tired of inculcating the same idea. A deep spirit of "reverence towards the God-indwelt souls around one" was instilled in the Noviceship as a preventive against rudeness, selfishness, or even familiarity. A dizzy ideal; but definitely realizable by those whose lives are governed by standards of faith.

(2)

The question now, however, seemed to be, what, with another taxi approaching and the fat man just in front of me, I was going to do.

I lifted the heavier of my suitcases. Then, with such strength as I could muster, I bashed it as hard as I could against the bend behind the fat man's knees.

He curtsied profoundly. Before he could get his balance, I elbowed past him and, hurling my luggage into the taxi, fell headlong into the only vacant seat. A moment later we had left the station far behind.

Not a very edifying incident, you will say, considering the way I had been brought up. I couldn't agree more.

But then, I simply *had* to catch that train.

199

(3)

The last incident in this educative journey had Wigan for its setting.

I arrived there in the dark and small hours of the morning. My sense of humour was quiescent: my vitality extremely low. Moreover, I was so tired and sleepy that when a porter with a face like something in a horror tale by Edgar Allen Poe informed me that I must cross Wigan to another station, I nearly lifted up my voice and howled.

There was no transport. The porter advised me to "park" my baggage with an organization called "Luggage in Advance". It might, he told me, just possibly be delivered within a week or two; provided always that it didn't get bombed; which was, it seemed, as things were at the moment, almost too much to hope. The terms "parking" and "Luggage in Advance" were unfamiliar to me, but I implored the porter to do what he considered best.

I then set out, torchless and with no umbrella, into the cold and dripping fog.

To linger in Wigan is the very last thing I desire to do. My remembrance of it is too unpleasant. What befell me there shall in consequence be briefly told.

It was about as dark and foggy a night as you could wish for. For a while I floundered about, stumbling in and out of gutters and trying, unsuccessfully, to follow the porter's directions. The station, however, appeared

200

to have temporarily withdrawn itself from the map. At last, despairingly, I began to retrace my steps.

It was then that I realized that I had lost my way.

Now, ordinarily speaking, darkness and solitude do not alarm me. I don't think I'm psychic, though I still hope to see a ghost before I die. So it was all the more curious that for no reason that I could think of, I suddenly became aware that I had got The Creeps. A nightmare certainty took hold of me that in the surrounding darkness some evil Thing was lurking, soaking the night with horror as a dreadful odour saturates the air.

I stood still. My knees felt wobbly with terror. I went cold and my heart thumped so hard that I began to feel slightly sick.

All round I could hear the clippety-clop of clogs as they clattered past me. Factory-workers, I supposed, on their way to the early morning shift. But their neighbour-hood gave me no feeling of security. A rather frightening sense of isolation had come over me. Had an uninhabited continent separated us, I couldn't have felt more alone. And all the time the horror grew and grew.

I must here warn anyone who hopes for thrills that they will be disappointed. Because nothing happened. I simply stood there, petrified, sweating with terror, unable to move. For I knew, beyond all possibility of doubting, that this Thing, formless, horrible, malignant, was closing in on me. Somehow or other, I had got to get away.

Possibly, if I'd held on a little longer, quite an interesting contribution might have been made to the psychic literature of to-day.

But I didn't.

A moment came when I felt I couldn't endure it any longer. I was long past reasoning. I just yielded to instinct, and, when at last another pair of clogs came clattering past me in the darkness, I reached out with a mighty effort and clutched frantically at the invisible passer-by.

There was — not unnaturally — a screech. A torch flashed. An instant later, an outraged factory-hand and I were glaring into one another's eyes.

The preternatural withdrew.

With that, I'm afraid, all interest vanishes from the story. The woman at whom I'd grabbed turned out to be as kind as she was bulky — which was saying a lot. When I'd explained and apologized for my behaviour, she insisted on coming all the way to the station with me herself. For her sake I shall always feel tenderly towards the Lancastrians.

"Eee, luv," she said, "I've been lost in t'fog meself before t'night."

Well, you may, if you like, explain it by saying that my fears were due to imagination. But I don't believe anybody could have reached the pitch of terror that I experienced that night without some authentic and even formidable cause.

When I was still a nun, I sometimes wondered, as I recited Compline, what exactly the psalmist had in mind when he spoke of the protection promised from the Noonday Devil — *daemonio meridiano* — and its opposite number — *Negotio perambulante in tenebris* — the Business That Stalketh About in the Dark.

To me there was something sinister in the way in which, instead of being described, these things were only hinted at. And I used to wonder, as I passed down the dim arched cloisters in the twilight or braved the darkness of the ancient creaking garrets on a winter night, what exactly it would feel like if one were to meet that Business alone on its perambulations.

Well, I knew now. And I had no wish at all to repeat the experience. All the same, it still strikes me as a little comic that it should have been in Wigan — of all prosaic places — that initiation should have been vouchsafed.

(4)

I reached Scoreswick at about seven in the morning.

A ticket collector with a broad Lancashire accent indicated a crowded workmen's bus. Room was made for me, and presently we were rattling through the narrow streets of the mean little town.

I had never seen a place quite like it. Before the war, it had been a depressed area. But enemy bombs had driven an important arsenal northwards and comparative prosperity had followed. Traces of the lean years, however, still scarred its poor shops and the jerry-built houses along the ugly hill-road leading out of the town.

After passing some allotments, a cemetery and some bleak and hideous council-houses, the bus stopped at the gate of a large enclosure surrounded by a high fence of netting and barbed wire.

"Flower Gardens," said the conductor. "You get off here."

So I did.

My first impression was of surprise. I'd expected one hostel. Instead I found thirty. For Flower Gardens — (the name puzzled me, for neither bed nor blossom was visible) — was an enormous camp of huts. One of the great War Ministries had erected it about two years previously, to house some of the thousand or so girls conscripted for munition making at the factory on the other side of the town.

Beyond the gates I could see the huts dotted here and there on either side of the road that curved round the camp like a cinder-coloured snake. Built of rough, greyish brick, they had flat roofs, long low windows, and an outhouse for coal storage and central heating at the back. The place was honeycombed with ditches, crossed precariously by little bridges made of planks. Rank, muddy-looking field grass grew everywhere. The soil, newly turned up along the ditches, lay in moist heaps, like mouldy chocolate.

I went forward to investigate.

Everything at Flower Gardens was so strange and unfamiliar that my first days there were invested with a dream-like quality which makes them difficult to describe. Shock followed shock with a machine-gun rapidity. Before I had recovered from the first half-dozen, a hundred more were on their way.

Little by little I began to sort out certain basic facts.

Flower Gardens appeared to be run — though it actually belonged to the Ministry which financed it — by a well-known philanthropic society. This last, I was told, held itself more or less responsible for the physical and moral well-being of the girls. It owed its name to the lady who had been at the head of things since the place began. We will call her Mrs. Todd.

"Flower Gardens," she told me, "is really England in the making. The perfect democracy . . . I gave it its name because the girls work all day in such hideous surroundings: so one likes the poor dears to come back to a place which is at least beautiful in name."

She showed me a coloured diagram pinned up on the office wall.

"You see? Each hut is called after a different flower: Bluebell Bank; Primrose Park; Crocus Cottage . . . just the sort of names that people like that choose when they have houses of their own."

I asked her whether the girls belonged more or less to the same social class.

She said: "They're an age-group, so are, of course, conscripted from different surroundings. You'll find servants, shop-girls, flower-sellers, laundry-hands, quite a lot of mixed Irish, some thieves, a lady or two and several prostitutes. Most of them belong to what are called the working classes. One has to try and handle them according to their kind."

We continued our tour of the camp.

The organization of the place was simple. Mrs. Todd, as Chief Warden, had as her underlings four Matrons, each responsible for several huts of girls. Every hut had its Steward — a woman supposed to combine the offices of mother and nanny, and a girl Orderly who came in daily to help with the domestic work.

There was also an enormous staff consisting of clerks, secretaries, typists, messengers, electricians, A.R.P. personnel, firemen, plumbers, carpenters, car and lorry drivers, gate porters, night-watchmen and heaven knows what besides. The sick bay had its staff of nurses and the canteen a regiment of cooks, caterers, cleaners, waitresses and workers of every kind.

Besides the girls' huts, there were large offices and stores. The more important heads of departments had small bungalows of their own. The four Matrons, with several other officials, had quarters in the Staff Hut, where I also was given a room.

The large central building contained, besides the canteen, a dance-hall with a high curtained stage at one end; a lounge, with deep arm-chairs and cosy little tables where the girls could entertain their visitors, and a workshop in which trained teachers gave lessons in dressmaking, toymaking, leather-work and other handicrafts. The laundry, fitted with every imaginable labour-saving device for washing and drying, was a housewife's paradise. Further on were a post and telegraph office, a store where sweets, make-up, cigarettes and papers could always be obtained, and a hairdressers' shop where shampoos and permanent waves could be had for a nominal price.

Theatricals and games were taught and organized by experts. Really, it was not surprising that the munition-workers were called the pampered darlings of the Government.

(5)

As "relief", my job was to do the work of whichever Matron might be taking her weekly day off.

After breakfasting in the canteen, one settled down in one of the Matrons' offices to "see" the Stewards. Attendance sheets, on which the girls' pay depended, had to be checked carefully and excuses for absenteeism examined. By following up the explanations invented by these young women for their non-appearance at the factory, I learned things about their private lives and about human nature in general which I could never otherwise have believed.

I liked the Stewards. Some of them had been nannies in "good" families. These knew what was what, stood no nonsense from anyone and had an excellent influence on the girls. One or two of the others were less admirable. They appeared to be feathering their nests very comfortably with a view to retirement at the end of the war.

I discovered this when they presented their "Requirements Lists" at the beginning of the week for me to sign or censor. These were long catalogues of curiously named things such as Vim, Roo, Rinso, Brasso and so on which, of course, I'd never heard of before. I'd been cautioned to check these carefully, because rumour had it that certain Stewards who had relatives in Scoreswick tended to supply them so lavishly at the Government's expense that they seldom needed to enter a shop.

I remember especially one Steward who asked every week on her list for a new chamois leather. I suggested that this was excessive. She replied that she used them for window-cleaning and that they had never before been refused to her. In the end, I found out that she made rather attractive gloves with them, which she sold for fancy prices in the town.

I remarked that I thought this dishonest, which made her very angry. Her argument was that, as a taxpayer, she helped to finance the Government and had therefore a right to anything she wanted "off the place". Nothing I said could make her alter her point of view.

Sometimes the Stewards brought in hair-raising stories of the girls' behaviour. At least, they raised my hair for the first few weeks; after which, I suppose my skin thickened, for I was able to listen without blenching to the most crudely worded tales.

I had never before seen or dreamed of anything like those girls. I used to gaze in amazement at their over-elaborate hairdressing, tight slacks and heavily made-up skins. Apparently, the ambition of every working girl in Scoreswick was to resemble as much as possible what in 1914 would have been primly and disapprovingly described as a "person of the *demi-monde*."

Later, of course, I discovered that the prototypes on which they modelled themselves were the Hollywood cuties who happened to be the idols of the hour.

"*Cutie*" . . . a terrible word for a terrible thing. None the less, into my rapidly growing vocabulary it had to go.

The girls worked in three shifts, of which the night-shift was the best-paid but the most unpopular. When not at work, a large part of their time was spent in capering round the dance-hall to the strains of the radiogram. *Jealousy* was their favourite. Even now, a few bars of that orange-coloured tango recalls memories of plump forms bursting out of oyster satin blouses, tight-seated slacks or attenuated skirts. Beneath these, stockingless legs pranced and wriggled with unfamiliar caperings.

How those legs appalled me. Strange as it may appear, I was not yet accustomed to the length of stocking that modern fashions revealed. But naked legs . . .

I could hardly endure to look at them.

Now and again a troupe of ENSA artists would arrive, tightly packed into enormous buses, spend a night or two at Flower Gardens and give a performance in the dance-hall for the benefit of the Camp.

On one such occasion I found myself sitting in the canteen next to a lively dark-haired woman with a good deal of make-up on her face. I like highly vitalized people, so we started talking; and, though I was faintly appalled at the amount of lipstick that stayed on her coffee-cup when she had finished drinking, I found her excellent company.

Afterwards, someone told me that my neighbour had been the famous Bebe Daniels: a fact which at that time impressed me not at all, because — believe it or not — I had never heard her name.

To my relief, I got on rather well with the girls.

Most of them were young, flighty, man-mad and excessively home-sick. Their one aim was to get as far as possible from Flower Gardens whenever their turn came round for a long week-end. They did not care how long the journey lasted provided that Mum and Dad were at the end of it. The alternative was to go off with a boy-friend to the nearest seaside town. Neither Matrons nor Stewards seemed able to prevent these lapses on the part of their Shirleys, Lily-Ivys and Marlenes.

"They're of age," a Steward said to me, "so you can't control them. Once outside the camp, all they care for is to get off with their boy-friends."

It was she who told me the story of That Eileen Hotchkiss. Six months gone she was, and nobody the wiser, till, only the other night, the Steward had grown suspicious and wormed the story out of her when she was in bed.

"And when I asked her who the father was, she had the face to tell me that it might be any of them chaps she'd been going with since the Yankee Camp was set up. Five or six of them, there was; and what she said to me was, 'the more the merrier'. Brazen, that's what those girls are: leastways, some of them . . ."

Such cases were not, I was told, infrequent. When discovered, they were reported to the Chief Warden, who then made what were called the "necessary arrangements" for mother and child.

On the whole, though, my impression was that most of the girls were good and steady. I have said more concerning those who were not because, naturally, they gave me more to think about.

It was not really surprising that, in a place like Flower Gardens, people found it difficult to get away from sex. The atmosphere was at once tense and enervating. Everyone was living under a physical and emotional strain. It was an unnatural existence; not only the girls, but the Matrons and Stewards were entirely cut off from male companionship. People were worried to death about fathers and brothers, husbands, lovers and sons. Many were suffering keenly over the recent loss of some near relation, and, during the periods of intensive bombing, they were desperately anxious about the safety of their homes. The majority of the girls disliked their work and made little or no attempt to settle down. Was it, after all, so very surprising that, feeling as they did, herded together in a place they hated — despite the attractions provided by a Government whose slaves they had temporarily become — they often reacted regrettably to circumstances from which they were unable to escape?

One of the Matrons said to me:
"Haven't you noticed? The people here are feverish. They *must* find some escape from the strain under

which they live. We of the older sort find relief in Bridge and gossip. The younger ones chain-smoke, haunt the pictures, and get all the kick they know how to — and do they know how! — out of men."

A little way up the road was a camp of American soldiers. This did not particularly help things. In fact, it provided opportunities for all that the authorities were trying to avoid.

Nobody could ignore the way those girls chased after the Americans. It revolted me. They would hang around the lanes, in groups or alone, and try, by means of eye-play, cock-shrieks, giggling and other alluring behaviour to attract the attention of the men.

Not that the Yankees required encouragement. They were quite as forthcoming as the ladies, though their technique was different. What they liked best was to conceal themselves in unfrequented corners of the grounds and buildings, to emerge at nightfall for appointments with adventurous girl-friends. Time and again I discovered khaki-clad Romeos lurking behind the curtains in the dance-hall, crouching in the coal-hole, skulking among the little stunted bushes at the top of the camp. As a rule, they were not difficult to deal with. It was enough to link a request for their immediate departure from the premises with a mention of the Military Police . . .

One day, a woman in the Catering Department whom I cultivated because she so often let fall useful information, said to me:

212

"Listen. If you want to see where most of the trouble in this place starts, go and look at the Bottom Pinchers' Parade on a Saturday night."

"The *what?*" I said, aghast.

So she explained to me that the noble sport of Bottom Pinching (introduced, it was said, into this blameless country by the wicked Americans) was Scoreswick's most popular outdoor game.

Its focal point was the churchyard *en route* to the town. Here, especially on Saturday evenings when the girls walked down to Scoreswick to the pictures, the soldiers would lie in ambush among the graves. And, as they passed by, giggling and squawking according to the manner of their kind, the men would pussy-foot after them and then, suddenly and unexpectedly, nip their behinds.

When the welkin had ceased to ring with their laughter and screeches, it was customary for pinched and pinchers to join forces and proceed arm-in-arm to spend the evening in the town.

"Come along with me one night and watch them at it," my informant suggested. "It'll open your eyes to quite a lot of things."

In the end I allowed myself to be persuaded.

She was perfectly right. It did.

(6)

Once a week, every Matron had to take her turn as Night Sentinel.

This meant a twelve-hour vigil, beginning at 7.30 p.m.

Part One consisted of four hours spent in the small and stuffy Matrons' office. One had to sign chits, answer telephone calls, give out passes and permissions, check arrivals and departures and cope with any problem that might arise.

About half an hour before midnight, you locked up the office, tucked the Log Book (in which everything that took place during the night had to be meticulously recorded) under your arm and embarked upon Part Two.

Your first job was to empty the Central Building. This meant chasing the girls from the dance-hall to their respective huts. After that, you took over the keys from various officials, extinguished the lights and shut the doors. Then, by the light of your carefully shaded government lantern, you had to go back and search the dance-hall, workshops, lounge and recreation rooms, lest Young America, intent upon amorous adventure, had attempted concealment in some ingenious hiding-place.

Only when this was accomplished might the Central Building be locked for the night.

Part the Third opened with a nerve-shattering walk across the camp in all but utter darkness. The night-noises were too sinister for words. Long, low sighs. (The wind, of course.) Faint moanings. (Girls, probably having nightmares, inside the huts.) Soft footsteps that padded after one and then scurried away into the dark. (Dogs? Cats? Imagination? Poltergeists?)

214

Queer, scuffling sounds inside the ditches, as though someone were splashing softly in the water. (Rats? Burglars?) And now and again a blood-curdling screech which might — or might not — have been an owl. A horrible little walk. I generally covered the last dozen yards at a run.

The final and most trying part of the vigil had for its setting Cactus Cottage, near the Porter's Lodge, by the entrance-gate. Any girl who broke rules by coming in without a permit after lock-up had to spend the night there; an arrangement intended to safeguard the sleep of those in the hut to which the offender belonged. Though not strictly speaking a punishment hut, a certain disgrace was attached to having slept at Cactus Cottage. The girls loathed it. The beds were hard, the floors rugless, and there were no mirrors on the walls.

Here, in a sort of office that smelt abominably of black-out curtains, the Night Sentinel had to spend the following seven hours, in order to deal with any delinquents whom the Night Porter might bring in.

They had to be interviewed carefully. When you had judged whether they were drunk or sober, you had to find out what they had been doing, take down the excuses they gave for their behaviour and see them off to bed.

Sometimes — though very rarely — there were no late arrivals. One then had to sit there for the whole night, reading, smoking, sometimes even dozing a little, till morning came.

The windy nights were the worst. The hut would become the centre of curious noises. Cracks and creakings in the wood-work; rattlings at the windows as though someone were desperately trying to get in; knocks and sighings in the passage; or a door would burst open suddenly, and, when you got up to close it, a sound as of softly withdrawing footsteps would send cold shivers down your spine. The whole place seemed thronged with unseen presences intent upon mysterious secret business of their own.

Now and again the girls would come in drunk. Generally I found them easy to manage, though their language, and occasionally their behaviour, was rather embarrassing. If I found a girl impossible to cope with, I summoned the Night Porter to lend a helping hand.

I had a high opinion of that Night Porter. He had several daughters of his own, which accounted, perhaps, for his sureness of touch in the regrettable situations which occasionally arose.

One incident still makes me heavy-hearted when I think of it.

At about 2 a.m. on a certain morning of wind and rain, the Porter brought into the office a very young girl. As she had apparently passed out, he had to carry her. He said that he had found her lying in a heap, unconscious, just outside the Porter's Lodge. He thought somebody must have dumped her down and left her. She was breathing in a queer, snoring way that rather frightened me.

Between us we carried her into one of the bedrooms. It took me some time to get her inert body out of her saturated clothes.

216

Everything she had on was not only drenched but torn and filthy. You would have said she had been thrown down and rolled about in the mud . . . I could have wept over her.

When I went back to the office, the Porter was standing gloomily on the hearth-rug.

I said I supposed she had had some sort of accident.

He said: "Accident, my elbow. There's been too many accidents of that kind since that camp got started up along the road. Takin' them kids out of an evening — couple of ports, a doped cigarette or two, and out they passes . . . And it's nobody's business what happens after that. Not the first time, it isn't, that I've seen a young lass left there at the gate when her boy-friend's done with her. Time something got done about it; that's what I tell Mrs. Todd whenever we meet."

"What *can* be done?" I said unhappily.

"You're askin' me!" he said.

Next day I reported what had happened. I was told that the authorities were "doing everything that they could to prevent such incidents."

During the afternoon I looked in to see the girl. She was humped up in bed, her lips swollen and with bloodshot eyes. I couldn't get a word out of her till just before I went away, when she muttered:

"I don't want my mum and dad to know what I done. They'd half-kill me. I can't never go home now." Then she turned her face to the wall and dragged the bedclothes over her head.

Not long after, she left Flower Gardens. She wouldn't give any address. One hates to think of what probably became of her.

Such are the by-products of war.

(7)

One day as I was whisking out of the bank in Scoreswick I almost collided with an elegant fur-coated woman who had just skipped out of a car.

"Darling!" she exclaimed. "What on earth are *you* doing up here?"

It was Gay.

We explained ourselves to each other and I learnt that she had only come north a few days previously to look after Maurice, her husband, who had been ill. He was, it appeared, in charge of some very hush-hush scientific research for the Government in a large country house which had been requisitioned as a laboratory.

"Come out and see us some afternoon," she suggested. "Maurice needs cheering up and we've got Wim — my brother-in-law — with us on a spot of leave. You and Wim would get on."

So, on my next day off, I accepted the invitation.

Acefield Court — the requisitioned house — stood in its own grounds on the other side of Scoreswick. It was so long since I'd seen an ancestral home that I'd almost forgotten what they looked like. This one reminded me of Albrighton Hall, the Shropshire home of my Sparrow aunt and uncle, where — in the spacious days before 1914 — some of the happiest hours of my life had been spent.

As we drove through the sentry-guarded gates I saw yew hedges and neglected lawns sloping to a wide lake patterned with bronze and silver water-fowl. A boat-house like a pagan temple stood against a dark background of elms and oaks. Probably, as things were, its former owners would never again be able to live there. Certainly, the world as I remembered it was changing day by day into something very different from everything that I'd known.

Gay led me through the rather flamboyant doorway into the wing where she and her husband had their rooms.

Maurice, resplendent in a yellow Chinese dressing-gown, lay propped up with pillows on the sofa. Wim, very English and correct, drifted in towards the end of tea. I thought he looked the type who would not suffer fools, gladly or otherwise. This made me apprehensive. I lay low.

I observed both men carefully. To me they were as strange and intriguing as an okapi or giant panda at the Zoo. I was much interested in Wim's garments. He wore a rough tweed sports coat, flannel trousers and a dark periwinkle shirt with socks and tie to match. What an improvement, I thought, on the narrow-legged, sombre-hued lounge-suits in which men had encased themselves for every possible occasion when I was a girl.

I don't remember who started it, but towards the end of tea we began talking about convents.

Gay said she wanted above all things to know what nuns were allowed to have for breakfast. (I suppose she had visualized a diet of pulse and rain-water or its equivalent for, when I told her that tea with bread and margarine was the usual fare, she looked disappointed.)

Maurice remarked primly that he'd always imagined that nuns were obliged to fast.

"They are," I replied, "but not always. The whole of Lent — two or three days a week in Advent, nearly every Friday in the year and the vigils of all the more important feasts — it works out at quite as much as most people can manage in these difficult days. On fasts, you get only a small slice of dry bread and half a cup of black coffee for breakfast, a full meal at midday and an eight-ounce collation at night."

I told them how astonished I'd been when I "came out" to see how important a place food seemed to hold in the lives of people in the world.

"In the convent," I explained, trying not to sound priggish, "you feed your body enough to get a certain amount of work out of it. If you eat things just because you happen to like them, it's considered gluttony. And one is taught in the Noviceship to mortify one's palate at least once during every meal."

Gay said: "How do you mean, mortify your palate?"

I explained that you could eat something that you didn't like or refuse something that you did. Or, if you were thirsty, you could put off drinking till the end of the meal or even not drink at all. Then, as an extreme

220

case, I told them how I had once seen a nun transfer to her own plate the bits of fat, gristle and other horrors from the "scrap-plate" which was passed round once during each meal to collect what nobody could eat.

"And what," Gay asked breathlessly, "did she do with it?"

"Swallowed it," I replied.

They all looked so shattered that I wished I had not told them. The horrified silence was broken by Gay. She said:

"Darling, of course it may be most frightfully holy and all that to go about devouring garbage, but to me it seems simply too, too revolting. And how it can possibly benefit anybody is quite beyond me."

I tried hard to think of some common ground on which to base an explanation. I could find none. It was like trying to discuss radar with a goldfish.

I said, despairingly, "Well, you see, the nun who did it believed that grace — if the term conveys anything to you — can be 'won' for souls by acts of self-conquest and self-sacrifice: the principle being that Christ saved the world by allowing his human nature to be crucified. Another motive for mortification, as it's called, is that the graces you receive in prayer depend largely upon the generosity with which you have mortified yourself between the times of prayer. Anybody who 'goes in' for prayer at all will soon discover this. The saints' lives were full of these 'self-crucifying' acts. Francis of Assissi kissed a leper; St. Francis Borgia, when he had to sleep on the floor of an overcrowded inn, deliberately chose to lie by the bed of a consumptive who didn't know he was there and who spent the whole night spitting on the saint's face. (And I may mention that when, in the morning, somebody discovered what he'd been enduring, he only said as an explanation, that he couldn't imagine a more suitable place on which anyone could spit.) And St. Margaret Mary's 'acts of mortification' were so appalling that they've only recently found their way into print."

Gay said: "Sounds completely bats to me. Also — forgive me for saying it, darling, quite too repulsive and unhygienic for words. People who do such things ought definitely to be shut up."

"Quite a lot of them are," I replied brightly. "You'd be surprised at the number of nuns with "missionary vocations" who deliberately enter enclosed orders. They feel, you see, that they'll find more opportunities for self-sacrifice there than on the mission field."

And I quoted Bishop Hedley, who insisted that conversion was not brought about by human means but by the grace of God; and that what really went to the root of the matter was "the prayer and self-sacrifice of a truly humble and crucified soul".

There followed another slightly uncomfortable pause.

Then Gay said: "Of course, my sweet, it's quite too marvellous, the way you hold forth about it all. But I'm afraid it leaves me *merely* baffled. You see, *your* line of approach to saying prayers and all that and mine are so, *so* different. In a fairly hectic existence, I've discovered that even a *murmur* to the Powers That Be about wanting or not wanting anything to happen, is *more*

222

than enough to start them coercing one in every imaginable way. Sort of perversity fixation, don't you know what I mean? — like the Air Ministry and the weather. And as for trying to convert sinners by swallowing other people's bits of gristle — well, it strikes me as being just the tiniest bit far-fetched, because one *does* so feel, *doesn't* one, that after all those millions of aeons — or whatever they're called — that They have been in charge of things, They probably know better than we do what's the best line to take; and anyhow, who can possibly hope to stop Them, once They've decided what They're going to do, especially when you think of all the people who are sure to be praying, just as hard as we are, in exactly the opposite direction. That is, of course, always supposing that there really *is* anyone there who has the slightest control over anything; which, when one looks at the *shatteringly* bloody mess that everyone has made of everything in the world to-day, oneself included, one feels definitely inclined to doubt."

With which interesting, if slightly involved, statement of her religious beliefs, Gay selected a cigarette from the blue enamelled box on the table, applied her jewelled lighter with a dash and elegance that filled me with envious admiration, and subsided into her chair.

The next attack was launched by Maurice.

He couldn't, he declared a little crossly, understand the mania that nuns appeared to have for shutting themselves up. If you wanted to live a good life, why fly from your fellow creatures to spend your existence skulking behind walls and bars?

"Listen," I said. "Nuns don't 'skulk'. Silence and solitude are such a help to a life of prayer that surely anybody who feels called to it is justified in securing them? Even scientists work better in peace and quiet. It's so difficult to combine contemplative life with life in the world that few people even attempt it. That was why so many fled into the Egyptian desert when the Roman Empire was at its most corrupt . . ."

Maurice insisted that to do that was in itself a confession of weakness.

"But of course!" I said. "Human nature *is* weak. It's because nuns are trying to lead a life in which yielding to weakness spells failure that they have to guard against it so ferociously. Hence the walls and bars."

"Sheer escapism!" said Maurice. "They should stay in the world and face their responsibilities. Good God! I'd like to know what would happen if everybody were to sneak off and hide away behind bars!"

"I shouldn't worry," I said, annoyed. "There's not much danger of that. And, incidentally, nuns don't 'sneak off'. If they hide themselves, it's in order to live harder lives and shoulder heavier responsibilities than people in the world. You don't enter a convent to escape hard things, but to do a job of work so exacting that it takes not only all the strength and courage you can muster but large extra supplies of the grace of God which can only be obtained by prayer. Without that, you could hardly hope to persevere to the end."

"Do explain yourself," said Maurice.

224

"Well," I said, "what a nun really offers herself for, when she makes her Vows at her Profession, is to '*fill up*' — as St. Paul calls it — '*what is wanting to the Passion of Christ*'. Though I don't suppose," I added, feeling faintly worried as I realized how deep were the waters upon which I was embarking, "that *that* conveys very much to any of you."

They admitted that it didn't. So I said:

"Well, short of preaching you a sermon on the Mystical Body of Christ, which I don't propose to do" (their relief was obvious), "I fail to see how I can make you understand. Unless, perhaps, what Huysmans said, in *St. Lidwine of Schiedam . . .*"

I had copied the passage from that rather repulsive masterpiece when, as quite a young nun, it had first come into my hands. And I'd read and re-read it so often that I knew it by heart. I quoted it now.

"Le Sauveur ne peut plus souffrir par lui-même depuis qu'il est remonté près de son Père: sa tâche redemptrice s'est epuisée avec son sang. Ses tortures ont fini avec sa mort. S'il veut encore pâtir ici-bas, ce ne peut être que dans son Eglise, dans les membres de son Corps Mystique . . ."

No one said anything. And as there didn't seem to be much that I could usefully add to M. Huysmans' remarks on the subject, we left it at that.

I am thankful to say that nobody asked me any more questions about nuns and convents during the rest of the afternoon.

Instead, Wim, whose mysterious job had apparently taken him up north for a month or two during the summer, entertained us with enraptured descriptions of Skye.

There must, I think, have been some special magic in his words, for what he said about the Cuillin, Lochs Coruisk and Scavaig, and the fey, strange atmosphere that haunts the island, so enchanted me that I was all for throwing up everything and starting away for Dunvegan that very evening.

I mention this because such was the spell he managed to cast over me that the place haunted my thoughts like an *idée fixe* for more than a year afterwards. In fact, when the time came for such decision, I very nearly settled there.

I suppose the fact of having been enclosed for so long made me especially susceptible to descriptions of fascinating places.

Even as I write this, I can't help wondering whether one day Skye may not draw me northwards after all.

(8)

I left Flower Gardens about half-way through November.

Gay and Maurice had been long advising me to do so. (They said the place was "too much like a convent" — a statement which left me so staggered that I made no attempt to contradict it.) So that when one day Mrs. Todd told me that in order to reduce expenses, large cuts were being made in the staff by the Ministry responsible for the place, I was, on the whole, relieved.

Before I left, Mrs. Todd, as Head Warden, presented me with a testimonial. As I had never seen or heard of such a thing before, I was perhaps unduly thrilled.

From it I learned that I was — among other agreeable things — "devotedly patriotic"; that I had "extremely high ideals" and that I "threw myself whole-heartedly into anything that I undertook".

All highly gratifying, even if a little inaccurate. But I couldn't help wondering, as I packed my few possessions once more into the two faithful suitcases, just how much this catalogue of virtues was going to help me when it came to hunting for another job.

CHAPTER
EIGHT

(1)

A fortnight later I travelled down to London.

Rail journeys had by now lost their terrors for me. This one would have been almost tediously uneventful had it not been for a minute incident which — as it turned out — propelled me along the path which was to lead me to my destiny.

Gay, who had risen at some unearthly hour to see me off at Scoreswick, cast a book in at the carriage window as the train moved out.

It was *Le Morte d'Arthur* by Sir Thomas Malory.

Now, I'm quite aware that *Le Morte d'Arthur* isn't everybody's fancy. It is, however, very definitely mine. And I met it again after nearly half a lifetime with a quickening of the heart.

I first read it when I was about fifteen, using the *Idylls of the King* and Swinburne's *Tristram of Lyonesse* to set the stage. From then onwards it always held for me a quite extraordinary charm. And when I say "charm", I mean it. Literally. The book was a door that opened into an enchanted world. Its humour might be archaic but it was irresistible. Its pathos wrung one's heart. Best of all, its closely printed pages positively effused romance.

228

I took all three books back with me to school. *Tristram of Lyonesse* and the *Idylls* were promptly confiscated by the nuns, though for some reason they saw fit to leave me my Malory. I used to escape into it when the classes were more than usually dull.

Was it Maeterlinck who said: "*Ne faites pas le rêve . . . faites les choses qui font rêver*"? Because, to me, that has always seemed Malory's supreme gift. His pages are so charged with life that they set the imagination tingling. A background of beauty springs up and weaves itself into the tale as it moves along.

The parts of the story I liked best were set in Cornwall.

Camelot, of course, with its magic gates carved by the wizardry of Merlin, its soaring towers and shadowy palaces, came straight from the *Idylls*. So did the sad, sea-sounding wastes of Lyonesse. The forests, too — Cornish counterparts of Sherwood and Bedegraine — dark with gnarled oaks and green-gloomed groves where deep fern grew like smouldering fire of emerald. But there were pictures which certainly hadn't come out of the *Idylls* — or indeed out of anything else that I've ever been able to trace. Stretches of lonely moor, stained with deep, quaggy marshes and sedgy streams; trackless uplands, where, gaunt against the skyline, huge granite blocks were piled in strange, fantastic shapes. Or, at the land's edge, strong cliff castles, sternly battlemented, towering above dark rocks where, far below, the surf boomed and sea-birds wheeled and cried. Or again, storm scenes, with Swinburne's terrible Atlantic breakers boiling and eddying, "ravening aloud

229

for ruin of lives", hurling themselves, wind-lashed in "rent white shreds and shattering storm" against the "high-towered hold" of "dark Tintagel by the Cornish sea" . . .

The odd thing was, of course, that I'd never set foot in Cornwall. And yet I could picture it all as though I'd lived there all my life.

And now, suddenly, here I was, after all these years, with the book in my hands again.

I paused: rather as one is apt to do before opening an important door.

I'd had so many disappointments over things and people remembered too ecstatically out of an impressionable youth. Somehow, when I'd met them again after the lapse of all those years, their glory had departed. How frightful, if, on re-reading this book which had been to me an archway into fairyland, I were to find that its magic, too, had fled. Shouldn't I, perhaps, be wiser to leave it unopened?

Of course, in the end, I risked it.

At the bottom of the first page I knew I need have no further fears.

"It befell in the days of King Uther Pendragon, when he was king of all England . . . that there was a mighty duke in Cornwall that held war against him long time. And the duke was called the duke of Tintagil. And so by means King Uther sent for this duke, charging him to bring his wife with him, for she was a passing fair lady, and a passing wise. And her name was called Igraine . . ."

230

With a shiver of delight I settled myself, book in hand, into my corner.

The old familiar witchery was at work.

It was like meeting old friends from whom I had been separated for too many years. Merlin the Enchanter, addicted to spasmodic fits of second sight (how perfectly he fitted in to Mr. Dunn's theories of the inseparability of time!); Sir Garlon, the black-faced gangster knight who "rode invisible"; the craven Mark of Cornwall; Sir Dinadan, most inveterate of japers; Breuse Saunce Pitié "that was the most mischievous knight living"; Palomides the Saracen, who, like Mr. Salteena, could never quite succeed in being a gentleman: the Beast Glatisant, last of this island's dinosaurs, and the long procession of lovely ladies from Elaine of Astolat to the selfish, mean-spirited, glamorous Queen Guinevere.

I spent the journey in a kind of ecstasy. Indeed, it was only when the train slowed down before steaming into Euston that I returned to earth.

And — believe it or not — it was at that precise moment, just as I was regretfully leaving Sir Tristram and La Beale Isoud to ride away to the tournament at Lonazep, that the Thing happened for which all this apparently pointless preamble had prepared the way.

Cornwall, like a lovely sleeping sorceress, bestirred herself, sat up, stretched forth a long, slim, beckoning hand and, in a voice like the sound of fairy harps across deep water, commanded me to come.

(2)

To leap straight out of the Court of King Arthur into the Ministry of Supply in Adam Street is, believe me, no laughing matter. Especially when a summons such as that which I had just received is ringing in your ears.

Following the uniformed underling up the ugly staircase to the music of clacking typewriters and scurrying feet, I tried hard to shake myself into the correct attitude of mind for an elderly spinster who is about to be interviewed for the post of Assistant in a scientific library. But without success. I just could not get back to the world where I belonged. Every bit of me that counted had been left behind on the rock-bound shores of Lyonesse.

Perhaps that is why my recollections of that particular interview are so hazy. Two details alone remain in my memory. One was the appalling stuffiness of the dark little hutch in which I was deposited to await my summons: the other, the curiously fifteenth-century face of a tall, pale young man whose profile was sharply outlined against the window-pane in front of which he sat. Exactly the kind of face, I reflected, that one would expect to see in the streets of Camelot or glancing from under a lifted vizor in the Forest of Bedegraine. A reincarnation, perhaps, of Sir Alesaunder le Orphelin or Griflet le Fise Dieu. (Good Heavens, I thought. Here I am again, still drooling about in a world of whimsy . . . I must get back to reality. And I gave myself another ferocious mental shake.)

★   ★   ★

About my interview, which followed directly on the heels of that for which the pale young man had been whisked away ten minutes previously, there is nothing to say except that the Ministry of Supply did not engage me. The committee before which I was summoned informed me that a wider knowledge of technical terms in French and German than I possessed was needed.

So that was the end of that.

I had warned A.B. that if I failed to get the job, I should descend upon her in Sussex for a while. I therefore took a taxi to Victoria.

All the way down I could think of nothing but Cornwall. The ideal setting for my Cottage in the Clouds had at last been revealed. With the eyes of my heart I watched it slowly begin to emerge from the mists of dream.

I decided I'd wait till the war was ended. But — come the Peace — I would set out immediately.

Cornwall had spoken. The spell of Merlin was beginning to weave itself about me. To all intents and purposes, I was already on my way.

(3)

For reasons which needn't be given here, since they could be of no interest to anybody, that particular visit to A.B. was not a success.

I was sorry, because my sister was staying there and I had been looking forward to our meeting. However, I

233

had not been twenty-four hours in the house before it became obvious that the sooner I removed myself, the better.

The tiresome thing was that I had nowhere else to go.

I'd had quite a lot of friends when I first went into the convent. But I'd been told to warn everyone when I said good-bye that, once inside, it would have to be the end. They were part of the "All" that one was renouncing. So that when I came out again, I had lost contact with almost everyone I had known.

On the Sunday after my arrival in Sussex, therefore, I set out for Mass in some perplexity as to what my next step had better be.

To my annoyance, no sooner did I attempt to marshal my thoughts into order than I discovered that I simply could not concentrate.

My nerves were jangled. Try as I would, I could think of nothing but certain rather annoying happenings which had darkened the last few days. Could it be that I had fallen into that distressing condition known in religious communities as having Lost One's Peace of Soul?

Anyone who enters a contemplative convent presumably does so in the hopes of achieving union with God by means of prayer. For this, it is essential that one's peace of soul should be preserved.

Now, as anyone who has attempted it will tell you, success in prayer depends very largely upon how you behave in between the times of prayer. If, for instance,

234

you allow yourself to be disturbed or agitated, you will find, when you return to prayer, that a barrier has arisen between your soul and God. So that one of the first things that has to be learnt in the Noviceship is, how to keep your thoughts and feelings well under control. Once allow your soul to be disturbed by any violent emotion and, like the waters of a tempest-tossed lake, it can no longer reflect the divine Image. St. John of the Cross says that such a soul becomes *ipso facto* incapable — for the time being — of "living spiritually". Interior tranquillity, he insists, can always be maintained by never allowing the memory or imagination to become "cumbered" or "dissipated".

Which sounds, of course, perfectly simple.

Actually, as those who have attempted it for any length of time are only too well aware, it is anything but that. For it means neither more nor less than a sustained and ruthless effort to repress one's "natural impulses" by a series of cold, calculated acts of the naked will. A gruelling process.

Suppose, for instance, that something happens which makes you *feel* very violently. It may be fear, anger, sorrow, indignation . . . even in convents such things do happen now and then, especially when one is young and sensitive and what is called "attached" to people and things.

Well — if the blow be really shattering — if one feels lacerated, shattered, explosive, the "natural" reaction will probably be to fly to one's cell, fling oneself down beside one's bed or on one's prie-dieu and let the tempest rage. Even a storm of tears may follow, leaving one exhausted though possibly physically relieved.

This may go on until one is recalled to oneself by hearing a bell ring somewhere in the monastery. One remembers that, no matter how bitter one's own personal suffering, the life of the community must go on. One is therefore obliged to pull oneself together and go back — quite possibly still half-dazed with misery — to one's place in the great machine.

In the world, people can escape — at least for a time — from their troubles. Things can be crowded out, forgotten, at a theatre or cinema. One may even get away for a change of scene.

But in an enclosed convent, none of these things are possible. There you are, and there you have to remain. You have got to face the fact that for a certain period of time — until, in fact, you have grown accustomed to what has happened to you — an intruder called Pain is going to be with you in every detail of your life. You will find it awaiting at the end of your bed to join itself to you every morning when you awaken; it will worm itself into your thoughts when you go to prayer: curl like a cold snake round your heart as you sit through your silent meals in the refectory: make you weary at work, morose at recreation, and even haunt the hours that should be spent in sleep.

Now, experts in the spiritual life will tell you that to meet suffering along these lines is fatal.

To begin with, it is purely "natural" as opposed to "supernatural" behaviour. Moreover, it is a lamentable waste of spiritual power.

I remember a very wise old nun explaining to me that suffering was one of the most valuable things in the spiritual life. Nothing, she declared, except, perhaps, humiliation, was even comparable to it.

"*Rien*", she quoted, "*ne porte aussi loin en avant que la souffrance: rien ne laisse après elle tant de bénédiction, tant de grâce!*"

It was, therefore, important to know exactly how to cope with it. Otherwise it would rush in, oust you from your rightful place as ruler of your soul and proceed to tyrannize over every department of your spiritual life.

The right way to deal with it, she said, was to rouse up your will and hold the thing at bay. Refuse it entrance, no matter in what guise it might present itself, to the citadel of your soul. Do that and it would immediately become your servant. You would then be able to harness it, like a kind of spiritual steam, to be used as a tremendous power at the very roots of your prayer. Properly managed, it would drive your prayer upwards, endowing it with a power, a quality, a value, which it could never otherwise have possessed.

"Suffering," she once told me, "if you accept it lovingly, can give an intensity to one's prayer which nothing else can give."

Another nun told me how she had once struggled for nearly a week to prevent a storm of suffering from entering her soul. She said that the effort of holding the door barred against it had been a kind of agony and that she had only managed to endure to the end by praying constantly and refusing to let her mind dwell for even an instant on what was distressing her. She surprised me by declaring that there was such a thing as *luxuriating in suffering*, and that what she called "real austerity of will" was needed to deny oneself the comfort of thinking about what was causing one pain.

Of course, suffering was not the only disturbance against which it was necessary to steel one's soul. Anger, jealousy, curiosity — in fact, any emotion strong enough to get hold of one was fatal to interior peace. And because, in the earlier stages of these struggles, "natural" reactions gave one very little respite, this business of guarding the citadel was, for anyone who went in for it seriously, an all-time job.

I remember the Novice Mistress telling us that the only weapons were a determined will and prayer. The former without the latter would be of little avail. As an incentive she quoted to us those haunting words of St. John of the Cross, which reveal nothing yet hint at so much: "*Interior recollection alone is able to open the fountain of spiritual delights.*"

That "fountain of spiritual delights"! There it was, at the end of every long dark tunnel, waiting to refresh one before one started off on the next phase of the ascent; not an end in itself but just a stimulus to the achievement of greater things. This nun also told me that she had always envisaged the business of acquiring peace of soul in terms of silence.

Exterior silence first: stillness, gentleness, absolute noiselessness in all her movements down to the very way she opened a door or laid down her scissors on the polished table in the community room. Next, the substitution of silence for speech. I never knew her break the smallest rule of silence, or even speak at all, unless it were demanded by charity or necessity. I thought this a pity, for her rare words were always well worth listening to. They seemed charged with some dynamic energy from the silence which had gone before.

The next degree of silence was interior. It had to be imposed upon one's memory and imagination, one's likes and dislikes, sufferings and joys . . . that strange gabble of voices that were always clamouring outside the gates. Even into her prayer this silence followed her. She spent it, she told me, chiefly in what she called "listening for God's voice". (Observe — not "*to*", but "*for*".) Because, sometimes for weeks and months at a time, God seemed to hide himself from her so that she had no means of apprehending him except the very bleakest kind of faith.

"Do tell me," I once said to her, "what you do when that happens."

Her answer impressed me.

"Well, I just fill my soul with his silence and . . . endure."

In this constant and universal effort after silence, a soul can find all the mortification it requires. Because silence can be harder than fasting. It can weigh you down like an iron chain. It can bore you almost to screaming point. And yet there can be no doubt that God exacts it from certain souls as a condition of union with himself.

When I was a young nun, Dom John Chapman, O.S.B., came to give a Retreat at the convent. He had just been made Abbot of Downside and was well known as one of the greatest English authorities on early Church History as well as a famous director of contemplatives. Though horribly nervous at the prospect of talking to so great a scholar, I went to the parlour one day to ask his advice.

When I told him how difficult I found it to keep my soul barred against the disturbances that, in my case, inevitably followed any kind of suffering, he nodded understandingly. (He was a large man with a proportionately enormous sense of humour and a kindness of heart which almost took one's breath away.)

"Probably," he said, "you are not going the right way about it."

He then explained how everything that happened to one was through the Will of God, and that God's Will, being the Will of One who loved us, was always best, however strange this might seem, because it intended our good. The thing to do, therefore, was to see God's Will in every tiniest detail of one's life and to lay one's will alongside his, so that his Will and ours became one thing.

Of course, he said a good deal more about it than that. But that was the gist of it. You had to *accept* everything, no matter whether it hurt or pleased you, as God's special choice for you. You had to take everything that came to you from God's hands, not only with reverence, but with love. You had to force yourself to say, no matter what happened: "I *want* this thing, because it is your will; I would not have it otherwise."

Another thing he said was (quoting, I believe, from de Caussade, who as is well known, was his master in the spiritual life): "Don't you see? — in all suffering, *c'est l'acceptation qui délivre.*" And again: "*C'est la volonté de Dieu qui opère la sainteté dans nos âmes . . . Ce qui nous arrive à chaque moment par la volonté de Dieu, est ce qu' il y a de plus saint et de plus sanctifiant pour nous.*"

He told me to read Cardinal Newman's *Sermon on Bodily Suffering.* It contained, he said, a complete programme of how to cope with the difficulties I'd described. I did so, and found it to be a compendium of the doctrine of de Caussade and St. John of the Cross. No better or briefer advice could be found for getting the best out of any kind of pain.

This is the passage he spoke of. (The arrangement under numbers is my own.)

To bear pain well, is:

(1) To meet it courageously: not to shrink or waver, but,

(2) To pray for God's help: then,

(3) To look at it steadfastly;

(4) To summon what nerve we have of mind or body to receive its attack, and

(5) To bear up against it (when strength is given to us) as against some visible enemy in close combat.

(6) When sent to us, we must make its presence (as it were) *our own voluntary act*, by the cheerful and ready concurrence of our will with the will of God.

Of course, I'm not suggesting that everyone in the convent strove after the attainment of peace of soul exactly along those lines. But somehow or other, if you wanted to get anywhere in the spiritual life, it had got to be achieved. It all depended upon what happened to be your *attrait*.

Now, *attraits* are things you hear a good deal about in contemplative communities. The word — as of course you are aware — signifies the special angle or aspect of the spiritual life towards which a soul feels particularly drawn. (The English word "attraction" doesn't convey exactly the same meaning.) You might almost say that an *attrait* was a vocation within a vocation. As a rule, if you followed your *attrait*, you became a specialist along some particular spiritual line.

Practically every nun in the convent had her *attrait*. It was usually discovered in the Noviceship, either by yourself or by the Mistress of Novices, who would then advise you as to the best method of following it up. Until you knew your *attrait*, you were inclined to beat the air a little purposelessly. Once, however, light had dawned, one forged ahead with a new and concentrated energy.

Most of the nuns tended, as life went on, to concentrate more and more upon their *attrait*. There were Souls of Silence, Souls of Penance, Liturgical Souls, Souls of Prayer, Souls of Charity, Souls of Humility and Souls of Faith. There were "*Ames d'Abandon*" — (which, incidentally, is not at all the same thing as "abandoned souls") — Souls of Sacrifice, and quite a number whose spiritual life centred round the Mystery of the Blessed Trinity. There was a nun to whom the doctrine of Grace as revealed in the Epistles of St. Paul was everything; and another who had offered her life, with its prayers, works, sufferings and joys, for the Sanctification of Priests. Another — an Apostolic Soul — lived only to win the graces necessary for the Conversion of Sinners; another for the Foreign Missions; another was wholly inspired by the idea of membership in the Mystical Body of Christ. And there was one rather prosaic old nun who used to say that she didn't hold with all this talk about "ways" and "*attraits*". For her part, she found everything she needed in exact fidelity to Rule.

Two of quite the nicest nuns in the community had as their *attrait* an intense devotion to the Blessed Virgin. The life of one of them seemed to consist largely of what Hilaire Belloc, in a curiously moving letter to G. K. Chesterton, at the time of the latter's conversion, calls "a *looking up* to Our Dear Lady, the Blessed Mother of God".

I don't know whether it is the same in all religious communities, but in that one, each nun seemed to be looking at God through a different facet of the million-faced jewel of religious life.

Naturally, just as people in the world enjoy talking about their hobbies, so the nuns liked to discuss their views upon the spiritual life.

The *choc des idées*, it was held, often engendered what were known as "lights", which sometimes had far-reaching consequences on people's lives. So that

243

now and again a group of nuns would get together when occasion offered and compare ideas.

The best — indeed, the only — time for doing this was during what were called the Lot Days.

This rather peculiar phrase had its origin in the old custom of "letting blood", which took place three times a year in all mediaeval monasteries.[1]

Four days were allowed for it, during which, in order that the victims of the lancet might more speedily regain their vigour, the Rule was considerably relaxed. And it has always struck me as a sign of great spiritual enlightenment on the part of Superiors that, even when blood-letting was discontinued, the Lot Days were still retained. Even in the early fourth century, Pachomius, that wise and saintly Abbot of the Desert Fathers, was heard to say that "no religious, least of all the younger, could persevere in virtue unless from time to time a certain relaxation were allowed to them".

I still remember the Mistress of Novices revealing to me the existence of the Lot Days. A certain amount of talking, she told me, would be permitted. Also, the nuns, instead of being obliged to sit and sew all day in the community room, would be free to go about the house and garden and to do — always within fairly strict limits — what they liked. In the refectory, too, the fare would be less austere than usual, and, during

---

[1] An interesting account of the mitigations of Rule practised at these seasons in the old Benedictine monasteries can be read in Abbot Gasquet's *Medieval Monasteries*, cf. especially the chapter on "The Infirmarian and His Work".

the autumn Lot Days, when the fruit trees were loaded with apples and cherries, special permission was sometimes given for the nuns to pick and even eat.

These revelations, I am ashamed to say, filled me with profound disapproval. With the odious priggishness of extreme youth, I held that such junketings were unfitted to the life I had embraced. And it was only after several sets of Lot Days had come and gone and I had observed for myself with what renewed vigour and enthusiasm the nuns took up once more their austere life when the Lot Days were over, that I understood how immensely helpful such a break in the ordinary routine can be. They were as braced by it as people in the world would be by a week at the sea.

(4)

It is, however, time that we returned to my departed Peace of Soul.

I was still lamenting its loss when I arrived at the little church of St. Teresa of Lisieux. If you have ever seen it, you will certainly remember the rather shattering coloured plaster statue of the saint which stands on guard in a sort of wooden sentry box outside the door. As I passed it, the thought came to me that probably no other saint in the calendar has been so consistently misunderstood. Of course, her appearance *is* rather misleading: a young, almost childlike figure in a rough brown habit and cream-coloured cloak, a rather simpering smile on her lips and one clumsily modelled hand clutching a bunch of cruelly deceptive roses to her heart. Unless you had read her life — (and if you haven't, do *please* be careful which you select from the two or three dozen, of which at least half are as stupid and unrevealing as the pictures and statues which abound) — well, you would find it difficult to believe that for sheer, stark, heroic courage, sustained at concert pitch throughout her short and hidden life, she would be difficult to surpass. "Little Flower", indeed! "Little Wedge of Iron" or "Bar of Steel" would be nearer the mark.

I pushed open the door. Groping in the darkness, I found, as I believed, the pew in which I usually knelt. I stepped into it, stumbled heavily over an invisible foreign body and just managed to save myself from falling prostrate over the kneeling legs of a lady in a fur coat. The scuffling noise of my agitated withdrawal caused somebody to switch on the electric light. The lady, instead of scowling angrily upon me, smiled kindly and made room for me beside her in the pew.

A minute incident that seems hardly worth recording. Which only shows how difficult it is to know which are the small and which the important things in life. For, as it happened, this early morning *recontre* was in reality the beginning of another Push from Providence along the road to my Cottage-in-the-Clouds.

By the end of Mass, I was feeling a good deal better. My Peace of Soul had miraculously returned, bringing with it the idea of a plan which I determined I'd work out that very day.

I would make a patriotic gesture. I would go into Brighton, visit the Labour Exchange and offer myself to do the kind of war work the authorities there considered my country needed most.

(5)

I'm afraid I wasn't wildly enthusiastic about the job they offered me. However, since the masterful lady in uniform who interviewed me kept repeating that "the country was yelling out loud for women to serve the Services", I had the satisfaction of feeling that at least I was filling up a gap.

So I produced my birth and baptism certificates, answered a long list of peculiarly irrelevant questions, filled up a dozen or so of variously tinted forms, signed a document giving the address of my next-of-kin and another to say that I didn't object to working in a danger-zone and went forth in a somewhat exalted state of mind as an employee of an organization which we will call the British Army Canteen Service. Headquarters would inform me, I was told, within a day or so, where I should finally be sent.

On my homeward journey I stepped off the bus into a darkness that baffles description. I was trying to find my way along the lane when for the second time that day I tumbled into the lady in the fur coat. She and her husband, taking compassion on my torchless condition, escorted me home. By the time we parted at the long white gate leading into my aunt's garden, we found we liked each other.

I dined with them once, and for two reasons I remember that evening rather clearly. One was my discovery that my hosts possessed a summer bungalow on the north-west coast of Cornwall; the other that my vis-à-vis at dinner was a nice young Irish priest from Donegal.

Now, this gave me a curious sensation because it was the first time that I had met a priest "socially" since I had been a secular.

You see, in the convent, one had been trained to look upon things and people from what was called a "purely supernatural" point of view. Thus, the view of a priest was so enhanced and glorified by the dignity and sanctity of his office that he was practically negligible as a man. A nun, happening to meet the convent chaplain in the cloister, immediately knelt at his feet for a blessing, and the same at the parlour if she went to see a priest. So that it felt just a little odd to meet one on an equal footing, and to shake hands, smoke, and so on, just as one would have done with anybody else.

One of the severest reproofs I ever received from a Superior was for having spoken critically about the convent chaplain.

He was an oldish man, with sharp little light-lashed eyes and a heavy jowl. In fact, he might almost have sat for Memling's *Man with a Carnation*, hands and all.

To me he was, and will always remain, a psychological mystery. One can't and mustn't judge one's neighbour: but how anyone could remain stationary at the stage of blameless mediocrity which he had apparently achieved was to me incomprehensible.

248

He had, moreover, a rare genius for infusing dullness into everything with which he dealt. After the spiritual conferences which the Rule ordained that he should, once a month, inflict upon the community, one came forth feeling so completely desiccated that it was sometimes several hours before one's spiritual energy began to work again. One felt, as one listened to him, that the Water of Life itself would dry into bone-dust if he so much as looked at it.

"I can't help it," I remember almost spluttering to the Reverend Mother after one of these appalling *séances*. "He simply withers me with dullness. Nobody ought to be *allowed* to bore other people like that about spiritual things. It's like being smothered in stale sawdust. If he really believed the things he talks to us about, he couldn't talk in the way he does . . . Anybody who's so obviously dead ought at least to be decently buried instead of being allowed to spread that awful blight of boredom over other people's souls!"

Reverend Mother was much displeased. She said that that was not the way to talk. The Chaplain was a very learned man, and I had better read the *Letters* and *Dialogues of St. Catherine of Siena*, who probably more than anyone in history had to criticize the ecclesiastics of her day.

Well, I did so; and, to be quite honest, before I had reached the end of those amazing volumes I had begun to change my point of view. The saint's method of coping with anything that was not as it should be was to envisage it through what she called "the eye of faith".

It didn't, however, explain to me the convent chaplain's curious mentality.

I wonder how many convents possess a really satisfactory chaplain?

In this country, where there are not nearly enough priests to go round, they must be hard to discover. Most of them appear to be drawn from one of two classes.

There are the delicate, sometimes slightly eccentric men, who are unfitted to cope with the exacting demands of a parish; and the unselfish, hard-working ones who can be called upon to combine a double service. Neither are, of course, really suitable for the job.

The ideal chaplain for a community of contemplatives would be a priest who was so "interior" that he could keep ahead of, or at least abreast with, the religious in their spiritual lives. Such hidden treasures, however, are rare. Which explains why many nuns look upon the chaplain only as a confessor. If they need a director, they go elsewhere.

I can never remember any difficulty about spiritual direction. The Church legislates quite admirably for this in the case of contemplatives. Besides the ordinary confessor, who is always most carefully chosen, another priest, known as the "confessor extraordinary", is deputed to hear the nuns' confessions at stated times. Besides this, there were two annual "Retreats" — one lasting for eight days or so in the summer, and a Lenten "triduum" intended to stimulate the nuns to greater fervour in the practice of their Vows. The priests who gave these retreats were men eminent for personal holiness and frequently distinguished directors in the spiritual life.

Some of the many people who have questioned me about convents appeared to have the most fantastic notions about the relations between chaplain and nuns. In reality, nothing could be more matter-of-fact or simple.

The priest's business is to celebrate daily Mass, hear the nuns' confessions once a week, administer the Last Sacraments when anyone is dying, and officiate at the burial of the dead. By special permission of the Bishop, he is allowed to enter the enclosure to visit the sick in the infirmary and to give occasional spiritual conferences to the nuns. And there his duties end.

If any nun wishes to consult him, she may always do so, though, of course, always behind grilles. As a rule, however, both he and they have little time to spare for conversation beyond what is strictly necessary. Nuns are taught to behave with the greatest respect in all their dealings with the clergy. The keynote is struck by the practice already mentioned of kneeling to ask a blessing whenever they meet a priest.

One of the nuns had a tale of how, going one day to the parlour to see Father Vincent MacNabb, who, as those who knew him best will assure you, was half genius and half saint, she knelt to ask his blessing. The holy old friar, however, suddenly overwhelmed by humility at seeing her thus abased before him, cast himself also on his knees on the other side of the grille and requested that she should rather bless *him*. Who finally blessed whom, or how the story ends, history does not relate. The whole episode, however, is fragrant with a spirit certainly not of this world.

(6)

Now and again a bishop visited the convent.

I find bishops difficult to write about, because, to be perfectly frank, the three I knew inspired me with dislike.

I am quite sure that all of them were excellent men in their way. Only — their way just didn't happen to be mine. Which — believe me — isn't really as arrogant as it sounds. Because, if ever a nun needed episcopal counsel, that nun was I. And get it I could *not*. Indeed, what earthly use was there in trying to explain things to them when everything they said and did proclaimed the fact that (1) they didn't understand convents; (2) they didn't understand women (indeed, if you come to think of it, how should they?); and (3) they didn't understand nuns.

I was once told that destructive criticism never got anybody anywhere. If you permit yourself the luxury of finding fault, you should suggest a remedy. Well, the only bright suggestion that I can think of in this connection is that a carefully selected staff of nuns — preferably not Reverend Mothers — should hold an annual Summer School which it should be obligatory for bishops to attend. Papers might be read on such subjects as Feminine Psychology; The Effects of Repression; How to Counteract the Disadvantages of Intensive Femininity in One's Surroundings; Community Pests and How to Deal with Them; Problems Peculiar to Enclosed Religious; Tact and Sympathy; How — and Especially How *Not* — to Conduct an Episcopal Visitation ... Others will readily suggest themselves to those concerned.

An Episcopal Visitation from the Bishop of the Diocese is an important event in a religious community. Normally I believe it takes place once a year. The Church's intention, I take it, is to provide the bishop with an opportunity for discovering whether everything is going as it should. He therefore makes a detailed inspection of the church and sacristy, visits the cemetery to make certain that the graves are kept in decent order, delivers an exhortation to the religious and then interviews everybody in the community from the Reverend Mother to the youngest Lay Sister postulant.

A wise, kind and understanding bishop can do an immense amount of good at a Visitation. Should he, however, be lacking in these qualities, his appearance is apt to be greeted with sinkings of the heart.

I remember a bishop who always began his exhortation by telling the nuns that if anyone had a little trouble and would like to confide it to him, he would do anything that he could to help. Were I, however, to relate what happened when a certain nun rashly took him at his word and laid a difficulty before him, you would immediately understand why it is that, on the whole, nuns prefer to keep their "little troubles" to themselves.

With which venomous remarks we will abandon the subject of bishops and proceed to the three cardinals who from time to time visited the convent when I was there.

The one who impressed me most was Cardinal Mercier. Tall, gaunt, immensely dignified and picturesque, breath-takingly humble, he might have stepped straight from the pages of a historical romance. I despair of describing him. He was the most individual person I've ever encountered; and individuality, like genius, is pretty well impossible to put into words. On the whole, what I remember most vividly about him is his hands. They were large and long, with curiously supple fingers; strong, delicate, powerful hands which you felt instinctively were fashioned not only for healing and consolation but for strong government and the chastisement of enemies. To me, however, they appeared above all as hands of prayer. Suppliant hands, which still might have wrestled with an angel: hands that were made for offering and pleading and pouring forth again in a largesse of benediction the good things that they had received.

When he spoke to the community, it was always about prayer and mortification. Once, when a nun asked him how much time one ought to spend on prayer, he replied:

"*Il faut donner a l'oraison autant de temps que l'on peut.*" And to another nun he said:

254

"Ce n'est qu'après trois ou quatre heures de prière que viennent les grandes lumières . . ."

A statement which carried considerable weight if there is any truth in the report that he invariably ended his long and arduous days with several hours spent in his private chapel before the Blessed Sacrament.

A greater contrast to the Belgian cardinal could hardly be imagined than the characteristically British Cardinal Bourne, whose stocky, spectacled figure was held in such affectionate reverence by the community. His spirituality had been modelled on the lines laid down by Cardinal de Bérulle, and his conferences had about them a recognizably Sulpician ring. I remember him giving a particularly lucid explanation of a method of prayer which he himself had used, so he said, since his seminary days.

"La prière", he once quoted — I forget from whom, though the words made a dint in my memory — *"est plus forte que Dieu. Never forget that, you whose lives have prayer as their raison d'être."*

One day, when the Cardinal was paying a visit to the convent, the nuns, with the Prioress at their head, were just about to enter the choir after saying Grace. At that precise moment, a mother mouse, followed by a family of almost microscopic mouselings, appeared suddenly from nowhere and proceeded to trot, with an air of almost indescribable pomposity, into the choir. The spectacle of these minute creatures bustling along in single file was so comic and unexpected that the nuns, startled out of the usual reactions, paused until the absurd procession had gone by. When, however, I knelt

255

down in my stall, I found that one of the mouselings had taken refuge there. It made no effort to move, so I picked it up and took it with me when I went to my cell. I fancy it must have been the runt of that particular litter, for it was quite the thinnest mouse I'd ever seen. It lay perfectly still in the palm of my hand and showed not the slightest desire to escape. I was just wondering what possible substitute I could find for mouse-milk on which to nourish it when, to my horror, I heard the "tings" sounding for me in the cloister below.

I may here mention for the benefit of those who are not familiar with monastic customs that the "tings" are used to summon a nun who might otherwise be difficult to find. They consist of two bars of steel, about six inches in length, which when struck sharply together give out a clear, bell-like sound that can be heard all over the monastery. Each nun has her own morse-like combination of "knocks" and "tings", to which, when she hears it rung out by anyone who may need to summon her, she must immediately reply in a voice loud enough to be heard by whoever has "tinged" — or, if you prefer it, "tung" — her, the mystic words: "*Deo gratias!*"

Mouse in hand, I went forth to be told that the Cardinal had sent for me. He had, it appeared, just met or was about to meet my uncle, who had recently become Prime Minister. And he wanted some detail about him corroborated. I forget what it was.

As I couldn't think what on earth to do with the mouse, I took it with me. And I still remember the quiet interest with which the Cardinal examined it when I shepherded it very carefully through the grille into his hand. When it washed its minute whiskers with an infinitesimal paw, we both sat spell-bound.

The Cardinal, as he returned it to me, said:

"And to think that there are people who refuse to believe in the existence of God . . . How could anything so mirrraculously" — he had a curious way of pronouncing his r's — "small and perfect have come into being unless it were the concept of an infinite Mind!"

I'm afraid that the excitement of that interview was too much for the mouse, because it died that same afternoon, still curled up in the palm of my hand.

Anyhow, it is nice to think that its last hours were spent in such exalted company.

The third on my catalogue of cardinals was Cardinal Hinsley.

He visited the convent during the First World War. In those days, he was still a bishop. But although I had already begun to develop what Mrs. Angela Thirkell would call "a thing" about bishops, I felt somehow that this one was "different".

The Second World War was in progress when next he came to see the nuns. Now he was a Cardinal, a Prince of the Church. Monsignor Elwes (son of the famous singer, Gervase Elwes, and the indomitable Lady Winifred) was in attendance.

The Cardinal sat at the top of the long, polished table in the community room, looking exactly like the portrait painted of him by Neville Lytton. On his left, tactful and self-effaced, the discreet Monsignor sat in silence until such time as his services might be required.

"Those Nazis . . . those Nazis!"

The Cardinal's voice had an almost anguished ring in it as he pronounced the words. His strong, bony face was creased into an expression of indignant suffering: behind his spectacles his eyes flashed. Something about him, while he was talking to the nuns about the war, suggested an avenging archangel standing, sword in hand, ready to strike down the hosts of darkness into the abyss from which they were endeavouring to rise. This Cardinal, it appeared, was a man of action, a fighter, even, for all his deeply spiritual outlook upon life.

Presently Monsignor Elwes approached a faintly hawk-like profile to the Cardinal's ear.

"Eminence . . ." — (I wondered why he so carefully pronounced it "Emeenens") — "we are going to be most dreadfully late for supper if we don't start soon."

But it was only after I had left the convent that I really got to know him.

It is a pity that the subject-matter of our three conversations can't be reproduced, because it would show, so much better than anything I could say about his kindness, that it had to be experienced to be believed. He had a way of turning his whole attention on to any problems submitted to him which was immensely reassuring when it came to asking him for advice.

The last time I saw him, however, he said something which I should like to record. He told me, quite definitely, after hearing and examining all the circumstances, that the step I had taken was, in his opinion, the only one that it was possible for me to take.

I felt enormously encouraged to face the various difficulties that lay before me when I heard him say those words.

I walked back to my aunt's house late that night feeling both thrilled and apprehensive.

The thrill was due to an invitation from the lady in the fur coat to stay with them in their Cornish bungalow; the apprehension to the prospect of the new adventure which was to begin the following day.

(7)

I suppose I had only myself to thank for my next adventure.

The woman at the Labour Exchange had warned me that the job would be hard. But I was too inexperienced even to guess at what this hardness might involve. Could I have foreseen what was coming to me, I should never have attempted it. For a job more unsuited to the peculiar and uncomfortable creature that I felt myself to be would have been difficult to find.

Indeed, the qualities required by a British Army Canteen Service hand were just those that I most conspicuously lacked.

The physical strength of an ox, for example. The hide of a rhinoceros. A gift for the kind of back-chat that makes, I should imagine, the most successful kind of barmaid, with sufficient knowledge of the speech, habits and general outlook of the ordinary British private to safeguard one against becoming hot and bothered in the canteen. Most essential of all was, perhaps, the peculiar brand of courage that can take not only bombs, shells and flying shrapnel in its stride but remains undismayed at the appearance and subsequent attacks of — (well, sooner or later the things must be mentioned) — fleas, bed-bugs and lice.

The austerity of religious life had accustomed me to many kinds of hardness. But austerity and "roughing it" are two very different things. What is more, the Vow of Enclosure segregates nuns so completely from worldly happenings that when I found myself hurled into the back-kitchen, rough-and-tumble life of a barracks canteen, I felt like a toy boat of folded tissue paper tossed about in an Atlantic gale.

It was a grey December afternoon when I arrived at Wisthaven.

At the station, a kindly policeman demanded my "papers" (what, I wondered, could "papers" possibly consist of?) and identity card. I fumbled clumsily in my handbag. An inexperienced traveller, I had none of those business-like habits which distinguish the woman of to-day.

The policeman, probably concluding that such a bewildered half-wit was beneath suspicion, glanced cursorily at the travelling instructions provided by the B.A.C.S. — the only "papers" I could produce.

"Bus-stop just up the road," he called after me as I drifted out of the station. "Canteen's at the Royal Barracks, two miles outside the town. Tell them to put you down at Joker's Lane."

Wisthaven, huddled untidily along the white cliffs of Kent, stares grimly out of a war-ravaged face across the sea at France. On that particular afternoon, the place made me think of an Early Flemish *grisaille*. Grey sea; silver-grey gulls wheeling and swooping against a sky the colour of ashes; the sea-wind blowing icily from the harbour to whirl grey clouds of rubble out of shell-holes where shops and houses had been standing only a day or two before. It seemed an earthquake-stricken scene.

An unconscious relapse into my inconvenient habit of keeping my eyes turned earthwards caused me nearly to miss the bus-stop. Annoyed, I reacted so violently with the technique I'd acquired in the taxi-queue in Glasgow that when the bus eventually arrived, people made way for me with respect. Once inside, however, I was assailed by an unpleasant feeling of deflation. Physically, there could be no doubt that I had succeeded. But — spiritually —?

I was not so sure.

★ ★ ★

After dragging my heavy suitcase for about half a mile along Joker's Lane, in which camouflaged army-lorries made queer clots of darkness under the faintly moonlit sky, I reached the Barracks.

Continuous bell-ringing at various wrong doors brought me finally to a long, low building with a two-storied house at one end of it.

I tried again.

A girl answered the door, blinking doubtfully among the shadows in a carefully blacked-out hall.

Yes, this was the B.A.C.S. billets. Expecting me? No, nobody hadn't been told nothing about my being sent. (She examined the travelling instructions.) She'd have to ask Maudie about it. If I liked, I could wait there while she went to find out what was to be done.

Maudie — with whom she presently returned — struck me as a particularly nasty piece of work. She had a mean little face and wore thick glasses through which she looked me coldly up and down. She appeared unimpressed. The Commandant, she explained, had gone out, but if I cared to, I could come in and wait till she returned.

"Though when *that'll* be," she added nastily to the other girl, who giggled sycophantishly, "seeing that it's her afternoon off, I'm sure it's not for *me* to say."

The kitchen into which I followed them was bright and cosy. Two girls were rolling pastry in front of an old-fashioned range; others sat round a bare deal table, talking and laughing together over their tea. As I came in, they glanced up but took no further notice of me.

262

I stood there for a while, feeling faintly idiotic. At last, advancing to the table, I asked politely what I was supposed to do.

This produced an embarrassing silence. Then Maudie remarked:

"It's the new 'and. Better give her a cupper tea, girls."

A blonde girl with an appalling squint in one eye then made room for me beside her. The conversation continued as before.

As nobody spoke to me, I felt it was wiser to keep silence. Unaccustomed to look after myself, I'd not thought of providing food for the journey and in consequence had eaten nothing since breakfast, seven hours earlier in the day. I therefore quietly consumed enormous quantities of tea and buns, examining the girls meanwhile out of the corner of my eye.

They looked to me extremely young. From their language and behaviour, I judged that most of them belonged to the class from which kitchen maids — in the days before such luxuries became legendary — were usually drawn. They wore overalls of blue drill, with scarlet buttons and an arm-band with the B.A.C.S. monogram in red.

After tea, Maudie, who appeared to hold some undefinable position of authority, ordered me to help Lily — the squint-eyed girl — with the washing-up. We were still at it, aided by a good-looking girl called Iris, with soft eyes like a Jersey cow, when Lily squeaked suddenly:

"Coo! If it isn't the Commandant!"

A dim-looking young woman in khaki was standing in the doorway. She said:

"Well, girls! Back sooner than you expected? Don't ask me why!" She giggled foolishly. Then, catching sight of me: "And is this the new hand?"

Assuming a suitable air of deference, I went forward to explain.

The Commandant didn't seem particularly pleased to see me. Headquarters, she admitted, had mentioned something about sending somebody along, and she'd intended to phone them up and say not to because *reelly* this place was what you might call crowded out; but what with this and that she'd had so much to do it had slipped her memory. Anyway, they'd find plenty of jobs for me now I was here. Young Ireen had sprained her knee and wouldn't mind a hand with the scrubbing and of course there was always the potatoes to peel. Though, come to think of it, where I was to be put to sleep with not a spare inch in the place since the hostel was bombed a fortnight ago, and this only tempery quarters where they was now, she reely hadn't an idea. She'd have a word with Maudie on the subject and see what they could do.

"Silly twerp," remarked Iris. "Forgets every darned thing since she got off with that ossifer. Bet he drove her home in his car. Makes me sick, the ways she goes on."

The love-smitten condition of the Commandant, I was soon to discover, was the explanation of a good many minor hitches in the workings of the canteen.

★ ★ ★

264

Presently Maudie bustled in and explained that as there was nothing for me to sleep on, I should just have to make do with whatever could be obtained. A red-haired young private who appeared, like the Slave of the Lamp, whenever anyone shouted "Badger!" long and loud enough to be heard outside the canteen, was then commanded by Maudie to "go out and requisition a bed". It being his week on fatigue, explained Lily (I did not like to reveal my ignorance by inquiring what that expression meant), little jobs of that kind fell automatically to his lot.

Lily having been allowed an evening off the canteen service to initiate me, we waited together in one of the bedrooms till his return. The fire by which we sat was permitted, it appeared, since the bombing of the hostel, because the girls had nowhere else to sit when not at work. Here we were joined presently by a girl with the strangest eyes I'd ever seen. Blue as hyacinths, they were vacant as the eyes of a corpse. The effect was startling and rather sinister.

She stood before us, fumbling vaguely with the top of her stocking. From it she presently produced a greasy book of tickets. These she held out to me.

"Lottery," she remarked. "Winner gets one of me brother's rabbits. Want one? Price one shilling each."

Not quite knowing how to refuse, I handed over the shilling and received a crumpled pink ticket in exchange; upon which she silently withdrew.

"Rabbit my foot," said Lily, when she was out of earshot. "She ain't got no brother, nor he ain't got no rabbits. Most of us gives her a shilling, though, when she comes around like that. Sends it to her kids."

"Kids?"

I was incredulous. The girl had looked about fifteen.

"Uh-huh. Two on 'em, she got. Twins. And black as the pots, if you believe me. Got off with one of them nigger chaps as was billeted down where she come from and that's where he landed her. Bit gone in the 'ead, she is, too, pore kid, so you can't blame 'er, not reelly. 'As fits, too, now and again: something crool to see when she reelly gets worked up. Doesn't do to cross her."

I digested these revelations.

Lily warned me that owing to shortage of cupboard space, each girl had to keep everything she possessed locked up in her suitcase under her bed. If you left anything about, young Ireen would be sure to nab it, pop it and send the proceeds to Auntie for her twins.

Presently Badger reappeared, staggering beneath a camp-bed, two doubtfully clean-looking sleeping-bags to serve as mattresses, some grey army blankets and an armful of cushions which smelt of cheese. With these, the three of us made up a kind of litter, in which it appeared that I was to spend the night.

The only bright spot I could discover in my surroundings was a bathroom. Hot water has always had a most stimulating effect on my morale. Unfortunately, however, my ablutions only helped to emphasize the contrast between my freshly washed self and the revoltingly frowsty malodorous bedding into which I was about to creep.

266

Three beds would have been too many in so small a room. And it contained seven. They were placed so close together that the occupants could only get in and out by climbing over the ends.

The windows had to be kept tightly closed because of the blackout; and if you opened so much as a chink of the door, the fire smoked.

It was not long before the atmosphere became asphyxiating.

I had never before slept in a room with other people. It embarrassed me. The girls made peculiar and unpleasing noises in their sleep. Most of them snored. One or two chattered and grunted. Another ground her teeth. Poor Lily, who seemed to be suffering from bronchitis, coughed incessantly and without restraint. It was like sleeping among a herd of pigs.

The occupant of the bed on my right seemed particularly restless. I had not seen who she was as she had only crept in after the lights were out. She gibbered frightfully, tossed, turned and finally began to moan as though in the throes of some horrible dream. Hoping to rouse her from her nightmare, I sat up and flashed my torch into her face.

To my horror, I discovered that it was young Ireen.

What on earth should I do if this vacant-eyed mother of twin negroes were to take it into her head to have a fit?

Desperately alarmed, I began — as is my custom when disaster threatens — to invoke the saints of paradise.

The reply vouchsafed, though certainly according to the letter, was hardly in sympathy with the spirit of my request. It helped, however, to confirm a certain suspicion which, during the last few years, had been rapidly developing into a certainty. This was that, on the whole, it is better not to send out an S.O.S. to heaven whenever a difficulty looms on the horizon. Better to square one's shoulders, set one's teeth and take what is coming to one. Endeavours to cajole Providence into smoothing one's path through life are apt to end in the frying-pan being substituted for the fire.

What followed was a case in point.

Ireen — who, if left to herself, would probably just have had a clean tidy fit and no damage done — now sat up suddenly, uttered a short, sharp screech that awakened everybody in the room, and was noisily and abundantly sick . . .

When the agitation had subsided and we had finished clearing up the mess, the girls rolled back into bed and immediately went to sleep again. I, however, was less fortunate.

Lying there in the stuffy darkness, sickened and revolted by the frowst that rose like a disgusting miasma from my bedding, I tried to think up some idea that would help me not only to endure but to accept.

In the Noviceship one had been taught that the best thing to do when anything went against the grain was to "offer it up" for the people or "intentions" that were nearest to one's heart.

268

"The more to suffer, the more to offer", was a favourite saying of an old nun who certainly knew what she was talking about and to whom I had often gone for counsel in my youth. "Suffering", she once told me, "is sent to us to make use of in whatever way we choose. It can sour us; but it can also save and sanctify. *Value suffering.*"

Looking back, it now seems to me that the whole business of Religious Life — that is to say, whether one made a success or failure of it — depended upon one's attitude towards suffering. From the outset, one was taught the immense value of "mortification" — the painful, monotonous job of putting to death one's "natural inclinations" so that the "supernatural" life of grace might take complete possession of one's soul.

There was no getting away from it, no royal road or easy way. You could only develop "supernaturally" at the expense of what was "natural"; if you wanted to attain the summits of the spiritual life — to be what the saints and mystics call "transformed into Christ" — well, not only sin, self-indulgence, pleasure, comfort and ease, but even the smallest gratification of the "natural man" had to go. That, of course, was why so few — so *terribly* few — persevered in absolute self-denial to the end.

The fact is that Religious Life, lived fully and generously, as it should be lived, is a life of heroism. That is because it is a call to sanctity; and no one can be a saint who does not live spiritually always at concert pitch. This is an arduous and exhausting business; anyone who has attempted it will tell you it is not surprising that so many begin to feel a little tired before the end of the race.

Just how much dogged courage is required by those who undertake the adventure of Religious Life may be gathered from the spiritual diary of a young Irish Jesuit who was killed while acting as chaplain to the Forces in the First World War.

This young priest, who, if heroism is one of the marks of sanctity, was surely as near to that enviable condition as most of us are likely to get, declared in this diary (it was published after his death, in spite of his explicit directions that all his papers should be burnt) that he felt God demanded of him the complete sacrifice always and in everything, of every human pleasure and comfort, and the embracing — so far as the Rule allowed and without injuring his health or work — of every possible discomfort or pain. His aim, said the diary, was: (a) never to avoid suffering; e.g. heat, cold, unpleasant people; (b) of two alternatives, always to choose the harder: e.g. ordinary or arm-chair; (c) to try and let pass absolutely no occasion of self-denial; (d) as far as possible not to omit his ordinary penances when he was not well.

Certainly this was "mortification" with a vengeance; an "emptying of self" that would create a capacity into which the grace of God could flow in an impetuous stream.

And, apparently, that was exactly what happened. When a soul really gives everything to God, the great transforming graces of the saints are not withheld.

270

I have quoted the above because it gives such an excellent bird's-eye view of the lines on which, in an enclosed contemplative community, the idea of penance and mortification is ordinarily worked out. Without any extraordinary means, people are able to live lives of the most complete and utter self-denial — hardly observed, perhaps, by those around them unless they too happen to be working on similar lines. Not everyone, of course, aspires to the same degree of heroism; but total war against "natural desires and inclinations" is, on the whole, what everybody is trying to achieve.

This is no place in which to set forth the motives which inspire the penitential practices of the religious orders. It is, however, interesting to note that the extraordinary penances of the saints were not so much the outcome of a desire for their own sanctification as a tremendous urge to help and save and if possible atone for the sins and sufferings of a world which has very largely lost the true idea of God. The life itself — hard, silent, rigorous, austere — is packed with opportunities for self-denial. And yet, for many souls, even that does not seem to be enough.

Therefore, in the old religious orders, besides silence, fasting and vigils, the use of the "discipline" is also enjoined by Rule.

Most people, I suppose, would be horrified if they were shown the small scourge made of thin waxed cord to which five or six little knotted tails are attached and told that it was used by almost all religious to inflict upon themselves a considerable amount of pain.

The metal "discipline" is an even more vicious-looking instrument. Its slender, snake-like tails can cut and sting quite cruelly.

For those who have a definite *attrait* for penitential practices, other ingenious torments have been devised. There are bracelets of steel, wide-linked and studded with points, which, although not sharp enough to draw blood, are none the less extremely painful when fastened tightly round an arm or leg. Chain girdles on the same lines are also worn occasionally; and a little flat wooden cross, set with short, slightly blunted nails, can cause — when worn, for example, on the shoulder under a heavily pressing choir mantle — almost excruciating pain.

Haircloths — the favourite garment of the Fathers of the Desert — were desperately uncomfortable things. There were two styles: one, a kind of sleeveless tunic like a herald's tabard; the other, a wide belt, strapped about the loins. They were made of knotted horsehair with as many ends as possible left loose to prick the wearer. My recollections of the hours I spent inside them are best left undescribed.

With the exception of the discipline, nobody is obliged to use any of these instruments of torture. During Lent, however, on the vigils of the greater festivals and at other times when the spirit of penance is in the air, most religious, I imagine, go in for something of the kind.

And it is a positive fact that these penances, when wisely practised, produce remarkable results. Performed under obedience, they do a very great deal to bring

272

about that subjection of the body to the spirit without which the highest adventures in the spiritual life can never be achieved.

We will now return to the canteen.

The last thing I mentioned, you may remember, was my lying awake in the stifling and densely populated room.

By now, the atmosphere had become positively fetid. Feeling that suffocation was imminent, I was just about to decamp to the bathroom for the remainder of the night when suddenly a long, screaming whistle followed by the familiar crump that to the initiated could only mean one thing, came hurtling through the air. A split second later, a deafening explosion made the house curtsy and sway before it staggered back into immobility. Then the sirens began.

"O Gawd," said Maudie, crossly, sitting up in bed with her skinny arms clasping her bony knees. "Landmine, I shouldn't wonder. Blast that 'Itler! Can't 'e let a pore girl sleep in peace?"

On the whole, alarm was less noticeable among the girls than irritation. Presently the Commandant, obviously nervous, looked in and suggested the shelter. The girls, however, declared that they couldn't be bothered, and when, after about an hour, the bombardment from overseas stopped as suddenly as it had begun, they rolled back into bed again and automatically fell asleep.

I observed that Ireen, alone out of the whole roomful, had slept undisturbed throughout the din.

An hour passed . . . half an hour . . . and then, just as a faint sensation of drowsiness was at last beginning to steal over me, I was roused by a dreadful sensation of something hurrying along my spine. I ignored it. An instant later, there it was again, this time in the region of my shoulder.

Groaning inwardly, I reached out in the darkness and found my torch . . .

Investigations revealed that two large and exceedingly muscular fleas were careering about my person.

I was unable to catch either of them.

Three-quarters of an hour later, somebody's alarm went off in the passage outside.

It was time to get up.

(8)

Life in the B.A.C.S. billets started at seven in the morning.

The girls rolled out of bed, smeared over their faces with a damp washing glove, shook out their hair and then went down to breakfast in the kitchen. As the excellent food was apparently unlimited, this took a certain amount of time. They then washed up and dispersed to get the housework done.

Their beds, which they never dreamed of stripping and seldom opened, were quickly finished. After that, the food for the canteen had to be prepared.

Just before ten o'clock, there was a frantic scurry to the bedroom. Here they removed the curlers from their hair, anointed their faces with skin-cream, rouge, powder, mascara, lipstick and what-not and came forth so resplendent as to be hardly recognizable.

I had consigned them to the kitchen-maid stratum of society. But on comparing them with the down-at-heel untouchables who, in my early youth, had relieved my mother's admirable cooks of such arduous tasks as potato-peeling and the scouring of the innumerable saucepans exacted by the luxurious cookery of that bygone age, I could only shake my head. The world, in the last thirty years or so, had done more than alter. It had become a completely different place.

Three times a day the canteen opened for a couple of hours. In consequence, three times daily, the kitchen and scullery floors had to be scoured on hands and knees. This job was allotted to me. And as my labour was unskilled, I came in for a good deal of contumely from Maudie, who had made up her mind that I considered myself superior to the other girls.

"If you think them lah-di-dah airs you gives yourself is going to get you anywhere," she would declare venomously before the assembled staff, "you're wrong. You've got to scrub them floors same as anybody else. Lady nor no lady, I won't have no work shirked in my kitchen, so back you just go and scrub that bit over by the coal bucket: see?"

Had she but known how despairingly un-lah-di-dah my opinion of my own accomplishments was fast becoming, she might have been more merciful. As for being a "lady" — well, if there is anything in the Brains Trust definition of a lady as one who is invariably kind and thoughtful with regard to other people's feelings — few of us, I suppose, could pass the test.

Washing-up was an occupation that I particularly detested. Iris and Badger were supposed to help me but as a rule were too much occupied in making love to attend to anything else.

A large proportion of the time was spent in peeling potatoes; a depressing job, as it had to be done in the scullery which was dark as hell and smelt of cheese. Or did it? Perhaps it was just the faint aroma of tired Camembert which hung tenaciously about those cushions (scrounged from heaven alone knows where for me by the kindly Badger) which followed me, no matter where I went, throughout the day . . .

Try as I would, it had been impossible to rouse the Commandant to take action about my bedding. When I'd mentioned the fleas, she had merely lifted her eyebrows and asked me whether I realized that there was a War On. In consequence, the creatures had so increased and multiplied that they now caused me infinitely more discomfort than the nightly shelling from enemy batteries across the sea. Worse, Iris — admittedly a more competent authority than I was on such matters — declared that certain bites on my neck and arms had been inflicted by an even more sinister insect than the flea.

Once more I appealed to the Commandant. The moment was ill-chosen, for I saw — though only when it was too late — that the Ossifer was waiting in the lobby to take her out. In vain did I strip my sleeve and show my scars. My petition for proper bedding was turned down. As for the insects, the Commandant said she didn't believe there was anything of the sort anywhere in the billets and if there was, I must have brought them with me. Upon which she joined the Ossifer and was seen no more that day.

Besides one free afternoon a week, we were allowed two hours off after dinner when we had finished the washing-up.

Most of this time was spent by me in the yard outside the kitchen, trying desperately to dislodge any possible occupant from the curious assortment of bags and blankets of which my bed was made. When I'd finished my shaking, brushing and beating, I'd leave everything out on the clothes-line to flap a while in the piercing north-east blast that blew with almost unparalleled force during the whole time I was there. I would then withdraw to the bathroom, light a cigarette to drown the odour of cabbage that always seeped through from the kitchen and escape into the *Morte d' Arthur*. It was the only book I had.

The bathroom was the one place in which I could hope for any sort of privacy. Pleasantly warmed by the hot-water tank, it was not at all a bad spot in which to take refuge from the horrors of the canteen. What was more, the book possessed certain magical qualities which affected me almost as though it were hashish.

I'd only to open it and there I was, standing on enchanted ground, the song of the sea echoing in my ears and the long pageant of the ancient legends unfolding themselves before my eyes. Each place-name had its picture, especially in Cornwall: but most of all

Tintagel and the stretch of coast that guards it like a fortress above the sea.

To me the very name was evocative as the Shepherd's Call in the Third Act of *Tristan*; a charmed word that caused visions to materialize. One saw the flash of armour; heard the breaking of lances; felt the anguish shot with radiance, the secret life, the almost intangible silence that soaked its walls.

Owing to my distressing lack of any time-sense (due, possibly, to having always lived the same kind of life and relied on the sound of a bell for every change of occupation), I now and again omitted to appear for tea. Lily, therefore, who seemed to have a kind of nannie-complex where I was concerned, used to bang on the bathroom door when she herself went down. I was thus saved from vituperation on the part of Maudie as well as from what was considerably more distressing — a hungry afternoon.

Lily was one of those wingless angels whom Providence has set upon my path at various stages of my misspent life to safeguard me from calamities which would otherwise have been inevitable. She could have been my granddaughter; her superior knowledge of life, however, caused our positions to be reversed.

Lily's home was in Poplar. (I'd no idea where that was: from her description, it sounded pretty awful.) Her father — killed by a bomb at the beginning of the blitzkrieg — had been a dustman. Her mother was a cleaner who rose at 5 a.m. to prepare breakfast for her seven children before setting out for the Government office in the City which had to be "done out" before the staff arrived at eight.

Lily was the salt of the earth. She sent home every penny of her weekly wages except eighteen-pence for the necessities of life. Now and again her mother sent back to her a shilling or two; otherwise she never had a farthing to spend on what she liked. Her judgment was one of the soundest I've encountered; her heart was unalloyed gold. Every girl in the canteen told her their troubles and went to her for counsel. The whole time I was there I never heard her say a word against man, woman or child.

"Tell you what, Judy," she remarked to me one day (they had seen on a letter the nickname by which I was known to certain of my friends, since when I had been "Jee-oody" to the whole canteen) "this here ain't reelly your cupper tea."

I couldn't have agreed more. I was sorry, however, that it was so evident, for I'd tried hard to throw myself whole-bodiedly, if not always, perhaps, whole-heartedly — into the job.

No, Lily continued. I wasn't, she considered, the sort for domestic work. An office job, she suggested, would be ever so much more in my line. She, Maudie and Iris, she explained to me, didn't mind it because scrubbing and washing-up and peeling spuds came natural to them, they having been brought up to it. Seven in a room, too — or, for that matter, three in a bed — just didn't mean a thing to them, nor yet insects running about on you when you was in bed. And as for the rough edge of Maudie's tongue — well, it was no worse than most of them was used to from their mums. They all liked the canteen because the food was lovely, ever so much better than they'd get at home. The work wasn't too hard, either: and then, there was no denying, they did have a smashing good time with the boys.

That night, lying awake after the usual enemy bombardment after midnight, I thought upon these things.

Lily, I reflected, had been right when she declared so emphatically that the B.A.C.S. was no place for me. I hated it with everything in me. The complete lack of privacy. The crowded sleeping-quarters. The coarse talk and sometimes revolting behaviour of certain of the girls. The exhausting work — consisting, in my case, uniquely of peeling potatoes, scouring saucepans and scrubbing floors. The petty bullying and spiteful abuse of Maudie, recognized by everyone as "having got her knife into me", and the stuffy, sleepless, bomb-and-shell-infested nights.

Not that the raids alarmed me. I'd grown accustomed to bombs before leaving the convent. Besides, I hadn't the slightest objection to being killed. But night after night of those endless, ear-splitting explosions all round, and as often as not very nearly on the top of one, coupled with the all but total lack of sleep, began slowly to wear me down. My nerves began to fray. I found that I no longer possessed the resilience of youth.

On the whole, I think that what I most hated (next, of course, to the incursions of insect life — a perpetual torture) was having to serve in the canteen.

To-day, after nearly eight years of battering by the world, my skin has thickened so that I see things differently. Then, however, I was still fresh from my twenty-eight years of enclosure; sensitive, almost unbelievably inhibited, still looking at everything from the angle of religious life.

Now I wish I knew how to convey to you the almost brutal violence of the contrast between the convent and the canteen. Actually, I doubt whether anyone who had not themselves lived "enclosed" for many years could ever fully grasp it.

Nuns, you see, are the most devastatingly neat, clean, quiet, tidy, well-behaved creatures in existence. Every one of their movements is studiedly "religious"; every one of their words is careful, accurate and suitably refined. (Anyone who receives letters from nuns cannot but be struck by the stereotyped phrases which embellish them; the "religious" endings — "Yours devotedly in Xto", "Yours sincerely in Christ", and so on . . . all a part of the same system by which a religious is moulded into something completely alien to the spirit of this world.) They move about gently and quietly, hands joined, heads a little bowed and eyes cast down. What is more, the atmosphere which surrounds them is intensely and peculiarly *feminine;* an atmosphere from which anything even remotely associated with the masculine element of life has been inexorably expelled. Try to picture a row of exquisitely symmetrical madonna lilies (from which, of course, the perfume has been carefully removed), growing inside a shaded glass-house and watered daily with an elixir composed of milk (pasteurized) and snow. That may give you a notion of what I am trying to convey; though even that is a very poor symbol of the reality.

Judge, then, of my feelings when, for the first time, I found myself serving in the canteen separated by only a wooden counter from what appeared to me as a horde of excited hooligans.

They were young; they were rowdy: they were bursting with animal spirits and they were determined to give and to get as much fun as they possibly could with the girls. Their hands and nails were grimy and smelt of nicotine; their persons exhaled an odour of sweat and khaki which, with their hot breath and dubbined boots, produced a slightly overpowering atmosphere. They upset their tea, roared with laughter, thumped one another, danced about, leaned across the counter to help themselves to anything they fancied, swore, sang and bellowed cheerfully for tea, cakes, chocolate, potato chips and cigarettes. It was Bedlam. I felt like the man in the psalms when the fat bulls of Bashan — *vituli multi, tauri pingues* — encircled him.

I had the shock of my life when, on my first appearance, I was saluted on every side with friendly roars of "'Ullo, ducks!"

I had never before been so addressed. I was scandalized.

Soon, however, I discovered that the men never dreamed of calling the canteen hands anything else, unless perhaps it might be "sugar" or "sweety-pie" or some such revolting endearment imported from overseas. I managed, however, to camouflage my alarm and embarrassment by assuming a sphinx-like if slightly crooked smile and saying nothing. This, to my relief, produced a great impression. My prestige was ensured.

Another thing that made me dread serving in the canteen was my stupidity about arithmetic. Both at home and at school I'd so hated sums that I'd refused to have anything to do with them. Now I had to pay for my folly. I was perpetually in difficulties about giving change. Maudie soon discovered this and added to my confusion by acid comments. Humiliation became my daily bread.

Among the soldiers was one who, from the first, attracted my attention.

The men called him "Yippy". His face struck me as the saddest I had ever seen. His extreme youth, and the cheeky, almost impish cast of his features, made the bleak tragedy in his eyes the more remarkable.

I have sometimes wondered whether there may not be some vague, physical sympathy between the rootless members of the human race; those who have been completely severed from their backgrounds by the guillotine of circumstance. They are a small minority; ghosts who flit through life detached from everything being, fortunately, rare. Their solitude of spirit is, however, so intense as to be sometimes physically evident. It was so with Yippy. I recognized it at once.

I got to know him because it was always to me that he applied when he wanted anything at the canteen. Then, one day when I'd been down to Wisthaven we got off the same bus and walked back together in the cold and windy darkness of Joker's Lane. It was then that he told me his story.

Only two months ago, his entire family — parents, sisters, wife and three small children — had been blown to atoms by a land-mine that had fallen on his home. It had destroyed not only everything but everybody that he possessed.

Now, when anybody confides to one a tragedy of that magnitude, there really isn't very much that one can say. All the same, I did — very diffidently — try to get through to him in his terrible loneliness. And I somehow believe — though as likely as not, I am mistaken — that the philosophy of life that I tried to suggest to him (simply because it alone had saved me from shipwreck) did bring him a certain amount of comfort. Or perhaps what was at the moment more useful to him — a glimmer or two of hope.

He was a childlike person. In our subsequent conversations it became increasingly evident to me that of such is the Kingdom of Heaven.

(9)

Some months after all this, I was talking to a certain holy Jesuit about my adventures at the Royal Barracks. (At least, I suppose he was holy; one has only to read the Life of St. Ignatius to see at once that an *unholy* Jesuit would be a contradiction in terms.)

"Do tell me," he asked, "what it was that made you finally throw up the job at Wisthaven?"

284

So I explained.

I told him that I was too old to be dumped down to work with a crowd of girls young enough to be my grandchildren. I felt like Methuselah among the Innocents: the squarest of pegs in the roundest of possible holes. Moreover, what was the point of holding down a job that I detested when my country — so far as I was aware — could gain absolutely nothing by my sacrifice? The canteen already had too many girls at work there. Indeed, the only members of the community who stood to gain anything from my presence in Wisthaven were the bugs and fleas.

The moment I'd uttered the words I felt that I'd been too realist. For in all my life I've never seen a man look more shocked and horrified. He couldn't have worn a more appalled expression if I'd said something flagrantly obscene.

"You . . . you don't mean to say . . ."

"Yes, I do, Father!" I replied emphatically. "There were simply armies of them. All night and every night. And — well, the fact is, it was rather more than I could stand."

He looked at me with a kind of pained horror that was far more eloquent than words.

I have mentioned that little incident because, strange to say, it did a lot to reassure me. (I had wondered more than once whether perhaps I ought to have put up a tougher fight against the insect life of the canteen.) If, however, merely to mention the names of these revolting creatures was sufficient to make a strong man wilt, it could not, after all, have been so very blameworthy on my part to let myself be driven away by the ferocity of their attack.

There was a spice of adventure about my departure from Wisthaven which caused me considerable glee.

It began on the day I gave notice, after going for my weekly wages to the office of the Commandant.

"But you can't do that," she snapped crossly. "You've signed on for the duration. Notice indeed! I never heard of such a thing!"

This annoyed me, because I had been careful to do nothing of the sort. Besides, I was long past the age-limit of the last group called up for compulsory war work and was therefore free to do as I chose. As, however, it was the Commandant's Saturday Off and the Ossifer was kicking his heels in the hall till she should be ready to join him, I held my peace. (In my family, we are always most dangerous when we say least.)

The moment the Commandant was out of the house, I packed my suitcase. I then descended to the kitchen, where the girls were gossiping over their mid-morning buns and tea.

They appeared to be much impressed by my daring in what they called "'oppin' it" without permission from the Commandant. Some of them seemed so sorry to say good-bye that I was touched. The tender-hearted Lily produced a pocket-handkerchief. Iris raided the Commandant's locked office by the open window to get me my ration book. Even Maudie was galvanized into temporary amiability and fried me a sausage so that I should have, as she expressed it, "something inside of me" before I went.

We discussed my plan of action. The great snag was the trouble I'd had over my identity card the previous day. I forget exactly why it was, but the official who always boarded the bus at the barrier and examined those tiresome bits of cardboard every time one went to Wisthaven had told me he couldn't let me through again until the matter had been rectified. And as the Food Office shut at midday on Saturdays and it was already nearly dinner-time, it seemed that I was in rather a fix.

I said my good-byes, wondering how I should fare if I risked it and just tried my luck once again at the barrier. It was while I was crossing the courtyard that the great idea came to me.

I made a bee-line for the spot in which I knew Yippy was usually to be found at this hour.

Unfortunately, when discovered, Yippy was a little difficult to persuade. I didn't realize, he insisted, the kind of stink — (that, if I remember rightly, was the expression he used) — there'd be if he was copped. 'E'd 'ave the 'ole ruddy Wore Roffice about 'is ears.

However, I went on and on at him till at last he gave in. (Most people do this, I've discovered, if one is careful to use the right technique.)

Ten minutes later, he was driving the enormous army lorry with which his uncomfortable existence was so inseparably bound up, down the road into Wisthaven. Nobody guessed that inside, neatly curled up between two packing cases and concealed beneath a large and evil-smelling sheet of tarpaulin, was a fugitive from the canteen.

My aunt and uncle looked more surprised than pleased to see me when I marched yet once again into their house in Portland Place.

They listened sympathetically, however, to the story of my adventures and very kindly offered to put me up until I had discovered another job.

CHAPTER
NINE

1

The next few weeks were the blackest patch in my post-conventual career. Even to look back at them after three years gives me a faint sensation of nightmare.

Various domestic upsets induced an atmosphere of depression which air-raids, prolonged visits to the dentist, suppressed influenza and a fortnight of fog and icy drizzle did nothing to alleviate.

Worse, the squalor of the Wisthaven episode had entered deeply into my soul. I felt *smirched*. Carbolic baths and the fresh fragrance of immaculate sheets helped, to a certain extent, to restore my morale; but something had gone from me. Whether I should ever regain it remained to be seen.

My first concern was to find another job. No matter how kind and hospitable one's relations might be, one couldn't plant oneself indefinitely upon them. So once more the little honey-coloured forms from the Ministry of Labour began fluttering in through the letter-box.

An interesting job was offered to me at the Ministry of Information. One had to hunt up facts and figures to be used in speeches for overseas propaganda. When, however, I turned up at Malet Street for the interview, I was so overawed by the gigantic building, honeycombed with offices and passages down which important-looking people scurried incessantly to and fro, that I was in no condition to cope with the barrage of questions that came my way. As might have been expected, my curious ignorance of what had been happening between the wars proved too serious a handicap. I still remember the perplexed, incredulous expression on the interviewer's face when he discovered that I'd never heard of P.G. Wodehouse, Mr. Gandhi, or Suzanne Lenglen.

Another bleak remembrance is of the day when, half-stupefied by influenza and the freezing fog that seemed to penetrate the inmost back recesses of one's soul, I presented myself with extreme diffidence at the Redbourne Hotel, then a war-time annexe of the B.B.C.

Mr. Reginald Beckwith the playwright, a friend of my aunt's, was doing special broadcasts for the B.B.C., and, being the kindest of men, had provided me with a letter of introduction. From this — since it contained a remarkable catalogue of my accomplishments — my optimist uncle and aunt hoped great things.

Unfortunately, the brisk, elderly recruiting officer who put me through my paces appeared unimpressed. Specialized in Fourth-century History, did I? She was sorry, but at the moment, the B.B.C. were more interested in the Twentieth. What about languages? In these days, of course, everybody knew French, German and Italian: it seemed, however, that if my Greek, Russian, Turkish and Spanish were fairly fluent, she might perhaps find something for me as a — I believe

290

"monitor" was the word she used. It conveyed nothing to me.

A few more searching questions revealed how destitute I was of the necessary qualifications, and I found myself being politely dismissed with a murmured promise that the B.B.C. would "let me know".

Once more I'd drawn a blank.

Had Gay or Barbara been in town, I should have fled to them for counsel. As it was, I paid a call on the uncle who had initiated me in the mysteries of modern music when first I came forth into the world.

Though kind, he was not particularly helpful. This, I think, was because he regarded me as what he himself would have called the lowest type of mutt . . . a new word which I hastened to add to my rapidly increasing vocabulary.

As a result, after an hour or two of his companionship, I felt so mournful that I could have run round the city howling, like the dog in the psalms.

Like most of my family, he had a very poor opinion of nuns. It was true, he knew little about them; but this in no way prevented him from criticizing their behaviour whenever he got the chance.

Convents, he declared, were filled with herds of semi-demented spinsters whose repressed and abnormal existences induced a warped, unhealthy attitude towards life. The perpetual introspection which, he insisted, was their principal occupation could only bring about a frustrated, inhibited, even perverted state of mind.

It was useless to argue with him; he despised me too much even to listen to what I said.

However, I really couldn't allow such statements to go unchallenged. So, now and again, I used to unwind my coils like a cobra and strike back.

I explained to him that, on the subject of religious life, though quite possibly on no other in the world, I was qualified to speak. And he must forgive me if I told him that his outlook on the matter was prejudiced and absurd.

Nuns and monks were *not* — as he seemed to think — unhinged old maids and desiccated bachelors who had shuffled off their responsibilities in order to live lives of soured virginity. If he wanted the right angle on the subject, he should read the lives and writings of the saints and mystics: Catherine of Siena, Francis of Assisi, Angela of Foligno, Bernard of Clairvaux . . . Nobody who studied them could fail to see that, far from being either negative or diminished, the life lived by monks and nuns was one of intense and — in the case of the saints — even passionate love. Only, this love, instead of being "natural" and human, was "supernatural" and divine.

My uncle was scandalized.

As by now, however, I was in it up to the neck, I thought I might as well say everything I wanted to and have done with it.

So I suggested that, as a starting point, we'd take it that he admitted God to be a living person. Very well, then. Suppose that it were possible — as the saints and mystics declared it was — to get into conscious, vital contact with him; as surely and certainly (though, of

292

course, in an entirely different way) as with somebody at the opposite end of a telephone.

Well, God being who and what he was (among other things "the Man Who Made the World", as Chesterton somewhere calls him), wouldn't this business of getting into touch — this setting up of a personal, intimate relation with such a being — be the most stupendous, ineffable adventure within the possibility of human experience? And wouldn't those prepared to undertake the conditions imposed before success could be hoped for in this transcendent experiment, be a thousand times justified in doing so and in living the kind of life that would most help them to the attainment of their end?

What was more — and I pointed out that whether or no he believed it, made not the smallest difference to the objective reality of the fact — if people in the world had any idea of what that which the mystics describe as a life of union with God could really mean — well, the queues of people begging for admittance outside convent doors would stretch for miles.

As I might have foreseen, this burst of eloquence produced not the slightest effect upon my uncle.

There was a short, slightly embarrassing pause. Then he gave one of those little patronizing laughs that can be so supremely aggravating.

"I'm afraid," he said, "I've got too much common sense to take that kind of nonsense seriously. But I'm quite ready to believe that *you* believe it. Do help yourself to another cup of tea!"

My aunt and uncle being the kind of people who had always, so to speak, dwelt in marble halls, it was useless to ask their opinion as to where inexpensive lodgings could be sought.

It was, in the end, my uncle's secretary who told me of a periodical called *Dalton's Weekly* in which long lists of every possible kind of lodgings were to be found.

Armed with this, I set out for the Marylebone Public Library — always my haven of refuge in times of tribulation — borrowed the largest street map of London that was to be had and sat down with it spread out on the table before me to plan, like Napoleon, my campaign of the next few days.

As I had no idea how to find my way round London and knew little about the personal character of the various localities, I had nothing to guide me in my choice. I therefore picked out the addresses nearest the various jobs suggested by the indefatigable directors of Labour at Sardinia Street and set out with the list tucked under my wing to explore.

One of the small things to which I'd found it hardest to grow accustomed when I left the convent was the business of balancing myself in high-heeled shoes.

The kind worn by nuns are square-toed, flat-heeled and deliberately clumping, so it was months before I felt really at home in the elegant things my sister had helped me to buy. Which helps to explain how I came to twist my ankle rather viciously soon after my return to Portland Place.

A limp and a dropsical-looking ankle was not going to be exactly an asset in the surfeit of walking and talking that was to fill the next few days. Remembering, however, what I'd been taught in the convent about suppressing one's "natural reactions", I fought down the despondent mood induced by fog and influenza and set out to try my luck.

A job as assistant librarian at Guildhall had been suggested by Sardinia Street. This appealed to my historical imagination. As, however, I felt doubtful whether, with my peculiar limitations, I could secure so exalted a post, I tried, as I limped along Cheapside to my interview, to enlist the sympathies of the Saints of Paradise. It struck me that such holy doctors as Ambrose, Augustine and Jerome, who had spent every available moment in writing or studying books, might well take some interest in my affairs. *Omnes sancti doctores, orate pro nobis.* I invoked them passionately.

The head librarian, a large, kind, impressive person who rather overawed me, drew up a chair to the blazing fire in his comfortable room. To my relief, he had no trace of the slick, new-world manner which always so petrified me. Eyeing me thoughtfully, he began to talk.

And here I may mention that one of the things which has impressed me about the men I've seen since I left my cloister is their genius for comfort. I could say quite a lot about this, but at the moment it will be enough to remark that physical well-being seems far more essential to them than to us. Men just will not put up with the things that women take quite simply in their stride. In fact, men strike me as being — if I may so express it without seeming offensive — more "bodily" in every way. This may very well explain why nuns are far more numerous than monks and why statistics show that the percentage of women-mystics so far exceeds that of men.

One would not, of course, dare to suggest that men are more selfish than women; but it does rather look as though they were less inclined to cut loose from what "flatters the senses" than women, who step out with comparative ease into those draughty, uncomfortable regions in which the highest spiritual adventures normally take place.

However, we must return to Guildhall.

The job sounded ideal. And indeed, had I but understood more about the intricacies of the Dewey system, I believe it would have been mine. As it was, this — to me — new and quite incomprehensible method of classification was quite beyond me. I was therefore told kindly that if no one with higher qualifications applied within the next few days, the head librarian would Let Me Know. The interview was at an end.

As I followed him to be shown the charred ruins of the ancient building, yet another invocation from the Litany of the Saints soared up to heaven. The blitz scars were recent: the wreckage terrible. Brought up in the convent to an almost excessive reverence for things ancient, I looked upon the havoc wrought with indignation smouldering in my heart. *Ut inimicos nostrae* — I adjusted the words to present needs — *humiliare digneris, Te rogamus audi nos.* Apparently my reactions to the spectacle were much the same as those of the men who had composed that Litany more than fifteen hundred years before, perhaps with similar provocation. Genseric — Attila — Hitler — their mentality seems to have been very much the same.

I wandered about Holborn, staggered by the immensity of the desolation. In my tidy, well-ordered religious life, such a spectacle would have been quite inconceivable. Whole areas had been entirely flattened. Hideous bomb-craters yawned amid grey heaps of rubble and twisted metal. Here and there stood a smoke-scorched, partially shattered house whose sides, roof or front had been completely ripped away. I was appalled.

Just in case the Guildhall job should, after all, materialize, I decided to explore the surrounding neighbourhood and discover what were my chances of a lodging.

I tried twenty-two addresses. Having no previous experience to tell me what lodgings ought to look like, I took it for granted that what I saw was the usual thing. They were all dreadful, and abominably expensive; worse, almost every inquiry elicited the brief and unamiable answer that they were full up; and the door was shut in my face. By the end of the afternoon I was feeling so weary and dreary that I could have sat on a doorstep and wept.

And it was at this point that a wave of something not very unlike the revolt that precedes despair began slowly to creep over me. Loneliness and fatigue were beginning to break down my defences. But there was

297

more to it than that. The temptation — if that is the proper word for it — was to give way to a savage feeling of resentment against the Powers That Be for having cast my lot where it had fallen. Why, oh, why had I not been given a place among the ranks of the Fortunate Women — the *comfortable* ones of this earth — rich, elegant, capable, influential, with a family, home, friends, possessions, achievements; a car to take me anywhere I wanted, and, in the background, a large, pleasant, important and reasonably companionable husband to come between me and the wind?

Why had things so turned out as to end in the failure of my mighty effort to follow the way of life that I had once so honestly believed it my duty to embrace? And now, here I was — simply one of ten million or so unwanted elderly spinsters: dull, hard up, dressed in other people's clothes, without background, belongings or home and debarred by my queer limitations from refashioning my life into any pleasant or profitable shape.

What was it all *for*? What was the use of anything? Why had one been born into such a world of frustration and despair?

It was not the first assault I had experienced from that particular quarter. And my heart failed me as I realized the interior struggle I should now have to face.

(3)

This depressing account of my attack of gloom has been dragged in to introduce something I want to say

298

about a state of mind experienced by most of those who undertake the adventure of Religious Life.

It is known as Spiritual Desolation.

Like influenza, you are not absolutely bound to get it. Some people only have mild attacks; others suffer so acutely that they all but pass out. Mild or severe, however, the experience is universally acknowledged to be among the most gruelling of the spiritual life.

Generally speaking, this is more or less what happens.

As a rule, one is first attracted to prayer by the joy and sweetness that one finds in it. (People who never pray will obviously think that this is nonsense. Well, they are mistaken. It is a fact that there is no happiness on earth which can be compared to the happiness that is to be found in prayer. How, indeed, should it be otherwise if prayer is what the saints declare it to be — conscious contact with a Being whose very nature is Love?) And the first months or even years in the Noviceship are often spent in a state which is the spiritual equivalent for being in love. As a result, nothing is hard; one is carried along by a kind of romantic enthusiasm which makes of Religious Life an earthly paradise.

And then — often suddenly and for no apparent reason — the sunshine vanishes. Instead of the warmth and colour that have hitherto permeated everything, a dreadful depressing greyness — a dyspepsia of the soul — blights every detail of one's life like a bleak east wind. The almost rapturous sense of God's love and of his presence which made of each hard thing simply an opportunity to prove one's love, gives place to a feeling of terrifying solitude in which one becomes dismally aware only of the stark realities of life. The entire spiritual world seems meaningless and unreal; even one's own most vivid spiritual experiences fade out like half-forgotten dreams. One becomes keenly, sometimes agonizingly aware of everything prosaic: heat, cold, stuffy rooms, the acute discomfort of one's open chilblains: excessive weariness, the irritation of the heavy, un-comfortable garments that one is obliged to wear: other people's maddening "little ways"; the "sinking feeling" and depression that are inseparable from fasting: the appalling monotony of the rule-imposed routine . . .

Worse, one's condition is often aggravated by odd, inexplicable stupidities of hand and mind. One drops, spills, breaks, upsets and loses things: forgets one's duties; does one's work badly and finds oneself in awkward situations that lead to humiliation and reproof. Bitterest of all, one is beset by horrible temptations to see in Religious Life the most fantastic of all delusions and oneself as a pathetic fool for having undertaken it.

Normally one would turn to prayer as an escape from all these tribulations. But to those in the grip of real spiritual desolation, the hours of prayer are perhaps the hardest of the whole depressing day. One spends them in a dreary struggle against distractions, temptations and often over-powering sleep.

A novice who consults her Mistress about this melancholy state of things will be told that she should rejoice at these signs that God is now Treating Her As A

Strong Soul instead of as a Babe Who Must Be Fed On Milk. It will be explained to her that souls aiming at union with God must be prepared to undergo at his hands the process of purification which will "detach them from the idolatries of all that is not him".

Well, all this, of course, is quite true. But it is hardly calculated to encourage anyone in the throes of their first real taste of Desolation. Strong souls might be braced: but the average type — especially those who tend to be irritated by time-worn *clichés* — come forth feeling considerably worse than when they went in. Usually, by the time one has lashed oneself up to the point of revealing one's deplorable condition to one's Superior, one has reached such a pitch of gibbering misery as to be incapable of response to any further stimulus. And to be told that *"Un moine triste est un triste moine"*, or that, "It is the God of consolations and not the consolations of God that a true religious should seek" or that "Ten minutes' prayer in Desolation is worth a hundred in Consolation" merely makes one's hackles rise.

And when, on the top of all the rest, it is pointed out that to moan because all consolation in prayer has been withdrawn proves one to be a Spiritual Glutton . . . well, really, I ask you!

Souls in this state often go through real agonies. Having nothing to distract them from their wretchedness only intensifies the suffering. If one could only get away for a week-end or seek refuge in different companionship. But that, of course, is unthinkable. So one just drags along with the harness always galling in the same spot until such time as God sees fit to deliver one. Sometimes the trial lasts for long periods. St. Teresa is reported to have endured it for over twenty years. It appears to be the process by which souls normally advance in spiritual living: a blaze of light, followed by a long dark tunnel, at the end of which — provided always that one perseveres with the necessary courage — light is again vouchsafed. One then enters upon a new phase of the adventure, on a higher plane, fitted for new experiences. Then comes another spell of darkness and suffering, followed by an interval of light. And so the process of purification goes on.

All this has been analysed in detail by St. John of the Cross in his classic *The Dark Night of the Soul*. It is, however, unlikely that anyone who hasn't actually known at least the preliminary stages of the soul-searing happenings therein described will be able to grasp what it is all about.

Now, whether the fit of depression that so suddenly came down upon me in Holborn had or had not anything to do with the Dark Night of the Soul, it would be difficult to say. But there could be no doubt at all that for me it was the beginning of a very Dark Night indeed of everything else. For the next month or two I had to struggle on bereft of that spirit of adventure which had hitherto helped me to overcome every obstacle. Instead I was left feeling as though a cold sponge had been inserted into the space between the waistband and the heart.

Long experience had taught me that there was only one thing to be done in such circumstances. This was to set one's teeth grimly and just carry on by the will, without paying the slightest attention to how one felt.

And this I more or less successfully now endeavoured to do.

(4)

Next morning, my uncle, who almost always followed up cantankerousness by kindness, rang up and suggested some addresses as a stand-by in case the Guildhall job fell through.

The first of these landed me in the London Library, where a harassed librarian regretted politely that the vacancy I was after had just been filled. Should, however, any other suitable post in the Library fall vacant, he would certainly Let Me Know. I was, of course, a member of the Library Association? . . . No? . . . In that case, he was very much afraid . . .

I drifted out again into St. James's Square.

Address Number Two was in Oxford Street. It took me a long time to get there as I had stupidly left my map of London at home; I was therefore reduced to interrogating passers-by. All of these appeared to be foreigners. A policeman in those days was rare as a dodo, and all the directions given me seemed to be contradictory. I had, moreover, no idea which bus to take. Just to make things more difficult, it was raining rather heavily. Evidently, it was going to be One of Those Days.

The place, when at last I found it, turned out to be a sort of bureau in which women who wanted to join the Forces went through a preliminary sorting. The people who ran it seemed, for once, even more anxious to get hold of me than I was to join them; which made me, not unnaturally, suspicious.

A heavily made-up girl in khaki — I forget which branch of the Services she represented — sat at a table conducting interviews. She murmured:

"Ow! You reelly ought to join up, you know; they *do* (pronounced "dee-oo") give you such *wizard* pyjamas!"

But even had this bait succeeded, it would have been useless, for I was past the age limit. I withdrew, feeling even more on-the-shelf and obsolete than before.

Incredible as it may sound, the Times Book Club in Wigmore Street didn't appear to want me either, though they promised me that should a suitable vacancy occur, they too would be very pleased to Let Me Know.

By this time I was beginning to feel that if anyone else promised to Let Me Know, there would be murder . . .

Not knowing in the least how to conduct myself, I drifted into a shop in Oxford Street and nervously treated myself to lunch. (Should I ever learn how to walk into a proper restaurant and command a meal as nearly worth the eating as could be obtained in war-time? I doubted it.)

The third address on my list was a well-known firm of gramophone makers who had advertised for an assistant in their record library. Unfortunately, the place had been bombed only the evening before and chaos reigned. Judging that it would be futile to seek employment in a building that mainly consisted of rubble, I withdrew.

The last address on the list had been culled from one of that morning's daily papers. It was for an assistant in what was described as a "photographic business" in St. John's Wood. As previous experience was stated to be unnecessary, I thought I might perhaps stand a chance.

I hadn't visited St. John's Wood since the spacious days before the First World War; but the name still held memories of thrilling happenings at Lords. The house I sought was in a heavily bombed locality and when found struck me as quite the most unprepossessing in the long, dull, deserted road. With its shuttered windows and neglected garden overgrown with blasted-looking shrubs, it appeared to me as the sort of house in which positively anything might happen if the wrong sort of people were to get together inside.

Long after I'd pulled it, the old-fashioned bell went on echoing through what sounded like perfectly empty rooms. Most creepy. I began to regret that I'd ever come.

I regretted it even more when after a long wait, the door was opened by a Quilp-ish looking person with the shape and movements of a gorilla. He led me into a dark, damp room without so much as a chair to sit on. When he opened the shutters, I observed that the dingy paper hung in strips from the damp and leprous-looking walls.

"I gonduct my business in ze basement," he informed me, with the guttural intonation that one associates instinctively with villainous types. "Gome! I vill show you!" and he led me down a flight of dark and twisting stairs.

The big room which he unlocked at the bottom had blackout screens across the windows. It was lighted by green, heavily shaded electric bulbs. A large table which filled almost the entire room was covered with trays full of evil-smelling chemicals in which floated photographic negatives and prints. The atmosphere was poisonous.

"You vill help me mit the photographs down here," explained Mr. Quilp, "effery day from nine till six. I vill gif you four pound effery week. It is good pay."

I objected that the smell would make me sick.

"Ach, you soon get use to dat," he assured me.

Then I asked him what the photographs were. This appeared to amuse him.

"Look, I show you vone!" he said, then held up a negative against the light. It was the most disgustingly indecent thing that I had ever seen.

I didn't say anything, because I could think of no remark to make. I suppose Quilp misunderstood my silence, for, still chuckling, he began holding up other choice specimens of his art for me to admire.

I forget what excuse I eventually made to get away, but he was not pleased about it and began muttering at me rather threateningly.

I scuttled up the stairs and across the hall, murmuring something about having to catch a bus, and had just got the front door open when he put out a hand to detain me. At that moment, by the mercy of heaven, the post-man opened the garden gate and came up the steps.

306

I fled past him and a moment later was scurrying down the street as though the hounds of hell were at my heels.

That incident rather put me off applying for jobs advertised in newspapers. Henceforward I confined myself to addresses recommended by Sardinia Street.

A whole chapter might be written about the interviews and adventures that filled the next few days. I became quite an adept at the art of form-filling and at evading inconvenient questions as to what I had been up to in the years before the War.

In between times, I scoured the streets of London — unsuccessfully — for lodgings. And every day my mood of black despondency grew more profound.

(5)

There came a day when it was unmistakably borne in upon me that the time had come for me to evacuate the spare-room in my uncle's house in Portland Place.

I had taken my courage in both hands and gone down to Winchester on a wild goose chase after a job as receptionist to a partnership of doctors who saw their patients in a dank old house full of telephones and stairs.

On that particular day, when I returned to Portland Place rather late in the evening (I had taken the wrong bus at Waterloo and got lost in the black-out — an experience I shan't easily forget) — it was to find a domestic crisis on the verge of bubbling over. In the course of this, I realized that my departure had already been too long delayed.

Once again, therefore, I packed up my few belongings, and set out next morning, grimly determined to find another roof to shelter me before night fell or die in the attempt.

According to *Dalton's Weekly*, there seemed to be three localities in which lodgings were most likely to be found; Bloomsbury had refused to be my washpot; over Kensington, therefore, I would now cast my shoe. Failing that, there would still remain Victoria, though the glimpses I'd had of that neighbourhood during my wanderings in London made me feel that it was the last region in which I'd care to live.

Over my adventures in Kensington we may draw a veil. They were not very interesting and by two o'clock in the afternoon — I had been knocking at doors since soon after eight in the morning — the marble hardness of the pavements and the indignant refusals of the eighteen landladies whom I'd tried to persuade into lowering their extortionate terms had entered rather deeply into my bones. It was, of course, raining, and to say that I wished myself dead would be an understatement of the way I was beginning to feel.

The worst of London is that the distances between place and place are so enormous. By the time I'd bused from Kensington to Victoria Station, the streets were already beginning to grow dark. However, a lodging had got to be found, so, black-out or no black-out, I had to continue my search.

Now, I don't suppose that the streets and squares and terraces round Victoria are in reality much worse than any other collection of old-fashioned, blitz-scarred houses that have obviously come down in the world. My remembrance, however, of the whole locality is of a neighbourhood so dreary, depressing and dingy that my mood of desolation seemed to be reflected back from everything upon which I looked.

St. George's Drive ... Eccleston Square ... Belgrave Road ... up and down I wandered, footsore and weary, past the long bleak rows of drab front doors through which, whenever I pressed a bell or rapped a knocker, unfriendly faces scowled upon me, naming terms which were far beyond what I felt I could pay.

(I don't know why I had such a desperate fixation about economy. I suppose it sprang from the cold fear that used to haunt me lest I shouldn't be able to find a job and that my income would prove too small to live upon. When you lack Experience of Life, you have no standard by which to measure things. I therefore counted my halfpence like a miser, going without everything except the sheerest necessities. I even walked everywhere instead of taking buses, till I discovered that shoe-leather was the more expensive item of the two.)

The climax of this odious day occurred just as it was growing dark.

I had drifted into one of those dingy terraces off the sinister Wilton Road and was standing near a street-lamp, so footsore that I felt incapable of taking another step. I had found nothing and it appeared

309

unlikely that I should do so. To cast myself upon my family was unthinkable.

What in the world was I going to do?

Now, if this book were one of those pious biographies which infest the shelves of convent libraries, what followed would probably be described in such words as these:

> Recollecting herself profoundly, she placed herself devoutly in the presence of her Creator, and, inspired by the remembrance of the many occasions on which, in answer to fervent prayer, the aid of Heaven had been vouchsafed, she once more invoked the Divine Assistance with earnest confidence and hope.

Well, of course, if people *must* write about God like that they *must*. But I wish it could be prevented. For, to write about anything from that angle automatically invests it with an atmosphere of dullness which is too deadly to be endured. Isn't it bad enough to think of God as an inconveniently omniscient Old Gentleman in a cope, cloud-enthroned, only waiting till people start really enjoying themselves to leap out on them and spoil the fun? Or as a meek, white-night-gowned Personage with long hair, neatly parted down the middle, looking out upon the agonizing world with an expression of pained melancholy? And yet, dreadful as are both these crimes against the truth, there is another which strikes me as the worst of all. It is, to surround the idea of God with an atmosphere of dullness.

310

After all, wouldn't you yourself prefer to know that the thought of you roused fear or even dislike in other people, than that they simply looked upon you as a crashing bore?

The fact that so many people can still say, even after the Incarnation (how often, indeed, I've heard them!): "Sorry, but I'm just not interested in religion", seems to me to indicate that the devil has done his job extremely well. I had not been many months out of the convent before it became evident to me that if you discussed art, books, music, sport, sex, films, clothes, ghosts or personalities, you could always be sure of a response from someone. But mention God, and a vague atmosphere of discomfort immediately made itself felt. Rather as though you had dropped some sort of social brick. People simply weren't interested. And yet — wouldn't you have thought dullness was the last quality to be associated with the Man Who Made the World?

Even in the convent, where God permeated life almost like the air one breathed, its vestiges occasionally appeared. A nun's *vie intérieure* — known colloquially as her "spirituality" — could be devastatingly dull. Some of the priests, too, who came to give Retreats (though to be honest, this was the exception) generated a spiritual atmosphere that was dry as desert dust. They were such bores that it was all one could do to sit still and listen to their sermons.

After long reflection, I have come to the conclusion that this spiritual dullness must be the outcome of having little or no "personal relations" — if that is the proper name for it — with God. The boring preachers

311

were those who, instead of discussing God's ways and works as a man speaks about the doings of his friend, dished up second-hand material and served it up with rhetoric as sauce to hide the staleness of the taste. Just the difference between someone who reads aloud extracts from a book of travels and somebody who has actually visited the spot.

The fact is, the closer you get to God and the more intimately you know him, the more thrilling and absorbing does he become. It is only those who do not know him who find him dull.

What I actually did on this occasion was to send out as desperate an S.O.S. to Heaven as I had uttered for quite a number of years.

The result was what would have been described in the convent as "a miraculous answer to prayer".[1] For, believe it or not, I was suddenly inspired to look round

---

[1] Why answers to prayer should so often be described as "miraculous", I have yet to learn. Abbot Chapman once said to me that our prayers were invariably answered: the only thing was that since God concerned himself more with our spiritual than our temporal good, he didn't always do things in the way that *we* should consider best. But as any parent of small and not very far-seeing children will tell you, *No* is just as authentic an answer as *Yes*. God, explained the Abbot, being who and what he is, sees all round everything: whereas we, being of time, can only see our own little dot in the infinite and eternal scheme of things. At the time, I remember thinking it was a rather stodgy explanation. Now, having realized my own tendency to make mistakes about the things I pray for, I am completely satisfied.

at the house behind me. And, as I did so, a hand drew back the lace curtains of a ground floor window and put up a large card on which was printed the one word which of all others in the world I most desired to see:

APARTMENTS.

I dragged myself up the steps to the blitz-scarred front door and rang the bell.

(6)

I can still think of no explanation as to why the landlady asked so small a sum for the room she let to me. I suppose it was just part of the miracle.

She was a Lithuanian, yellow-haired, blue-eyed and married to an English ex-butler whose dazzlingly respectable appearance filled me with awe. Both of them were so kind to me that I gave them a permanent place on my list of Wingless Angels.

Though my small room was dark and gloomy, it had excellent furniture. The only snag was that they couldn't supply me with food. So, three times a day I had to trot out — almost invariably in rain or sleet — to the Empire Restaurant near Victoria. Here I stood patiently in the cafeteria queue for my breakfast, lunch and the tea-supper which was one of my economies.

I doubt whether my meals cost more than half a crown a day. Yet I felt sure that if I could "do for" myself, I should be able to live on even less.

The first Sunday I spent in my new surroundings is a day I shall never forget.

I had been to Mass at Westminster Cathedral and had felt overwhelmed by the beauty in which that greatest of all Acts had been enshrined. The vast building was flooded with rose-coloured light that streamed in through the sanctuary windows from the fiery, fog-veiled disc of the January sun. The dim side-chapels and the dark roof-space behind the gigantic crucifix were realms of sombre shadow, against which the pale clouds of ascending incense showed like drifting veils of mist. An unseen choir chanted from behind the altar, the unaccompanied plain-chant of the *Kyrie* and *Gloria in Excelsis* rising and falling like voices from another world.

Out in the street, the cold stabbed through one like a rapier. Bemused and dizzy, it seemed to me that a cup of hot coffee was the most desirable thing in life.

It was, therefore, rather a blow to discover that not only the Empire Restaurant, but apparently every other place at which food could be obtained was shuttered and barred.

I suppose that if I'd had the wit of a worm I should have gone to a hotel. It was, however, the first time I'd had to fend for myself on a Sunday in London and the idea didn't occur to me. I took it for granted that the same law applied everywhere. Depressed and frozen, I wandered back to Bettingdon Terrace.

It was unfortunate that my landlady and her husband had gone out for the day. It seemed that there was nothing to be done but to tighten my belt and endure.

Just about what should have normally been tea-time, I suddenly remembered some pea-nut butter that I had brought from Portland Place. The trouble was that, as I didn't possess a spoon, I couldn't imagine how to eat it. In the end, I decided that my shoe-horn would have to be used as a substitute. So I said my grace, sat down on the bed and set to work.

I will make no attempt to describe what I felt like on waking the following morning. Instead, I will utter a warning. Should you ever, after a fairly long fast, feel inclined to replenish your interior with shoe-hornfuls of peanut butter, take my advice and DON'T.

The next few days were taken up with intensive job-hunting. Some of my adventures were diverting; all helped to enrich my Experience of Life.

Unfortunately, in almost every case, the snag was my lack of previous experience. Now and again, however, I myself declined a job simply because I felt so sure that I should never be able to hold it down. This was, of course, a despicable line to take. But the truth was that since my experiment at Wisthaven, a sort of diffidence had begun to sap my courage. Lately, too, all the spring and bounce seemed to have gone out of me. I began to lose the good I might have won by fearing the attempt; a state of mind which has always struck me as particularly deplorable. And since inner darkness had come down upon me in Holborn, I no longer had the power to find wonder and delight in common things. Even the vision of my Cornish Cottage had receded into the universal fog and refused to emerge as a source of consolation.

Things, in fact, were looking about as black as they could be.

To add to the general atmosphere of *accidie*, sleep also began to desert me. Even by day the neighbourhood was noisy; but after midnight, when the house opposite began to eject its inmates, there was a Comus-like din. Shouts, shrieks, shrill giggling and drunken laughter made sleep impossible. When I mentioned it to my landlady, she merely shook her flaxen head and explained in her funny clipped English that it was a Bad House and that one of these days undoubtedly Something Would Happen there.

Possibly my complaints may have had something to do with speeding up the crisis, for a few nights later I was roused by an energetic knocking at the door. I hopped out of bed to find my landlady with a huge and apologetic-looking policeman. Between them they bore a folding screen which they proceeded to hoist into my room.

Should I very much object, my landlady inquired, if the police officer were to come in and sit at my window for a little while? He wanted to keep an eye on the comings and goings in the house over the way and from my room he would be able to observe everything without being himself visible.

I did object, and said so. This, however, appeared to distress them both so much that in the end there seemed nothing for it but to give in. Accordingly, the screen was placed all round my bed to provide a semblance of privacy. The Law then marched in, switched off the light, drew back an inch or so of curtain and then sat down, like puss at a mousehole, to observe its prey.

It must have been shortly after midnight that he sprang to his feet, muttered an apology for having what he described as "incommodated" me and darted out into the street.

I looked out of the window but it was too dark to see much of what happened. Two cars drew up; there was the sound of a police whistle — then voices, some angry, some laughing. Then some scuffling followed by the sound of running feet. Presently the cars drove off and there was silence. I waited a little but as nothing further happened, I went to bed.

Next morning, my landlady told me that there had been a police raid. After which, I am glad to say, sounds of revelry were heard no more across the street.

(7)

"If you will allow me to say so," observed Mr. Home — he had already done so twice during the interview, so that I was getting used to it — "you are *quite* the best-preserved lady for your years that I've ever seen!"

It *did* just flash through my mind that the compliment — if compliment you could call it — might have been more felicitously worded. But at forty-nine one is thankful for even the smallest mercies. I therefore said nothing. Thirty years back, I reflected, not without amusement, what a different story it would have been!

And here, if I may, before explaining who Mr. Home was and why I was sitting in that cosy armchair in his inner sanctuary, I will digress again.

From the age of about seventeen onwards, I had been, so I am told, what would now be described as "easy to look at". There can be no vanity in saying this. To-day, *Vogue* patterns, permanent waves, make-up and film-star technique have put glamour pretty well within the reach of everybody. In my youth, it was otherwise. Good-looking girls were far rarer then than now. So that if nature had blessed you with blue eyes, curly hair, a good complexion and the attractiveness that is inseparable from youth, you were bound to draw admiring glances from the average male.

When I first left school, I was considerably thrilled by this eye-homage. After a time, however, I grew so accustomed to it that I accepted it simply as my due.

Most women, I suppose, lose their looks and physical attraction gradually. And because this fading-out is a slow-motion process, it hurts less than if it happened all at once.

With me it was different.

I Went In young and good-looking. I Came Out elderly and plain. And I disliked this. Very much indeed.

In my youth, when I entered a room, bus or railway carriage, eyes had a way of straying round in my direction and of returning there over and over again. *Now* nobody ever bothered to glance at me. Or if they did, they looked away again so swiftly that it was almost worse than not being scrutinized at all.

I found it humiliating. It gave me a feeling of being inexpressibly old and dull.

We will now return to the inner sanctum of the Head Librarian at the Royal Society of Medicine, where Mr. Home was interviewing me for the job of temporary assistant in the Library.

After all the unpleasant people I'd been up against during the past few weeks, I found something very soothing about the kindliness of Mr. Home. This elderly semi-invalid, who liked Spain and played the cello in his leisure moments, seemed curiously uninfluenced by the jagged rhythms of modern life. To my astonishment, he never even mentioned the Library Association and accepted what I told him of my previous experience without undue probing into pre-war activities. So that, although he warned me that I must wait for a final decision till after a committee meeting in a fortnight's time, I went forth feeling not only full of courage but more cheerful than I'd done for weeks.

Just for safety, however, I thought it best to provide myself with at least one alternative job. Gay and Barbara had talked about the British Council: why shouldn't I call there and find out whether any vacancy existed which I might fill? So away I sped to their headquarters in Hanover Street.

On the whole, I think the most important thing I learnt from my invasion of their premises was that one can sometimes get farther by a judicious use of bluff and blarney than by keeping to the more conventional methods of the *chemin des vâches*. Thanks to a technique I'd evolved in the light of previous failures, I successfully managed to worm my way into the presence of a very important personage indeed.

Mr. Hampden, was, if I remember rightly, something high up in the British Council's Library Department. Though young, he gave the impression of being remarkably efficient. His manners, too, were charming. In fact, we should have got on very well had he not completely upset my poise by offering me a cigarette.

The moment I'd accepted it, I remembered how Gay had once declared that a man could find out Everything That Mattered about a woman by observing the way she dealt with a cigarette. This shook me rather badly. I reflected, however, that he probably wouldn't discover much from my antics: since it was unlikely that he'd ever seen anything remotely resembling the way I dealt with mine.

To my astonishment, the interview concluded with Mr. Hampden offering me a three months' trial in the library department of one of the British Council's headquarters in the provinces.

I was so overcome that I blinked at him for several seconds before I could think of anything to say. A blind instinct suggested that I should do well to get out of the place before he had time to change his mind. So, trying to conceal the exultation that was beginning to overwhelm me, I rose from my chair and, with as much

320

dignity and detachment as I could summon, held out my hand.

"Thank you," I said. "Thank you so very much. If I may, I will think over your offer. And when I've made up my mind, I will Let You Know . . ."

The other job for which I tried was at the Admiralty.

This involved several visits to the Labour Exchange, a considerable amount of queueing and the filling up of yet another lengthy autobiographical form. About ten days later I was summoned to report at certain temporary offices in Whitehall. Here, in a cold, badly lighted room I found about twenty rather dingy-looking women and one man waiting, apparently, on the same business as myself.

Presently two bewilderingly bright and competent young women of the school-teacher type appeared and ushered us into a room packed with rows of small wooden desks. I slipped into one in the back row between an elderly woman in glasses and a frail little wisp of a girl whose squint had apparently preserved her from being press-ganged into the Forces; and the ordeal began.

Now, I take it that what the Admiralty wanted to find out was the degree of intelligence possessed by the various candidates for the job. And — in the majority of cases — the General Information Quiz which formed the subject matter of most of the questions was as good a method as any other of separating the sheep from the goats.

For me, however, it would have been hard to find a more unfortunate system. Apart from the arithmetical problems, which I was totally incapable of solving, they nearly all dealt with things about which I'd never even heard.

It looked rather as though I should have to spend the morning twiddling my thumbs.

Then an idea struck me.

I composed an introductory note in which I explained the situation. In it I stated that I'd had a rather peculiar career but that although I couldn't answer just the questions that had been set, I hoped that what I was about to write below would serve as a proof that I possessed a certain amount of education.

I then wrote out in the form of questions and answers some fairly erudite facts about the Roman Empire in the fourth and fifth centuries. I drew up several neat little tables of dates and a genealogy of the rather complicated family of the Emperor Constantine. And I ended with an essay entitled *Points of Contrast Between London in 1913 and 1943*. One and a half hours' work in all; and though I say it who shouldn't, quite a tidy little sampler of my own particular type of mind.

Unfortunately, I shall never know what the examiners thought of it. Some days later, however, I received an official communication which stated with reference to my recent interview, that the Lords Commissioners of the Admiralty regretted to inform me that there was no suitable vacancy in which my services could be utilized.

On the whole, I was not very much surprised.

(8)

In the end, I decided to turn down the British Council for the Royal Society of Medicine.

For my final interview, I had to go before a committee consisting of kind Mr. Home; a rather ferocious-looking old gentleman, whose name I don't remember, and a dynamic being in some kind of lavender uniform, who turned out to be Mr. Geoffrey Edwards, the secretary and moving spirit of the R.S.M.

I was extremely nervous. They were, however, so nice to me that I ended by feeling happier than I had done for weeks. And when at the end of the proceedings, kind Mr. Home invited me to celebrate my engagement as an employee of the Society by having tea in his book-lined lair in the back recesses of the important-looking building, I felt as though I had fallen among friends.

It may possibly be remembered that some weeks previously, while awaiting my turn for an interview at the Ministry of Supply in Adam Street, I had been struck by the appearance of a tall, pale young man who would have fitted better into the pages of the *Morte d'Arthur* than into the waiting-room of a twentieth-century War Ministry. Picture to yourself, then, my surprise, when I discovered him as my fellow-guest at tea. He looked more like Sir Alesaunder Le Orphelin than ever; very much a champion of the oppressed, despite the obvious fact that his physical strength was much inferior to the spirit within. He had not, I believe, been down very long from Cambridge and I felt at once that many of our values were the same. I liked him. His name, it seemed, was John. Mr. Home explained that he too had joined the staff of the Royal Society of Medicine that afternoon.

I mention the tea-party because it held for me a very *mauvais quart d'heure* which I still remember. Being the only female present, I was asked to preside over the teapot. And this was a thing which I hadn't done for close on thirty years. I could hardly have felt more at sea if I'd been asked to take the wheel on the *Queen Elizabeth*. Manners and customs had changed so astonishingly during my absence that I felt sure all kinds of new rules about tea, sugar and milk must have come into being while I was away. A remark of Barbara's, to the effect that there were two sorts of people in the world — those who poured out the milk first and those who poured out the tea first — floated disturbingly through my mind. Which ought I to do? And didn't one have to do something about filling up the teapot with hot water? It was all very confusing. Another agitated S.O.S. sped heavenwards for guidance to the Saints of Paradise . . .

In the end, I got out of the difficulty by repeating Barbara's statement and asking each of the two men to which school of thought they belonged. This, I felt, would at least relieve me of responsibility for the dreadful choice.

Meanwhile, my thoughts swung back instinctively to afternoon tea in the convent. This was a brief, austere

324

and essentially unsociable affair. Nobody was obliged to have it. But, should you feel it necessary, you might, when the cloister bell rang for strict silence just before three in the afternoon, slip in for the cup of tea and slice of bread and margarine that were provided in the refectory. The food was set out on a strip of oil-cloth at the end of one of the long oak tables: beside it were ranged the big earthenware mugs with their basin-shaped saucers that the nuns used for breakfast and tea. You might sit where you liked — except, of course, at the Prioress' table which was sacrosanct — but you must observe absolute silence and keep your eyes, as always, recollectedly cast down. As often as not I have sat there with no idea who happened to be sitting on either side of me.

When you had finished you polished up your place with the duster provided for the purpose, carried your cup along the cloister to the *lavatorium* where the nuns washed their hands, cleansed it scrupulously (everything had to be done as perfectly as possible) and put it away in a cupboard till breakfast next day.

(9)

About my work at the Royal Society of Medicine there isn't really very much to say. I was put as a kind of assistant into the Library department, where my job consisted chiefly of taking in, checking and giving out the books and papers required by the Fellows. I also occasionally answered queries on the telephone.

Those queries were nightmares. As often as not, I could make no sense of what the person at the other end was talking about. It must, I know, sound pitifully feeble, but for some reason the habits of mind and body induced by the life I had always lived made it curiously hard for me to adapt myself to what was now required of me. I knew nothing of medical terms and, as often as not, was hardly ready with pencil and paper to take down the inquiry before the voice at the other end had rung off. In the end, I avoided the telephone and applied myself to humbler jobs in which there were next to no "personal contacts". I thus earned for myself — in certain quarters — a reputation for shirking the more arduous part of the work.

During the months I spent there, a good deal was added to my Experience of Life. Some of it was due to such intercourse as my work gave me with the Fellows — who appeared to belong to every type and nationality under the sun; but most of it came to me from observing the behaviour of the other members of the staff.

The Great Ones — Mr. Home and the elusive secretary, Mr. Geoffrey Edwards — dwelt apart in Olympian sanctuaries of their own. In consequence they were very seldom seen. But there were lesser deities in charge of various sub-departments who fascinated me by their utter unlikeness to anyone I had ever met before.

It has been said that Librarians, as a class, tend to develop unusual personalities. I am sure that Mr. Kelson, who worked in a kind of eyrie at the top of a twisted iron staircase, will not mind my saying that I always looked on him as a case in point. You felt instinctively that his spirit roamed in regions unexplored by ordinary mortals. I loved asking him questions because his answers so often made me jump. This stimulated thought. It also opened one's eyes to the possibility of there being other points of view besides one's own. Time and again I have marvelled at the agility with which his bony figure would dart up and down that iron stair in search of some query (we pronounced it to rhyme with "cherry" at the R.S.M.) — or to give an opinion on some abstruse and learned subject to an enquirer on the telephone.

There was also Miss Jones, who presided over the large and luxurious Fellows' Reading Room. Her culture and learning would have petrified me if it had not been for the delightful friendliness she always showed. Now and again we lunched together, which gave me the opportunity of studying at close quarters the phenomenon of a Girton M.A. who did not disdain to unbend until she could meet me on common ground.

As for the two girls who ran the section in which I worked, I learnt from listening while they chattered to one another — and they were seldom silent — quite a lot of which I had been unaware before. Young, highly efficient, the possessors of husbands, university degrees and an enviable supply of brains, is it to be wondered that their companionship produced in me a paralysing sense of my own inferiority? And when I assure you that however low was my own opinion of myself (and it grew daily lower), it was high compared with the opinion they obviously held of me . . .

All of which combined to keep my soul with its nose more or less in the dust.

It was John who, at this time, did most to advance my retarded education.

He was the kind of young man that I should have selected — had Providence permitted me the choice — for a nephew. He possessed just those qualities most calculated to rejoice the heart of an elderly spinster aunt. He was kind, tactful, sympathetic and full of the species of humour that I most appreciate. We met occasionally over lunch and tea; later, when summer came, we now and again spent what remained of the lunch-hour in the cool shade of the gardens in Cavendish Square.

Owing to his admirable modesty, I only discovered gradually how learned he was about art, books, music, ballet, antiquities and a dozen other subjects concerning which I was terribly eager to know more. He himself, he explained to me, was of the type labelled "arty" — or even — which was much worse — "arty-crafty": a term which, though it conveyed very little to me, appeared to permit one a certain elegant latitude in the matter of dress. In my opinion John's clothes were most attractive. I told him so: upon which he enlightened me about what might be called the basic theories of men's attire. After that, I examined the un-uniformed section of the male population with

328

growing interest. At last, I felt, I was beginning to realize What was What.

One night, John invited me to see the Sadler's Wells Ballet at the New Theatre.

As a schoolgirl, I had seen Pavlova and Njinsky when the Russian ballet first invaded London. I had been so enraptured that for several days I had gone about in a kind of trance. The dancing of Margot Fonteyn and Robert Helpmann, however, produced a different effect. In a way, it was rather heart-breaking. Once again I was obliged to confess that, as a result of my life in the convent, something within me had become atrophied. I had grown incapable of apprehending ballet emotionally. It reached me no longer through the senses, but *drily*, if I may so express it, through the mind.

I watched the flitting *Sylphides* and the enchanting movements of *Coppelia* as though I were on the other side of a glass window. The waves of emotion that they are surely meant to stir no longer reached me. As Barbara had declared, through repression and disuse, certain sections of my being had simply withered and died.

CHAPTER
TEN

(1)

Everyone, I suppose, has his peculiarities.

One of mine is that when, in the street, I encounter nuns, I tend to scuttle across to the other side of the road.

This is not because I dislike them. Quite the contrary. As a class, I hold nuns in the highest esteem. But the sight of those starched wimples, long dark habits and low-heeled shoes rouses memories I've no use for. And that is why, when nuns show themselves on my horizon, I dart up side-streets, averting my eyes as though Gorgons lurked beneath their veils.

It may therefore surprise you to hear that when the day came on which I felt I could no longer endure to go out for my meals in every kind of weather, I moved my lodging from Bettingdon Terrace to a convent school in Notting Hill.

The explanation is quite simple.

At the beginning of the war, when all children were evacuated from London, two or three of the Sisters to whom the school belonged were, with their pupils, billeted for a short time on the convent in which I was then still a nun. I had liked them. They were wise, kind, sympathetic women. And it now seemed to me that, faced as I was with the hopeless business of finding myself another room in war-packed London, they might be excellent people from whom to ask advice.

The convent was a big red stone building at the corner of Chepstow Villas. The Government had taken it over and transformed it into the headquarters of the local Red Cross and A.R.P. A few of the Sisters still remained there, however, presumably to keep an eye on things and to look after the lady-boarders who inhabited the upper floors.

In the ordinary course of things, the very last place that I should have chosen to live in was a convent. There is, however, a good old English saying to the effect that Beggars can't be Choosers: and when the nuns offered me not only board and lodging but a gay little room with central heating and a window with a view of the chimney-pots of Bayswater that Whistler might have envied — all for less than I'd paid for my lodging alone at Bettingdon Terrace — is it to be wondered at that I accepted?

Of course, if I had wanted amusement or companion-ship, I should not have gone there. But I didn't. I needed peace and quiet. Absurd as it must sound, at the day's end, the strain of struggling through twelve plain hours of life had completely worn me down.

(2)

Meanwhile, I was picking up much interesting in-formation about doctors at the Royal Society of Medicine.

Mr. Edwards, the secretary, who was certainly in a position to know, had assured me that no nicer set of men were to be found on earth than English doctors. This I was quite ready to believe. Watching them as they hurried in and out on their way to lecture hall or reading room I was impressed by what I saw. These tired, busy-looking men with lined and thoughtful faces inspired one with confidence. They looked sincere and kind: completely dedicated to the tremendous work which absorbed their lives and energies.

Now and again the girls in the Returns Office would draw my attention to celebrities.

"Look — quickly! That's Lord Horder just getting into the lift!" or "There's the Radio Doctor button-holing the fat little R.A.F. type with the gongs on his chest!"

And a brief and sometimes spicy biography would perhaps be vouchsafed in husky whispers . . . All highly educative to one as ignorant of medical personalities as I.

One morning I arrived to find the hall so crowded that I had literally to fight my way to the stairs. Every known and unknown language was being jabbered by doctors — mostly in khaki — of every possible shape and size. A buzz as of swarming hornets made the air vibrate.

"It's an International Conference," I was told when I asked what was happening.

Later in the morning I again became entangled with the same gentlemen as they poured — gabbling more excitedly than ever — out of one of the lecture halls. I noticed an elderly man explaining something to a group of smart young Yankee officers. Their expressions struck me. One does not often see reverence in the eyes of young America.

Then the elderly man turned round and I recognized him. It was Lord Dawson of Penn, friend and doctor of King George V — the man who all unwittingly had warned the Empire of the end of an epoch in the famous phrase: "The King's life is moving peacefully towards its close."

The last time I had seen him had been at my bedside in the convent. This may sound a little surprising. Let me hasten to explain.

When necessary, leave can always be obtained for doctors to penetrate behind walls and grilles to see their patients. Now, it happened that Lord Dawson was Uncle Stan's doctor. And, after the frightful strain and worry of the abdication, he had helped him rather wonderfully back to health. Therefore, when I myself had been ill and my uncle had come to see me, he had suggested that what Lord Dawson had done for him, he might be able to do for me.

Accordingly, on a certain foggy winter evening, the famous doctor arrived. The Reverend Mother Prioress herself conducted him up the ghost-haunted panelled staircase to the tiny cell where I was lying in bed in the dark.

Reverend Mother put down the small oil lamp on the chest of drawers. Then, to my astonishment, she quietly withdrew. Lord Dawson and I were alone.

How he had managed to obtain this unheard-of concession remains a mystery. I have, however, observed that people with noses shaped like his very seldom fail to get their way.

Though it was easy to see that he knew nothing of nuns or of their peculiar problems, he was extraordinarily intuitive. We had a long and excellent conversation. Much of the advice he gave me I shall remember and follow till I die.

The last thing he said as he rose to go was:

"Look here: do promise me that if ever anything in your life begins to go as it shouldn't, you will let me know . . ."

And now, here he was again.

That night I wrote and told him that I'd left the convent and was now on a job at the Royal Society of Medicine.

Next morning, I had just started work when one of the girls called out to me that I was wanted on the telephone. It was Lord Dawson's secretary.

Could I, she wanted to know, meet him that same day for lunch or dinner at the Dorchester?

For some reason I was so staggered by this invitation that she had to repeat it a second time before I could really take it in.

"Um . . . er . . . well . . . let me see . . ." I heard myself murmuring as though rapidly referring to an overcrowded engagement list.

"He says," the secretary's voice continued, "that he would prefer dinner if you can make it because there would be more time for conversation afterwards."

So dinner it was.

★　★　★

The look that the receptionist bestowed on me at the Dorchester when I went up to inquire for Viscount Dawson was enough to spoil anybody's evening. Naturally, I was quite aware that I was far from elegant, but, after all, there *was* a War On and I really had done everything I knew how to in the way of tatts and bobs. I'd even summoned up courage to call at my sister's flat on my way back from work, for I hadn't the vaguest idea how to rig myself out for the occasion. Advice was imperative. And Gay and Barbara were still out of town.

Having prepared myself for scourges, I had been pleasantly surprised when both my sister and the Friend-That-She-Lived-With manifested quite a reasonable amount of interest and answered my agitated inquiries about costume and behaviour with far less contempt than I expected or deserved.

No; it appeared that evening clothes would, in the circumstances, be definitely *wrong*. An afternoon dress, with no hat and a smart coat, if I had such a thing? Yes: there would probably be cocktails — (*before* the meal, silly! — one never drank them *during*). I'd better not have more than *one*, and be sure to drink it *slowly*. I *must* remember not to stick my hands under the table like one used to do in the old days. One should keep *at least* one elbow firmly planted beside one's plate and rest one's chin on one's hand at intervals. And never, *never* in *any* circumstances, must one say "ever so". It had sounded quite sweet and enthusiastic in 1913, but to utter the phrase to-day, stamped one simply as *beyond the pale* . . .

335

Finally, my sister had lent me her fur coat and rather a nice pearl necklace. This filled me with so frightful a sense of opulence and luxury that I hardly dared venture into the street.

The dinner was a great success.

Lord Dawson had certainly determined that it should be so, for there were violets at my place and the food and wine would, I feel sure, have been judged excellent by a far more experienced palate than mine is ever likely to become. And when coffee was brought, and an orange-lipped young woman with long black silk legs and a short frilled tou-tou like a ballet dancer's, appeared before my astonished eyes with an elegantly arranged tray of every possible kind of cigarette, Lord Dawson picked out half a dozen or so of the largest packets and started to build them up round my place rather like a child with a box of bricks.

"I know more, I expect, about these things than you do," he explained. "Stuff them into your bag and try them out when you get home."

Presently he dived into a pocket and produced some apples. He rolled the largest and rosiest across to me.

"One each," he observed. "If people consumed more of these, my income, which, I may tell you, is at the moment not to be sniffed at, would proportionately diminish. Keep that, however, under your hat."

I'd never before seen anything quite like the Dorchester. Compared with the convent, every detail of whose architecture and furnishing was carefully designed to elevate the soul by suppressing all that could in any way indulge the body, this place seemed to have been planned to make that body as snug and comfortable as could possibly be conceived. How different, too, were the faces, clothes, and general behaviour of our fellow-diners from those of the people by whom I'd been surrounded for the greater part of my life! Lord Dawson entertained me by pointing out interesting people at the various little tables dotted about the large luxurious room.

"That woman" — he indicated a luscious person whose diamond ear-rings flashed with each movement of her head — "kept an old clothes shop in the Mile End Road till clothes-rationing started. Then she made a fortune. Nobody, you see, could check up on what went backwards and forwards across the counter. Now she lives in great style and has champagne with every meal."

Much impressed, I studied her in silence.

Quite at the other end of the room, two extremely sophisticated-looking women were deep in talk.

"That's an odd *ménage*," said Lord Dawson. "They are in love with each other and live together as if they were man and wife. What do you think of that?"

Before I could answer, a ravishing creature in one of those long, bare-backed gowns which I'd gathered from advertisements were the modern woman's evening dress, strolled past our table. She touched Lord Dawson lightly on the shoulder with an exquisitely tended hand. He introduced us and I realized that I was talking to the wife of one of our leading generals out in Africa. In the short conversation that followed, I had ample opportunity of realizing how deep was the abyss which now separated me from the "society woman" of the present day.

It was after she had drifted gracefully away that we really began to get down to what I believe are now known as brass tacks.

In a fatherly kind of way, Lord Dawson inquired whether I had any Expectations.

A little ruefully, I replied that if he meant rich relations from whom I had hopes of legacies, the answer was emphatically No.

Lord Dawson put down his cup and began to talk interestingly and urgently about Industry. What I needed, he told me, was a Career. Very well, then. He would help me to plan one.

He was, he said, deeply interested in what he called the Welfare Department of Industry. He sketched what his idea of the person in charge of such a department in a first-class industrial concern ought to be. He told me, that in his opinion, I was in many ways qualified for such a position. Of course, I should need training; it might even mean a year of intensive study in one of the London hospitals. But with him behind me, that could easily be arranged. In fact, if the details of the work (and he proceeded to explain them) appealed to me, he would not only see that I had the best possible training, but, if I made good, at the end of it, would guarantee me a first-class job. I was to think it over carefully, he said, and, when I'd made up my mind, was to let him know.

* ★ ★

At the end of the evening, Lord Dawson packed me into a prepaid taxi, reminding me that I was to write to him as soon as I had decided whether I wanted his help or not.

It was a wonderful night. There were stars everywhere, swarming like golden bees against the dark velvet of the sky. I stopped the taxi. Walking is conducive to meditation. And I certainly had plenty to meditate upon as, shining my torch along the kerb, I walked back the rest of the way. Yet somehow, I think I had already decided that Welfare, Industrial or otherwise, was not for me.

(3)

Of course, if I had accepted Lord Dawson's offer — as I was strongly urged to do by everyone of whom I asked advice — my life would probably have been more useful than it is to-day. Or — would it?

Knowing myself, I felt sure that no matter how hard I tried, I should never be able to hold down a job of that kind for long. Besides, did I honestly want to? Wasn't it rather unwise to tie oneself up again so soon to a job for which one felt not only no enthusiasm but even a vague repugnance. The very word Industry suggested everything in the modern world that I most disliked.

Heaven knows what fate might befall me were I to set down here the feelings which, since my exodus, had been inspired by contact with what in my youth had been known as "the lower classes". I had come forth from my convent with definitely socialist tendencies. But a year of cheek-by-jowl intercourse with the working people of to-day had changed all that. There had been, of course, plenty of exceptions, but on the whole, "the people" now impressed me as full of class prejudice and an almost vindictive envy-hatred-and-malice fixation towards anyone who was richer, cleverer or in any way superior to themselves.

A good illustration of what I mean occurs in Noel Coward's *Cavalcade*. His thumbnail sketch of the gradual change that takes place in the attitude of Fanny and her mother towards their employers during the years between the wars was most illuminating. Quite possibly, if I'd known more about the causes of that change I should have been less repelled by it. As it was, I merely noted what had happened with resentment and a certain puzzled regret.

All of which, it now appeared to me, didn't form a very promising foundation on which to build my services to Industry.

Another thing.

In reviewing my misspent life, I am increasingly impressed by the fact that all my worst mistakes have resulted from turning a deaf ear to Inward Urges.

I say "urge" rather than "inspiration", because an Urge is such a queer, inexplicable thing that one hesitates to think of it as strictly spiritual. Indeed, in my case, Urges usually begin to operate from a prosaic spot somewhere in the pit of the stomach. Like some blind, irresistible force, they take complete possession of one's

340

being, impelling one to follow or to refrain from, some particular course of action. Should one, however, struggle to resist, and continue resisting, the Urge gradually fades out and ends by disappearing altogether. When this happens, I have observed that the remembrance of it tends to haunt one uncomfortably in the years that follow.

All my life I have been subject to these Urges. Now and again, I have resisted them in order to follow what then sounded like excellent advice. I have invariably regretted it. When, however, I have obeyed my Urge, no matter how crazy the course of action may have seemed at the moment, it has always turned out for the best.

So that now, when Lord Dawson uttered the word "Industry" and my Inward Urge commanded me to leave it alone, I knew quite well that I should obey.

Now, it has always appeared to me that, to get the best out of life, there are two things to be done. The first is to make up your mind what it is that you want above all things; the second, to go all out to achieve your end.

At that particular moment, the thing I most craved for was freedom. And the way to it seemed to me to be my Cornish Cottage. The vision had been vouchsafed. The question was, did I believe in it sufficiently to turn my back doggedly upon every other manner of life and fight on until Peace was won and I could reach my goal?

I decided that I did.

(4)

Three weeks later I wrote and told Lord Dawson of my decision.

His reply was to invite me to drive down with him the following morning to the country. He said he had to visit a patient and we could talk things over on the way.

To my relief, he quite understood my reasons for refusing his offer. He said I was not to think any more about it but just follow where my Voices led.

The great argument of the day started on the way back. We were driving past the lovely ruins of a famous Cistercian abbey when Lord Dawson stopped the car.

"I always try to pause at this place," he said. "Come along and see whether it affects you as it does me."

Together we wandered among the roofless arches. Though the sun lay on the turf outside in pools of gold, the shadows inside the ruined cloisters were cold and grey. Silence, austere and absolute, brooded like a guardian spirit. When we spoke, it was instinctively in an undertone.

Back in the car, Lord Dawson asked me whether, as what he called an expert, I could explain the passion for building monasteries which had swept Europe in the Middle Ages. Surely it wasn't only to ensure prayers being said for the founder's soul?

I said I supposed the chief motive for building an abbey had always been the glory of God. Patriotism, too, might have had something to do with it.

He said he didn't see the connexion.

342

"But yes!" I insisted. "If you believe religious life to be a life of professional perfection (and therefore the best sort of life that can be lived on earth) and that a country is good or bad in proportion to the goodness or badness of the people in it, then — if you help to increase the numbers of those who lead "professionally perfect" lives, you are surely being very patriotic indeed."

He looked unconvinced. There was, he said, unfortunately abundant evidence to show that the people inside those abbeys had lived anything but perfect lives.

So then we argued about monastic morals in the Middle Ages. I held out that half the accusations made when Henry VIII suppressed the monasteries were based on a comparison with primitive fervour. Gasquet's carefully documented book on the subject was proof positive of how, for their own ends, the King's Commissioners had distorted the truth. What was more, when one reflected how terribly unsettled a period for the Church the fifteen-hundreds were, the marvel was that even more of the prevalent unrest hadn't seeped into the cloister from outside.

"And anyhow," I insisted, "even though some of them may have been wash-outs, there's no doubt that the general level of life in the monasteries was — and is — far above that of ordinary people living in the world."

I had hoped that would be the end of it. For — as the patient reader has had ample opportunity to observe — controversy is not my best thing. But no. Five minutes later we were at it again. This time the objection was to People Who Shut Themselves Up Behind Four Walls instead of staying in the world to Do Their Bit.

I marshalled my usual artillery . . .

What so surprised me was the obvious interest that lay behind his questionings. It encouraged me — though I felt like a sparrow twittering to an eagle — to let myself go.

For instance, when I assured him that nuns and monks did not enclose themselves to escape responsibilities, but to continue — (and would he please notice that "continue" meant a great deal more than merely "imitate") — the hidden life of Christ, he said:

"Now, what exactly do you mean by that?"

So I explained.

The idea that I tried to put across to him is, I suppose, one of the most dynamic dogmas of the Catholic faith. I make no apology for inserting it: it is one of the great foundation ideas of religious life. If theology bores you, you can skip the next paragraph or two: though if you do so, you will miss something that may throw light on what, even for certain devout Catholics, is only too often a stumbling-block.

It burst, bomb-like, into my own life while I was still hesitating as to whether or no I should become a nun. One had, of course, now and again encountered the phrase "Mystical Body of Christ" in sermons; but it was an address by Monsignor Robert Hugh Benson and what he afterwards said to me on the subject that set the concept ablaze with life. The doctrine, with its

344

tremendous and dizzying implications, swept me clean off my feet. There seemed only one possible thing to be done. So I did it. My hesitations were at an end.

And now I wanted to make Lord Dawson see it as it had been shown to me.

For a starting-point, Monsignor Benson had used the Incarnation.

God, he said, had taken a human body with which to do the work he came on earth to do. Very well. Just as two thousand years ago, Christ's human body was born and lived and taught and suffered and died and rose again from the dead, so to-day he went on doing just those same things in a "mystical body" formed out of the living human members of the Catholic Church.

Next, he had explained the figure of the vine and the branches. One couldn't think of the vine *as* a vine unless one thought of the branches too: because they and it were one thing. The vine, so to speak, *energized* through the branches; they were nothing except in so far as they were united to the vine. Well, that was a sort of type of the identity that existed between Christ and the Church. He had quoted St. Paul, whose Epistles, he declared, simply teemed with the same idea. One text had impressed me immensely: the one in which St. Paul says that he is "*filling up what is lacking of the sufferings of Christ.*" This meant, said Monsignor Benson, that he was carrying on — actually *continuing in his own person*, the agony and Passion of the Crucified.

He had pointed out, too, an analogy to help one grasp this concept of Christ's Mystical Body. Every form of life could be regarded under a twofold aspect. One's own body, for instance. It had its own bodily life, unique and simple; but *inside* that life, so to speak, were the innumerable cells which make up every body that exists. Each of these lives separately by its own individual life, but also contributes to the unity of the body as a whole.

Well, the same applied to that body in which Christ lives to-day — the Mystical Body of Christ. It too consisted of just such a unity of countless cells; each a human entity, separate and complete in itself, yet, at the same time, a cell in the very Body of Christ. In this last capacity it was, of course, infinitely more important and alive than if it only existed, as you might say, on its own.

Further, Monsignor Benson had insisted (and I can still remember how his light blue eyes had glared and his thatch of fair hair almost appeared to stand on end as he stressed the point) Christ still lives upon earth in the persons of those who truly keep his commandments. The manner of it is, of course, "mystical", but the fact is no less real than it was two thousand years ago. "'*I live*,'" he had quoted, "'*yet no longer I, but Christ lives in me*.'"

"It is a tremendous claim," Lord Dawson said, unconvinced but apparently still interested. I answered:

"Yes. And what's more, if you accept it, the consequences which follow automatically are greater still. Because, you see, if Christ really goes on living in his 'Mystical Body' the same life that he lived in the Gospels, every aspect of that life will naturally appear in the Church as well."

And I picked out, as examples, the absolute authority with which the Church invariably teaches; her way of dealing with suffering and sin and those material needs of her children which simply must be met. And I ended — since it concerned us rather particularly at the moment — by pointing out how Christ still continues, in certain of his members, that "hidden life" which is almost invariably objected to by people in the world.

So many people seemed to forget that the claims made by humanity upon man were not always paramount: God, too, had certain claims. Surely his rights to the love and service of mankind must come before all else? Naturally, it was important that some lives should be devoted to the service of mankind — and I mentioned Sisters of Charity and the religious orders whose lives were spent in missionary work, teaching, and nursing the sick. But the Church had always held that a hidden life of contemplation should not be given the second place. Indeed, it would not be too much to say that contemplatives were essential to the Church's life.

"People," I said, "will insist on imagining the Church to be a philanthropic society; whereas she is so infinitely more than that."

And I tried to explain how the Church was, in reality, a Person; and how that Person was Divine. In fact, the whole notion of a life dedicated to contemplation really sprang from the fact that the Church was — well, quite simply — Christ himself.

"If you study his life," I said, "you'll see that for thirty years it was obscure and hidden. And yet at the end of that time, what happened? God the Father spoke from the sky and said he was well pleased. And there were the forty days spent in the wilderness, utterly alone and absorbed in prayer. And even when the people crowded round him to be healed so that he hadn't even time for food, yet at sunset he used to go up to the mountain and spend the night in what the gospel calls 'the prayer of God'."

Lord Dawson leaned forward and I remember being struck by the curious mingling in his face of lines which suggested spiritual thoughtfulness with something which was unmistakably of this world. I continued.

Well, I asked, didn't all this point to how, in the Mystical Body of Christ, there must be certain cells whose whole business was to continue that prayer of Christ and his silent absorption in the Vision of God? Christ to-day went on living the different parts of his life in the different members of his Mystical Body. Like a division of labour. During his earthly life, it was from those hidden periods of solitude and prayer that he drew the tremendous spiritual force that lay behind all he said or did. Well, in the Catholic Church to-day the same thing was to be found. Teaching, preaching, nursing, missionary work and so on made up the "public life" of the Mystical Body; but behind all this activity were the power-houses of the great contemplative orders — Carthusians, Cistercians, Carmelites,

348

Benedictines and the rest — which, by their hidden lives of prayer and penance supplied the necessary dynamic spiritual force. The help that they brought to the world was practically unlimited, for they were at the very heart of things. People who were truly united to God were able, in virtue of that union, to do more for God in one second than during a lifetime of merely human activity. The contemplative's place in the Mystical Body was at the white-hot centre of the furnace: at the very source of that Infinite, Absolute Force that created and preserved the world. Indeed, their contact with It was so vital that they might almost be said, in a certain sense, to control It. When God raised a soul to the highest degree of contemplation, he refused it nothing. So that such a soul would be in a position to do really tremendous things for the salvation and sanctification of the world. That, of course, was the explanation of the "miraculous answers" so often granted to the prayers of the saints . . .

I shall never know what effect this torrent of eloquence had upon Lord Dawson. For at this point the car stopped in front of the important-looking entrance to my lodging in Chepstow Villas.

My last glimpse of him was leaning back comfortably in his corner, bare-headed, the wind ruffling the hair above his high, wide, nobly proportioned brow. He did not look a day more than sixty, though I believe he was actually then in his seventy-eighth year.

I never saw him again.

The next month or two at the Royal Society of Medicine was uneventful.

I worked in my dark little corner of the Returns Office, watched spring break through in the neglected sooty gardens of Cavendish Square, gulped down my sandwich lunch of stale bread, fish-paste and limp tomato and wondered how long the country would have to continue paying out £15,000,000 a day before the war was won.

Air raids provided the chief excitement. Like the rest of the staff I took my turn of fire watching. I remember especially one stuffy April night, when, between two particularly savage raids, I climbed the roof-ladder and spent an agitated hour among the chimney-pots. And, watching the searchlights jittering among the night-wrack, I reflected how very surprised I should have been if, five years previously, it had been revealed to me in my convent cell that before 1943 was out, I should find myself perched on the roof of a high house at the corner of Wimpole Street, tin-hatted and trouser-clad, watching for fire-bombs while the most frightful war in history raged madly on every side. Which just shows what a mistake it is *ever* to tuck in one's toes and declare that Life is Over. *Anything* may happen to anybody, and at any time. Provided you obey your Inward Urges, adventure follows as the night the day.

One dangerous temptation to abandon my plan for a Cornish cottage crossed my path about this time in the form of Wim, who, back in London for a few days' leave from his mysterious war job, invited me out to dine. Thanks to the technique that I had acquired at the Dorchester, I came through the ordeal without too many blunders and spent a more or less delightful evening listening to further lyric descriptions of Skye.

Places have always meant more to me than people. And because my sequestered life had prevented more than a glimpse of anything outside enclosure walls, Wim's word-pictures of what he declared was the most magical spot in Scotland, stirred my imagination to the depths.

I may here mention that the word "magic" has always held a peculiar fascination for me. I have been told, with contumely, that this is because I have never completely "grown up". Quite possibly this is so. All I know is that the faun-and-fairy-haunted world (at which it would now appear to be the fashion to jeer contemptuously) of my childhood is to-day just as real to me as it was then. Even the power of "seeing things", though atrophied by nearly thirty years of inhibition, is now beginning to return.

Another thing. Whenever I find myself where pebbles are — as on the sea-shore, or now and again as I wander along a drive — I begin instinctively to hunt for the equivalent of Mr. Bultitude's Garuda Stone. As for old junk shops, they are always to me potential treasure troves. Who knows what historic ring, lamp, mirror, amulet or bottle may not lie waiting, with its attendant djinn invisibly attached to it, in some dusty corner? And only the other day, some friends presented me with a carpet. A single glance told me that it was one of those which can transport you in a flash back to Baghdad, Ur of the Chaldees, Old Cathay — or whirl you forward to the utmost outposts of the Atomic Age ... At the moment, it is still standing, neatly rolled, in a corner of the bathroom. One day, however, I shall begin experimenting. Interesting phenomena may then be expected to occur.

But in spite of Wim's repeated assurances that in Skye I should "find myself" as in no other place on earth, the lure of Cornwall proved in the end to be too strong for me. Impelled by an Inward Urge of more than usual intensity, I began once more to fill my *moments perdus* with dreams about my Cottage-in-the-Clouds.

(6)

One of the most exciting presents I have ever received was given to me about this time.

It was a wireless; and it brought so many thrills into my life that I feel they ought to be recorded here.

Apart from the news (which just then was concerned chiefly with the first great victorious push in North Africa), what I most enjoyed listening to was music. I will say nothing here about the classics; a fairly severe and comprehensive musical education had made me familiar from childhood with many works of most of the great masters. What delighted me now was the lighter music of the years between the wars.

When I fled from the world, London was prancing gaily to the new syncopated music which had just come over from America. People called it "rag-time". In 1914 it was all the rage. The hit tunes of the day were: *On the Mississippi, Hitchy Coo, The Wedding Glide*, and *Oh! You Beautiful Doll!* And at my last ball, I had danced ecstatically to *Nights of Gladness, The Quaker Girl, Destiny*, and the lilting waltzes from *The Girl in the Taxi, The Merry Widow*, and *The Count of Luxembourg*. The tango had only just begun to show the tip of its nose and was still looked upon as faintly improper. I remember causing quite a sensation in a London ballroom by trying it out with a partner (whom I had trained carefully during the preceding afternoon) to the tune of *Tommy, Won't You Teach Me how to Tango?*

Probably nobody would believe it if I were to try and describe just how enraptured I was with the songs and tunes which had become favourites during my years of seclusion. My first encounter, for instance, with *The Lambeth Walk, The Song of the Volga Boatmen, Lady Be Good*, and the haunting *I'll See You Again*. All so hackneyed to-day that everybody hates them. And there were the gay, catchy songs from *The Bing Boys* and *The Maid of the Mountains* — new to me and oh, how completely delightful! Besides the ballets, with the enchanting waltzes from *Coppelia, Swan Lake*, and Tchaikovsky's *Sleeping Princess*. Eric Coates was another welcome discovery: even now I can never hear a number from the *London Suite* without wanting to cut capers in a manner alas, wholly unsuitable to my years.

There were also the soldier songs. In the old war I had heard them shouting *Tipperary* as the regiments marched past outside the walls of the enclosure. But *Keep the Home Fires Burning, Roses of Picardy*, and the more recent *Lili Marlene* I did not know. And I am not ashamed to confess that almost invariably, they still bring me to the verge of tears.

As for the jazz, boogie-woogie and that kind of stuff — for music I cannot call it — that dance-bands play, it filled me not only with horror but with foreboding. To my unsophisticated ears it seemed just one more dreadful proof of the universal formlessness which had begun to swallow up everything which had stood for beauty in my youth. And at the risk of calling down the contemptuous anger of the initiates, I will record that to me the tuneless bray and blare of saxophones, the spasmodic, endlessly repeated rhythms, banged, thrummed, and beaten out on heaven-or-hell-knows-what fantastic instruments of torture, suggested nothing so much as noises made by a horde of debased and drunken savages midway through an orgy. It was a danger-signal, and alarming.

What kind of a world, really, was this to which I had returned?

About mid-June a rather disquieting restlessness began to obsess me. For one thing, I had begun to realize that I had absorbed about as much from the Royal Society of Medicine as it was likely to offer. I was also

354

becoming increasingly aware that my ignorance of medical terms and generally gun-shy attitude towards the telephone made me hardly an asset to my fellow-workers. What was more, in the depths of my subconscious another Inward Urge was slowly but unmistakably beginning to take shape.

This time it drove me to seize the opportunity conveniently offered by an amusing minor crisis in the Returns Office and to give in my resignation to the authorities.

All this time I had been practising an almost quadragesimal austerity of life. I had determined to put aside every possible farthing for the cottage in Cornwall on which I had set my heart. Books, clothes, sweets, drinks, cigarettes and theatres — about the only indulgences to be had in England at that time — were severely vetoed. (The cinema I looked upon as essential to my education. Indeed, there can be no doubt that it taught me a great deal that I could have learnt in no other way.)

For most people, this would of course have meant an intolerably bleak existence. But for me, it was different. When you have lived for close on thirty years by the formula: "Not What can I allow myself, but Is there anything that I can possibly manage to do without?" your needs become extraordinarily simple. In fact, they diminish almost to vanishing point.

For, in Religious Life, you are freed by the Vow of Poverty from all those material things which would otherwise entangle you. One might almost say that it chops off, by the spiritual equivalent of a surgical operation, one's very capacity for possessing. Those who make it, strip themselves of everything that could hamper them, as a swimmer strips before plunging into the sea.

But please do not for a moment imagine that taking the vow makes you perfect in poverty. To do this would be to make a very grave mistake. The highest degree of poverty only clears the decks for action. The real struggle only begins when you set your face to achieve the kind of poverty which is known as "spiritual". And, as one who fared so ill in the encounter as to end by flying from the field of battle, I can assure you that it is indeed a struggle to the death.

There are several other names for spiritual poverty. One is self-abnegation; another, detachment; another, freedom from desire. Taken by and large, I think it is fairly accurate to say that what it works out into is simply the desire for nothing except God's Will as revealed in the circumstances of one's daily life.

Could anything sound simpler? Yet those few words contain the essence of exalted sanctity.

The amazing thing is that, quite often in convents you come up against people who have, so to speak, re-attached themselves to the oddest things.

It seems almost incredible, doesn't it? One performs the heroic act of which the Vow of Poverty is the outward sign and then allows oneself to become entangled by a hot-water bottle, a set of breviaries, a fountain pen. Or perhaps even some small exception in the way of rest or diet which for reasons of health may have been temporarily allowed. Or a nun may become so attached to a favourite hobby that a request for help from some overworked Sister rouses feelings of acute resentment at the interference with her treasured "free-time". And I once knew a nun so devoted to a particular chair in the community room that she tied a neat bow of blue ribbon to the back of it and glared with such ferocity at anyone who dared to monopolize it that people shrugged their shoulders, smiled and let her have her way.

Another attachment is that which nuns sometimes develop for the work given to them. A Superior, for instance — especially if she has been long in office, may become so completely absorbed by her job that when the day comes for her to return to the simple routine of the community, she finds it almost impossible to settle down to so dull and inactive a life.

But perhaps the thing from which it is most difficult to be detached is one's reputation. Now and again one may see in a religious community some really soul-searing humiliation descend out of the blue on some perfectly innocent person's head. If she "takes it" without excuse or fuss, quietly allowing it to do its work in her, you may be sure that she has gone far along the road of spiritual poverty. If, however, she is disturbed, and reacts to the disgrace by an indignant outburst of self-justification — well, the obvious conclusion may be drawn.

And if I have once again slithered away into what sounds like a pious homily, let me assure you that it is not irrelevant. One cannot write about nuns, whose outlook is — or ought to be — entirely spiritual —

without describing what makes up their lives. And no one who has not had to attempt it can imagine how difficult it was for at least the first year after my exodus, to adjust my convent-trained outlook on earthly possessions to the point of view held by so many people in the world to-day. So accustomed was I to the religious outlook, that most of the people I met struck me as dreadfully selfish, possessive, go-getting, take-all-and-give-nothing: not only desiring, but grabbing everything that they could get. It depressed me. In fact, it depresses me a little still.

(7)

In the far-away, almost forgotten period before 1914, a well-brought-up girl was taught that to discuss one's own or anyone else's health in public was "bad form". Presumably people endured illnesses and underwent operations then as they do to-day. Only, one did not talk about it. So that the complete lack of reticence with which I now heard almost everyone holding forth about their ailments really staggered me.

A day came, however, when this new attitude was rather a relief. This was when, soon after leaving the Royal Society of Medicine, a dreadful feeling of *unmeantness* — I do not know how else to describe it — began to sweep over me at rapidly decreasing intervals. It used to go on, *crescendo*, until it reached a kind of agonizing peak: after which, for quite a long time, I used to feel as though I simply were not there at all.

358

I endured it for a week or two and then began wondering dismally whether I was losing my mind. The possibility was agitating. But the prospect of consulting a doctor was more agitating still. I had never coped unaided with a doctor in my life. In the convent, an interview between doctor and patient was always conducted by the infirmarian; the diagnosis and remedies only being revealed to one after he had gone. How, I wondered, were these affairs managed in the world? Did one ask for an appointment, or just march in and demand advice? And the question of fees? How much did a doctor cost? And how did one pay him? Did one offer him a cheque? Or was it the thing to wait till he sent in a bill? I had not a notion how to proceed.

In the end, I rang up the uncle who lived in Lancaster Gate and extracted the necessary information.

"I do hope," he inquired politely, when my problems had been dealt with, "that there is nothing seriously wrong?"

"Oh dear, no!" I replied cheerfully. "Merely what in my convent would be described as 'a Little Misery'."

My uncle uttered a snort of disgust and hung up the receiver with a clatter.

Soon after, I set out to see the doctor. He was a lean, rather angry-looking Scot, with a mouth like a razor. He sat and looked at me for several seconds before saying anything at all. Then came a machine-gun fire of questions.

Some of them were impossible to answer unless I told him of my former life. So, after a little unsuccessful hedging, out it came. When I had finished, he leaned back, examining me again in silence.

"Delayed action. Not shock, but strain. That's what you are suffering from. It's har-rr-dly to be wonder-rr-rd at in the cir-rr-cumstances. How long did ye say it was (he was growing Scotch-er and Scotch-er) before ye realized the mistake ye had made in becoming a nun?"

I said that it was about ten years.

He fixed me with a fierce little Scotch blue eye and almost shouted: "Ye mean to tell me ye went on for another eighteen years, knowing all the time it was not the life ye were intended for?"

I nodded.

He made an angry little clucking sound and shook his head.

"The wicked waste of it!" he muttered. "Throwing away the best years of your life! What possessed ye not to come out before?"

I tried to explain that in my eyes a Vow to God was a very solemn matter. The discovery that one had made a mistake hardly seemed sufficient excuse for backing out of what one had taken on.

He said "Ah" thoughtfully and went on staring at me.

"I would be glad to know," he said presently, "what it was that made ye finally come back to the world again."

I said: "I suppose I'd reached breaking point. Anyhow, I knew that if I stayed there any longer, I should go mad."

He said: "But how was it that ye didn't find out sooner that it was not the life for ye? Did they not give ye a time of probation to try things out?"

I assured him that they did. I had had every opportunity of testing my vocation.

"Then how" — and again that piercing little blue eye bored through me — "can ye explain how ye came to do it?"

"I can't," I said unhappily. "I suppose it must have been — well, just one of those things."

The doctor snorted.

Wandering homewards along the Bayswater Road in scorching sunshine, I reflected that it must have been the tendency towards instability in the modern character that caused the Catholic Church to revise her laws concerning the taking of Vows in recent years.

Before that, a member of the religious orders whose Vows were "perpetual" made them at the end of their year or so of noviceship. After that they were fixed, irrevocably, for life. To-day, however, the taking of a life-vow is a much more complicated affair. In fact, if all the preliminary stages were prolonged to their utmost limits, six years, or even more, might elapse before the novice was allowed to take her final Vows.

In my convent, the upward ascent began with the reception of the postulant's habit. This took place as soon as possible after one's arrival. The "habit" was a thick black serge gown reaching to the heels and caught in at the waist with a narrow belt of its own material. Though the sleeves were long and loose, a second pair, longer and even more enormous had to be worn over the first on Sundays and feast-days as well as whenever the postulant went to the choir or parlour. The long, black, skewer-like pins which secured them to the shoulders were concealed by one's "kerchief" — a large, curiously pinned-and-folded piece of thick white linen, stiffly starched and faintly suggestive of a combined helmet and cuirass. A long dark blue cotton apron was worn for going about the house and garden. Whenever the postulant went to the choir or parlour this was removed, folded carefully according to a particular method and carried in one of the vast pockets which, rather like a pair of saddle-bags, were slung beneath the habit round one's waist.

In most cases, a postulant observed the Rule in a somewhat mitigated form, new arrivals being "let down" rather easily.

Normally, the postulant period lasted from six to eighteen months. In exceptional cases it might be prolonged for a few months more. While it lasted, no vow or promise of any kind was made. A postulant, being "only a secular" might leave quite freely or be dismissed if considered unsuitable for the life.

The second stage was that of white-veiled novice. It was preceded by the Clothing ceremony and lasted for a year and a day. The novice now counted as a "religious"; the black serge gown and linen kerchief were exchanged for a white veil and habit closely resembling that worn by the nuns who had made their Vows. The Rule now had to be observed in all its strictness; and since this year was essentially a time of trial, the novice was deliberately tested so that those in authority might see and judge the stuff of which she was made. If undeterred, however, by any hardness, she still persevered, at the end of this period she would be allowed to take triennial Vows.

It was extremely rare for this white-veiled period to be extended. Almost invariably, the novice either left or made her temporary Vows twelve months and a day after she had been "Clothed".

She now wore the short black veil of the "Temporarily Professed" and for three years was bound by the four Vows of Poverty, Chastity, Obedience and Enclosure. She still remained under the care of the Novice Mistress, though a certain amount of communication, prohibited to the white-veiled novices, was now allowed with members of the community.

At the end of the three years, her Vows expired. She was now free and for the last time was given the opportunity to leave. If, however, she still wished to persevere, she made her final Vows at the ceremony of perpetual Profession. By these Vows she was bound for life — unless, as in my own almost unprecedented case, she turned out, after all, to be so unsuited to the life as to find it impossible to continue in the convent. In such circumstances, she could apply to the ecclesiastical authorities for a dispensation by special rescript from Rome.

All of which goes to show, in my opinion (and I really do feel that I know something about it) that when, through some tragic misfortune, a square peg finds itself wedged tightly into an agonizingly round hole, the blame cannot be laid at the door of the Catholic Church.

And if you ask me at whose door I think one *ought* to lay it, I can only reply that I haven't the slightest idea.

CHAPTER
ELEVEN

(1)

We have now reached a point where we are confronted by a serious difficulty.

This is because the next eighteen months or so, though filled with what appeared to me as highly exciting happenings, would, if recorded, strike the reader as both trivial and dull.

I therefore think that the best way to proceed will be by a series of kangaroo leaps, pausing only when anything sticks out sufficiently to seem worth while.

After leaving the Royal Society of Medicine, I thought it might be a good idea to try the War Office. To tell the truth, two things had roused my feminine curiosity. I longed to know something about the inner workings of the war machine, and I was determined to discover why a Civil Servant was always looked upon as a legitimate butt for every kind of gibe.

Now, I have been warned that I must be terribly, terribly careful over what I write about the War Office. This is a pity. For I managed to get myself whisked in and out of at least five different sections, and had many amusing glimpses of the way in which things were done.

If I were to write what I thought about the military branch to which I was first directed, I should get into trouble. So I will merely state baldly how much I detested the place, work and people, and how intense was my relief when, after six gruelling months, I got myself transferred.

My plans for the future began to crystallize during this rather unpleasant period.

It would be an exaggeration to say that I finally cut out Skye for Cornwall because of a radio play to which I listened by chance one Sunday evening. It gave me, however, a tremendous list in that direction. It also helped to divert my thoughts from the news that the R.A.F. had just dropped 2,300 tons of explosive on Hamburg. This, said the papers, was the heaviest bombing raid of the war . . .

The play, by a new writer, Frank Baker, as yet unknown to me, was entitled *Challacombe*. It was a Cornish fantasy. I thought it enchanting. Indeed, it impressed me so much that I wrote to the B.B.C. and asked whether other writings by the same author were to be obtained. The answer was vague and unhelpful. This, however, in no way damped my enthusiasm; and I plunged into a kind of Cornish orgy, reading, thinking and making dream-plans during every spare moment of the next few weeks.

It "sticks out" in my memory almost as though I had gone down to the Duchy on a summer holiday.

I set about my Cornish orgy with method. First, geography. Cornwall, it appeared, was only prevented from being an island by the little three-mile neck of

366

land between Severn-mouth and the squashy bog in Morwenstow from which the Tamar oozes. North, west and south, the Atlantic breakers roar or ripple according to the season.

To me, this seemed almost too good to be true. You see, I have always thought of an island as an ideal setting for romance (Shakespeare knew it when he chose Prospero's Isle as a background for *The Tempest*). I felt, too, that it helped to explain the "differentness" of Cornwall from the rest of England. She was more than just one more lovely English county; she was a country apart, whose people had every right to call folk from the other side of Tamar "foreigners".

I discovered, too, that even the dry geographical bones of her were shrouded with romantic legend. There was the primeval forest that had been swept away when the sea rushed in and overwhelmed Mounts Bay; the shifting sands of the north coast that had piled themselves above the ancient churches. And, loveliest legend of all, lost Lyonnesse, whose lands once stretched from where the Longships Lighthouse stands to-day over to the Scilly Isles and eastward right away to Lizard Point.

One writer, suggesting that the vanished Cassiterides were once a part of Lyonnesse, insisted that, if you listened breathlessly on those rare still days when no waves disturbed the sea, you could hear drowned church bells chiming in the water far below.

Her history I found a trifle disappointing. There seemed so little of it. Or, possibly, I got hold of the wrong books. Anyhow, Cornwall appeared to have had next to no contacts with the history of England. As "Q" pointed out, a few sturdy insurrections against the imposition of taxes or the "reformed" liturgy — two or three gallant campaigns in the fated cause of Charles I, and — of course — the great revival of religion led by Wesley, made up most of the written tale.

To atone for this, however, every stone and mound held hints of her unwritten story. And it was this which, above all things, thrilled and stirred my imagination.

This kind of history was not to be learnt from books. You had to get into actual contact with the place itself; with the tombs, long-stones, dolmens, barrows and stone circles set up more than six thousand years ago by an unknown race. This was the secret Cornwall of the hill-tops, moors and ruined cliff-castles, all older than the earliest records that exist.

Instinctively I knew that the Old People had left something of themselves behind them; that each grim monolith contained its own dark life. In those fantastically shaped stones where so much blood had been outpoured, often in human sacrifice, "Something" still lived, mysteriously imprisoned — "Something" which could only communicate itself if one were able to receive what it had to give.

I must, I felt, I absolutely *must* get down there; preferably to that weird, rather menacing neighbourhood inland from Morvah and Land's End. For I felt sure that if I could only soak myself sufficiently in the atmosphere of such places as the Stone Circles of Tregaseal, or Carn Kenidzhek — "the Hooting Cairn"

— among whose boulders and holed stones the spirits of an even older people than the ancient Celts still lurk — well — I should have no difficulty about "tuning in" to their vibrations. I pictured myself leaning down over the deep, dark tarn of Cornwall's earliest history, watching each bubble as it rose slowly to the surface to break, releasing secret forces that were faintly sinister and belonged to an unknown, utterly primitive mode of life. Could anything on earth have been more fascinating? I could not wait to get away.

(2)

The third thing which sticks out from this unlively period is the *Quadriga*.

In case you do not happen to be a Londoner, I had better explain that this is the sculptured group above the archway leading into the Green Park at Hyde Park Corner. It was given to the nation by one of King Edward VII's admirers and has for its subject *The Triumph of Peace.*

It caught my eye, rather in the manner of a heavenly vision, as I walked, one cold March morning along Piccadilly on my way to work. Silhouetted against a sunrise sky of fierce cerise and dusky violet, the grace and poise of the lovely standing figure in the two-wheeled chariot suggested a triumphant Victory of ancient Greece. But what impressed me was the fact that the four madly prancing horses harnessed to the chariot were reinless.

369

"That," I reflected as for the first time I set eyes on it, "isn't *Peace* at all. It's *Adventure*. Being galloped away with, who knows where, by the horses of Destiny."

And after that, morning after morning, as I skipped off my bus at Hyde Park Corner in sun or rain or fog or frost or snow, I used to cast long upward glances at the *Quadriga*, finding inspiration in the attitude towards life that I felt it typified.

The odd thing was that, in the back recesses of my memory, I felt sure that the *Quadriga* and I had met before.

And then, one morning as I was stepping delicately across the bomb débris after a night of particularly savage raids, it all came back to me.

It had happened years ago, when I was still in the convent. Sext and None were just over and I was tip-toeing down the beautiful wide staircase that led from the landing outside the choir to the blue-grey cloister down below. As refectorian, it was my duty to ring the great iron bell outside the refectory for the community exercise known as "Examen of Conscience" which took place ten minutes before the midday Angelus.

And here I should like to pause again and explain to those who are unfamiliar with such matters, in what that exercise consists.

During my first few days as a postulant, I observed that when Sext and None were ended, a bell used to clang somewhere far away in the cloister. Upon which, the nuns — already kneeling, as was their custom, on the bare parquet floor of the choir, noses pressed against the corners of their stalls — would give a kind of little wriggle, indicating somehow an even greater application to the business in hand. Each would then draw forth from her pocket a small black note-book, in which the briefest of entries would be made. Book and pencil were then re-pocketed; after which, with another indescribable wriggle, suggesting that an unpleasant duty had been virtuously performed, they once more buried their noses in the corner of their stalls.

What on earth could it all be about?

"I wish," I murmured plaintively that evening at Recreation, "that someone would tell me what the nuns *do* with those funny little books and pencils after Hours!"

"Hush, my dear!"

A Polish postulant, whose kindness of heart had already saved me from several pitfalls, smothered a rather refreshing giggle and drew me rapidly aside. "Don't you know, one never talks about such things in public!" she whispered. "One saves them up and asks Mother" ('Mother' was the Mistress of Novices) "when next she Calls For One for a little Talk. I'll just mention it to her, shall I?"

Next morning I was Called For.

The little alcove in which the Novice Mistress interviewed her charges was so small as to be positively a cupboard. I found her seated on a low, rush-bottomed chair, her fine profile silhouetted against the latticed window, her fingers busy with a delicate piece of needlework. I knelt beside her on the bare boards, hands uncomfortably clasped at waist level, eyes resolutely cast down.

I should do better, she suggested, to keep custody of the eyes in choir instead of indulging my curiosity by gazing around to see what other people were about. However, being such a newcomer to the convent, my fault perhaps was not, after all, so grave. As for the matter of the little books and pencils, that was easily explained.

I then learnt that "Particular Examen" was a simple but most efficacious means of acquiring virtues or ridding oneself of faults.

Later on, when I tried myself to practise it, I discovered that it worked out more or less like this:

Suppose, for example, that a certain nun in the community was so constructed as to tempt you almost automatically to Unkind Thoughts. (You know the sort of person. Even in the best regulated religious communities they are to be found.) Very well. By means of the Particular Examen, this temptation could be rapidly overcome.

The method was simple. You had to tackle your temptation three times daily. You began at your morning prayers with a really terrific resolution that, no matter how maddening you might find the behaviour of Sister So-and-So, you would not allow one Unkind Thought to enter your mind. You would next, as far as possible, preview the morning, foreseeing those occasions when — as experience had taught you — only the toughest of struggles would enable your resolution to be kept. In conclusion, you would pray earnestly to God for grace to save you from a Fall.

During the morning, you would, of course, watch your step whenever Sister So-and-So appeared on the horizon. Should, however, a Fall occur, you would immediately arise, beat your breast, renew your early morning resolution and — continue as before. The pencil and paper performance which had so intrigued me was simply the totting up of how often Sister So-and-so had got you down.

Contrition over lapses — a forward glance over possible afternoon collisions with Sister So-and-so — a re-stiffening of the will and a prayer for help in time of tribulation, and the midday exercise was at an end.

The final exercise, at bed-time, was simply a repetition of what has just been described.

I myself obtained better results from the positive method of attack.

Suppose, for instance, that your weekly Confessions revealed a disquieting habit of picking holes in other people. Well, instead of dotting down the number of times you had made disparaging remarks you would count how often you had succeeded in transforming incipient criticism into thoughts and words that were *kind*.

Humility was a favourite subject for Particular Examen.

[And I do beg of you just to cast your eye upon what follows. If you do not there are two things you will find it difficult to understand. One is, why all the details of religious life — the Vows, especially that of Obedience;

the subjection to Rule; the penances — some of which are quite agonizingly humiliating — and a hundred other things are all ordained with a view to the promotion of humility. The second is, the curious passion for humiliation which seems to get hold of people once they have made substantial progress in the spiritual life.]

We will begin with a story.

I hadn't been for many weeks in the convent when I heard an enthusiastic novice declare in public that her life's ambition was to reach the tip-top rung of the ladder of humility.

The Novice Mistress eyed her thoughtfully.

"Begin," she suggested drily, "by seeing how often you can accept correction without excuse."

So the novice continued plodding away at this till she had schooled herself to accept anything and everything without a word. And at last the Novice Mistress told her that she was fit to make the second grade.

This time, she had to mark down in her little black book how many times morning and afternoon she had failed to *welcome* a humiliation. (And if you think that sounds comparatively easy, do just think back over the way that you yourself instinctively react to sneers, snubs, settings-down, insolent or arrogant behaviour . . . or, hardest of all, the bitterness of undeserved disgrace.)

That kept her busy for a year or so. Then came a Retreat preached by a Jesuit who urged the nuns to "go in" for humility as people in the world "go in" for sport.

Then the novice felt that Now Her Chance Had Come. She set her teeth and took a flying leap on to the heroic level. Henceforward, instead of merely "welcoming" humiliations, she counted how many she could possibly manage to squeeze into her day.

Well, the point of the story is that if anyone has the courage to persevere with a course of action like that, noteworthy things begin to happen in their spiritual life. Père Surin, the Jesuit mystic, says that love of contempt is the key which unlocks the treasure-house of God's gifts and graces. Once you get to the point when you honestly *want* to be humiliated and looked down upon, you will find your soul flooded with what are known as "spiritual delights".

Which probably sounds to you completely crazy.

And yet, you know, it's not . . .

To-day, when I look back on that strange phenomenon known as Religious Life, I see clearly that success or failure in it depends, in the end, on one thing only: one's attitude to humility.

I had better be honest and own that I myself was spiritually so obtuse that it was years before I realized how all-important was the acquisition of that virtue. And I regret to say that even when I did . . .

"You know," I remember once complaining to a fellow-postulant, "I don't somehow seem able to grasp the idea *behind* this business of humility."

The postulant, to whom this fact must have been glaringly apparent, did her best to look sympathetic.

"Sometimes," I continued gloomily, "I think I must be rather like St. Augustine. When he was a Manichee, you know. He simply couldn't get into his head the idea of a spiritual substance. Well, I feel like that about humility."

The postulant looked startled and said good gracious, she hoped I wasn't going to become a Manichee.

"I may," I hissed (the bell for silence was already ringing) "become something even worse than that unless somebody soon enlightens me about humility."

"I'll whisper a word to Mother," she hissed back at me. And, as we parted, I saw her take out her little black book and — presumably for having broken silence — mark down a "one".

Next morning I was Called For by the Mistress of Novices. You may like to know a few of the things she said to me.

(a) The reason why humility was so terribly important was that it had always been the characteristic virtue not only of Christians but of Christ.

(b) It was the spirit and life and very nature of prayer; so the humbler one was, the better one would be able to pray.

(c) It was by far the quickest way to holiness, because a corresponding increase in all the other virtues was brought about by every increase in humility.

(d) In the same way that impurity defiled the body, so the spirit was defiled by pride. Humility was the purity of the soul, just as chastity was the body's purity. And without purity, no holiness was possible.

(e) Humility was so essential a part of sanctity that when anyone was proposed for canonization, the first thing that the authorities investigated was always whether humility had been practised in a heroic degree. If that could not be proved, the rest fell automatically to the ground.

There was a good deal more besides, which I have unfortunately forgotten. What was still more unfortunate, however, was that even when everything had been said, the word "humility" *still* just didn't mean a thing to me.

Which only shows that the things of the spirit are not to be got at by merely human reasoning. Understanding is a gift of the Holy Spirit. And it wasn't until several years later that even a small measure of it was bestowed upon me.

It happened, oddly enough, when I was helping to hang up some wet pillow-cases in the garret very early on an icy January morning. There was snow on the roof and my mind was completely taken up with the problem of how to hang frozen-stiff linen with fingers that were numb with cold.

And then, suddenly, and for no apparent reason, it was made clear to me. I saw how each act of humility which one so laboriously and distastefully performed was, far from being an end in itself, simply a means by which one was able to hollow out within one's soul an ever-deepening capacity. And this capacity was immediately and unceasingly filled up to over-flowing by a torrent of God's grace.

So that the deeper the soul hollowed itself out by the self-slaying practice of humility, the greater became its capacity for receiving the graces and gifts of God.

Yes, really. It was as simple as all that.

(3)

We seem to have become enmeshed in such a herring-net of interpolations that I can think of no way out.

If you will allow me, therefore, I propose to lead you by the hand back to our first point of call after leaving the *Quadriga*.

This, as you may remember, was the great staircase leading from the choir landing to the cloister which contained the bell outside the refectory door. And it was at the bottom of this staircase that the queer little incident occurred.

Just as I stepped off the last stair into the cloister, something suddenly seemed to swoop down like a whirlwind and seize hold of me, sweeping me up out of myself on to a completely different plane. I felt as though I had been flung into a madly rocking chariot, drawn by reinless horses, and was being whirled rapidly away through space. I knew it wasn't actually what was happening to me; but that somehow symbolized what I felt was taking place. Just for one mad moment some terrific unknown force had got completely hold of me and had taken over the direction of my life. I was so thrilled I could have screamed out loud with sheer excitement. At the same time it was borne in upon me as convincingly as though an archangel had shouted the words in my ear, that adventures lay ahead. Real, positive adventures, of a kind about which I had hitherto never even dreamed.

And then, no less suddenly and inexplicably than it had happened, the whole thing vanished into the whirlwind out of which it had come. And I found myself standing at the other end of the cloister, feeling rather dizzy and with my nose within an inch of the bell outside the refectory door.

I never told anyone about it. Neither did I try to explain it to myself. As for the queer, almost ominous sense of impending adventure which for the next few days stabbed me repeatedly with illicit and inexplicable thrills, I finally got rid of it by reminding myself severely that even the mildest adventures were out of the question when, by taking perpetual vows one had buried oneself in the depths of a strictly enclosed convent for the remainder of one's life.

(4)

You will, I feel certain, agree that we have had more than enough in the way of attempts to describe the indescribable. What follows shall, I promise you, be on a more prosaic plane.

From February till the end of May I worked at the Prisoners of War Department of the War Office in Curzon Street.

This, formerly an enormous block of luxury flats, had been requisitioned when war broke out and transformed into a honeycomb of offices. Rumour had it that among the maze of passages was one leading to a private suite which had been prepared for the King and Queen in case the bombing — which was becoming more and more terrific — should make Buckingham Palace unfit for habitation.

I was happier in the P.O.W. section than I had been in any other job since I left the convent. My fellow-clerks were kind and friendly; the work was, for once, within my rather limited powers of comprehension, and in my off-time there was always the house in South Audley Street close at hand where Gay and Barbara with a perpetually changing crowd of relatives and friends of every age and nationality carried on the war effort according to their various capacities.

At the end of May, unfortunately, some eye trouble which had been threatening ever since I started work at the War Office, suddenly put me out of action. The Scots doctor, looking angrier than ever, muttered that worse things were in store for me unless I could get away for rest and change. Scared by the idea of possible illness when I had no one to look after me, I extricated myself — not without difficulty — from the Civil Service and began to think up plans. Letters and telegrams buzzed to and fro between myself and A.B. I packed my suitcases (by now they were beginning to show signs of wear) and took a taxi to Victoria. Another train journey. (Heavens, the amount I'd learnt since my first solitary venture down that line two years ago!) The London episode was ended. My aunt met me on her doorstep. And the frightful depression which inevitably assaults me when I set foot in Sussex took hold of me again.

(5)

Down in the country the hedgerows were bridal-white with hawthorn. The gardens blazed with lilac and laburnum flower. But the heat was overpowering. And the entire county gave one the impression of an armed camp.

Soldiers, tanks, lorries and the immense closed vehicles — large as houses — that had already begun to pour through London, blocked the roads. The heat-wave, joined to the appalling pre-invasion tension was at moments almost more than one could bear. At night, the enemy dropped bombs; the roar of incessant dog-fights overhead made sleep impossible and intensified the atmosphere of strain.

Almost immediately after my arrival in Sussex, such tremendous events started happening that one almost ceased to have any personal life of one's own. One simply sat there panting, eyes excitedly scanning the headlines, ears glued firmly to the wireless, from which, in thrill-smitten, feverish voices, the announcers proclaimed the heroic happenings of the last weeks of the war.

About mid-June, another of my aunts invited me to stay with her. She lived in Hove — a place I have always particularly detested — and was the kind of invalid who could only endure the society of other people at stated times.

Now, my dislike of Hove is so intense as to amount almost to a mania. So much so indeed, than when obliged to go there, I try as far as possible to keep my eyes shut. In that way, I avoid a good deal that I had rather not see. And this, as may well be imagined, tends to induce a somewhat introverted state of mind.

Picture to yourself, then, my excitement when, on withdrawing myself in horror from my surroundings and slamming the door of my interior citadel, I discovered therein, bubbling and seething like a witches' cauldron in the depths of what I believe is to-day known as the subconscious mind, something which obviously just couldn't wait another minute for its release.

There was only one way of effecting this.

I sat down, took up my pen and began to write . . .

And that, ladies and gentlemen, is how the first chapters of this book were born.

(6)

I must say that to me it was like heaven to know that I could sit down there, uninterrupted, and write for as long as I chose.

In the convent, one of the things that had tried me most was the incessant change of occupation which became obligatory at the first sound of the bell. The discipline, too, of the thoughts which the Rule exacted was a severe trial to anyone blessed — or cursed — with an imagination like mine. The worst struggles always took place during (a) mental prayer, (b) the long hours spent in the recital of the Divine Office and (c) the time before sleep came to one at night. All of which were, of course, occasions when the Rule demanded that one's thoughts should be wholly occupied with "spiritual" things.

There were times when the urge to yield was almost irresistible. To kneel down and apply oneself to prayer seemed the signal for an army of attractive ideas to invade one's mind. In my case they were generally in the form of plots for stories; notions for essays; chapter-openings and conclusions; exciting situations; scraps of entertaining dialogue; even verses and ideas for plays. The very air seemed charged with these amusing literary odds and ends. As Elgar once declared about music, it was there all round you; you had but to reach out your hand to grasp it and it became your own.

One day I complained about this to a wise old nun to whom the Mistress of Novices had sent me in accordance with an ancient custom of the house. This decreed that on vigils of the greater festivals the novices should be sent to certain of the more venerable members of the community with the request that they should tell them of their faults.

On the whole, I had rather a horror of these little interviews. Their extreme formality always made me shy and embarrassed; besides, one knew quite well that one's reactions to what was said were being carefully noted and would help to tip the balance when the time came for one to be voted for by the persons concerned.

With this particular nun, however, it was different. Though I only knew her slightly, there were things about her that I could not but admire. She was afflicted with what in the convent was known as a "distracted memory" and in consequence, was addicted to turning up late. As a result, the poor soul often found herself in awkward and humiliating situations. And my sharp young eyes had observed with admiration how eagerly she made the most of every humiliation that came her way.

When I plopped down on my knees at her side in the bare little cell where old paper, string and boxes were stored for the general use of the community, she drew her bushy grey eyebrows together with a little grimace of half-amused distaste.

I asked her, in the ancient formula which every postulant had to learn at her entrance into the noviceship, for God's sake to tell me of my faults.

I have never forgotten her answer. It was given in a slightly gruff and half-embarrassed kind of voice. She said:

"I was just thinking that it might be a better thing if instead *you* were to tell me about *mine*."

Which, of course, did far more to attract me to the virtue of humility than any amount of exhortation could have done.

When I consulted her about the dragon-fly ideas whose winged attacks so often prevented me from praying, she smiled and said:

"Innocent! That's a temptation of the devil. Father So-and so [she named a certain well-known Jesuit, long defunct, whose advice was rather too often, the younger members of the community considered, quoted by the older nuns whose spiritual director he had been] "always used to say that he made it a solemn rule never to act upon any 'bright ideas' that came to him when he should have been in prayer."

I would give a good deal to be able — honestly — to declare that from that day onwards I always imitated his excellent example. In this book, however, I have tried above all things to speak the truth. And the truth, I am sorry to say . . .

We had better leave it at that.

(7)

Somewhere about this time my hatred of Hove reached a point when I felt that it could no longer be endured.

That same feeling had visited me so often in the convent that I ought to have been inured to it. In a sense, I suppose, I was. But the difference between then and now was that to-day, if one felt that one's surroundings had become intolerable, one could escape.

There was, of course, only one spot upon earth that I wanted to escape to. What was more, my bones assured me that the hour had struck when the summons which had sounded in my heart on the journey down from Scoreswick must be obeyed.

Once more the enchanted country on the other side of Tamar had begun to magnetize me. There was clearly nothing to be done about it except fall in with what felt like one of the most terrific Inward Urges of my life.

(8)

The bags and suitcases on the overhead luggage-rack joggled dangerously. There were too many of them. You felt that a sudden jolt would bring them crashing down on their owners' heads. This, with the fact that the carriage contained more people than it had originally been built for, was all that from time to time reminded me that I was in a train.

You will perhaps be able to picture the state of mind in which I was journeying down to Cornwall when I tell you that, had I been hurtling through space in a chariot drawn by dragons, I could not have been more thrilled.

The very girders in the blitz-scarred roof at Paddington appeared transfigured: I saw them as fairy arches through which one passed out into the realm of gramarye.

"Gramarye." Yes: that, undoubtedly, was the word for it. And on that particular morning, it was everywhere. Now and again I had a definite physical feeling that it was beginning to break through from the invisible territory which I was trying to invade.

I settled myself into my corner and looked out through the broad plate-glass window of the Cornish Riviera express. If ever a magic casement, I reflected, had opened over a perilous fairy sea, it was to-day . . .

Blue skies and flowers in sunshine on the cliff-tops, with spars from a shipwreck floating in the cove below . . . to me that spelt the double personality of Cornwall. Half her charm lay in the number and unexpectedness of her contrasts. She communicated herself in a series of odd little shocks.

386

If I had to pick out the pair of contrasts which seemed to me the most characteristic of the double spirit which meets you at every turn in Cornwall, I should have no difficulty. I felt it long before I actually arrived. It was the subtle, almost sinister Tannhauser struggle between the two motifs of paganism and Christianity.

On the one side, you had the saints and hermits who, in the early centuries, had floated across from Ireland on a spread cloak or millstone of miraculous origin. From the little wave-side churches in the sand, from the holy wells beside which they had dwelt and to which they had given their names, rose their chant of prayer and praise strong and clear as a pilgrims' chorus down the years. And on the other . . . well, you might say what you liked . . . But there was no denying it; from among the trailing ivy and the gnarled tree-trunks in the wooded valleys, from the hillside boulders and the stone circles and the ancient burial-mounds, on a spring morning or when the moon was full at midsummer, the faint far-away fluting of the pipes of Pan could still be heard.

I kept my nose glued to my magic casement. But it was only after the train had rushed through Reading that the fun began.

It started with a sudden deepening of colour. The earth reddened. The fields grew lush and deep. The sky flamed to a more ardent blue. Streams and pools appeared and the woods and copses changed from burnt olive to emerald and gold.

387

At Exeter there was a long stop: long enough to let me hear for the first time the mellow, deep-voiced dialect of the West country. I liked it better than any speech I had ever heard.

After Exeter, a new rhythm crept into the melody. It was the rhythm of the sea. Along the miles of biscuit-coloured sand that stretch between Teignmouth and Dawlish, slow waves broke, in long ruled lines of silver. The milky, egg-shell blue of the water looked faint and feminine against the dark sorrel-red of the tunnelled rocks through which the train occasionally boomed. The sea was so close that now and again it seemed as though the waves would dash themselves across the line.

Plymouth — squalid beyond words, with its mean slums, war-wreckage and appalling devastation — was an unwelcome reminder of the civilization from which one was in flight.

"Look," somebody in the carriage called out excitedly, "we're just going over the viaduct at Saltash!"

And I knew that the gateway into the enchanted country had been reached.

A moment later and, with a rattle and a roar, the train was through it.

I was in Cornwall at last.

(9)

Now it is not the least use for prosaic people to insist that the "feeling" which comes upon you as you pass over from Devon into Cornwall is "imagination". Because it is nothing of the sort.

That first moment when you find yourself in "the land of the ancient kings and sorcerers and superstitions" is quite different from any other moment that you may have known. If you are properly prepared — if you are in the mood of sensitiveness and receptivity — if you are "tuned in" to accept what Cornwall has to give — then — well, as everybody knows, "anything may happen down in Cornwall". Whether, in your case, it will or not, depends very largely upon *you*.

The journey from Paddington to Saltash is only the prelude to Adventure. It is on the other side of Saltash Bridge that the Adventure begins . . .

The first thing that impressed me about Cornwall was that the landscape had grown sterner. Instead of the rich red soil and moist pastures of Devon, there were steep hills with scurrying streamlets and valleys filled with rocks and undergrowth. Now and again the train rumbled across a viaduct and, looking down, one saw the tops of trees far down in the gorge below.

Here were the forest tracks along which Sir Tristram must have ridden up to Camelot: the very woods, perhaps, through which King Mark fled, chased by Sir Dagonet the Fool . . . The whole country gave one a vague impression that it had lived through thrilling happenings. The very air was thick with story. It blew in through the open window like a breath of incense out of the forgotten past.

It was before Truro that a Cornish fellow-traveller started reciting the station names to his companion. After that, I knew for certain that I was in a foreign land. Menheniot; Doublebois; Lostwithiel; Carn Brea; Gulval . . . Here was gramarye indeed. Only to utter such words of power should surely be enough to summon buccas, spriggans, piskies from their lairs.

I had chosen this particular region of Cornwall because all I had read of it suggested that it would be the perfect setting for my Cottage-in-the-Clouds.

It bulged with ancient British villages. It crawled with prehistoric odds and ends. It contained more holed-stones, fogous, cromlechs, monoliths and stone circles than any other part of Cornwall. Mysterious presences and apparitions haunted it. People said that it was the last stronghold of the Cornish fairies. And in bygone days, it had been the chosen dwelling place of giants.

Could one ask more?

My plan was to explore the countryside in the hopes of discovering a cottage. Failing this, I meant to buy a plot of land and build.

It was late afternoon when my dragon-drawn chariot at last pulled in to Penzance. And — it was raining.

But what rain! To me it seemed almost lovelier than sunshine. The sky was a misted opal and the breeze from the sea like wine. And just across from Marazion, shrouded in veils of faintest lavender, St. Michael's Mount floated above the water, a dream palace on a fairy isle.

390

(10)

It was a pity that the state of my exchequer only allowed me to spend the inside of a week in Cornwall. However, the kind Vicar and his wife with whom I was staying drove me about quite a lot in their little blue Morris. This helped me to spy out more of the land than I could otherwise have done.

It was the first time I had ever stayed in anyone's house as a P.G. This bothered me. I felt certain I should do and say peculiar things. So, to safeguard myself against being thought "queer" I decided to give my host and hostess a brief outline of my career.

They had been charming to me from the outset. After that, however, their kindness deepened to solicitude. No one, in fact, had been nicer to me since I Came Out.

The Vicarage stood on the top of a hill with the sea at the bottom of it. When I woke on the morning of my arrival, warm, flower-scented air drifted in at the window. In the garden, fruit and palm trees made one think of the south of France. I floated downstairs in a kind of ecstasy.

At breakfast, the daughter of the house — a rather beautiful girl with the face and figure of an angelic Valkyrie — offered me a slice of ripe melon. After the sort of breakfast that I had grown accustomed to in London, I could hardly believe my eyes.

There was every sign that it was going to be a glorious day. For the first time since I left the convent,

I dared to wear a light summer dress which a friend had sent me from America. It felt inexpressibly frivolous. All the same, I couldn't help reflecting how much more sensible it seemed to be dressed according to the season instead of wearing the almost polar outfit which, summer or winter, had been obligatory while I was a nun.

Certain nightmarish memories still haunt me of the Fridays in June, July and August when the heat was very nearly unendurable in the choir. Friday, however, was the day on which the "choir sweep" had to be done. So, at nine in the morning, when the Subprioress rang the cloister bell for "Common Work", the head sacristan, followed by her two helps, would set out for the choir.

Even at that early hour, the heat was often tropical. Move an eyelash and a bath of perspiration would be the result. The heavy serge clothing and thick knitted stockings did not make things easier; and when one had girded on an all-enveloping apron there were at least six layers of various materials protecting — if that is the right word for it — one's torso from the air.

When the entire choir and carved stalls had been meticulously swept, dusted and brushed, the first polishing began. Beeswax and turpentine had to be rubbed in and then rubbed off again. Next came the final polishing. The wide parquet floor was the heaviest. You started on hands and knees, rubbing for all you were worth to get finished before the community arrived for their Visit to the Blessed Sacrament before Spiritual Reading at eleven o'clock. The ultimate mirror-like surface was not achieved without a struggle. One used a kind of long-handled broom with a heavily padded slab of concrete at the end; pushing it backwards and forwards until the desired perfection was obtained. It was really far too heavy for a woman to drag up the choir stairs from the distant cupboard in which it lived. Usually the two under-sacristans vied with one another for the distinction of hauling it to the choir without aid.

The whole business generally took about two hours of all-out effort. In the winter, it was an ideal way of restoring frozen circulation; but when the midsummer sun was overhead it was enough to fatigue an elephant. And if you happened to be fasting . . .

One day, early in my religious life when I was still full of Bright Ideas, I remember saying to the Reverend Mother:

"Sometimes, Reverend Mother, I can't help thinking that it would be so much less uncomfortable if, during the hot weather the sacristans were allowed to get up early and 'do' the choir before the community came in for Prime."

She looked at me thoughtfully. Then she said:

"And do you really think it so important to remove all discomfort from religious life?"

I said: "No, Reverend Mother: but to do the choir sweep in this weather means having to wash all over three times a day instead of twice. And that takes time . . ."

She drew her brows together in a way that made me wish I hadn't spoken.

"I call that exceedingly unmortified," she said. "Surely you can endure the discomfort of a little extra heat . . ."

I faded out.

I spent my first morning in consultation with an architect of whom I had heard through the simple expedient of writing to the Penzance Town Clerk. He was not encouraging. There were no Cornish cottages to be had anywhere, he assured me. As for the plans which I had sketched artlessly for my intended building, he clearly considered them beneath contempt. I walked up Market Jew Street feeling considerably deflated. It seemed that even the smallest conceivable cottage would cost more than I could afford.

The bus-ride back to Mousehole was, however, so lovely that it made me quickly forget my troubles. Beyond Mounts Bay the sea was a deep, blazing cornflower blue. St. Michael's Mount lifted delicate pinnacles against a Mediterranean sky. From the unhastening waves and the hot hillside, the Cornish magic distilled itself, slowly, almost imperceptibly, like a whispered spell.

(11)

That afternoon, they drove me out to Trevelioc.

To mention its real name would be, I feel, a betrayal. Too many visitors already break the silence of those lonely woods and desecrate the granite cliffs with

394

orange peel and cigarette cartons. I feel, too, that any attempt to describe it could only result in further purple patches. What is more, the curious spell which the place casts over those who visit it, springs from something which refuses to be translated into language.

So I must be content with the bald statement that of all the enchanted coves in the remote region which lies between Penzance and Zennor, Trevelioc is the most magical. Immediately I saw it, I recognized it as the one spot on earth in which I wanted to live. And although when the time came for me to return to England I had been unable to find even a foothold in the neighbourhood, I never for a moment yielded to discouragement. To do so, I felt, would weaken the intensity of my power to "want". And, as everybody knows, if you fail to get what you want, it is simply because you have not "wanted" it with sufficient passion and intensity.

It was in the convent that I learnt the tremendous importance of knowing how to "want" things. And as the only legitimate "want" of religious life is the object for which you embraced it, the whole thing really boils down to "wanting" God so tremendously that every other want fades out.

When I was a young nun, a kind and gentle Benedictine Father came to preach the Long Retreat to the community. He spoke simply, but his words left a very deep impression. I think it was because all he said was so obviously steeped in prayer.

One of his sermons was about mystical union with God; an aspect of the spiritual life which, under the

Novice Mistress of the moment, was practically taboo. As it also happened to be the subject in which above all others I was most keenly interested, this was rather unfortunate.

"You are too much preoccupied," she said to me one day when I had been Sent For, "with the whole subject of mysticism. Do remember, it is presumptuous to ask God to grant you mystical graces. There can be great danger of illusion for souls who try to force themselves along that way. The only safe way to divine union is through humility and the faithful performance of God's Will."

I thought to myself: Oh, how I hate "safe" ways! Aloud I said: "But, Mother, if mystical union with God is the end and aim of the contemplative life, like it says in *Sancta Sophia* . . ."

"And how did you get hold of *Sancta Sophia?*" she inquired, with a touch of severity.

I told her that I had taken it from the Noviceship cupboard one day when, being rather busy, she had given me leave to go and choose a book for myself.

"This is the bit I mean," I added. And, turning up the passage in question, I laid it open on her knee.

This is what Father Baker, well known as one of the greatest Benedictine contemplatives, has to say on the subject:

"The proper end of a contemplative life is the attaining unto an habitual and almost uninterrupted perfect union with God in the supreme point of the spirit . . . such a union as gives the soul a fruitive possession of

Him and a *real experimental perception* of His Divine Presence in the centre of the spirit."

She put on her glasses, read the passage, shut the book and put it away on the shelf beside which she was sitting.

"You can leave it here with me," she said.

"Oh, Mother!" I begged, "do let me have it back!"

She shook her head. All this preoccupation with mystic states of prayer, she insisted, was doing me no good. Far better leave such things to God and apply myself to obedience and humility.

Quite possibly, she was right. But I went away feeling rebellious. Surely, if union with God was one's object in entering the convent, and if mystical prayer was the shortest way to achieve it, not to go all out to become a "mystic" was simply to prove oneself a fool.

When the Retreat came, I had a word on the subject with the Benedictine Father.

I told him that I could never feel satisfied with just "talking to" God and thinking thoughts *about* him. What I wanted was God *himself*. And from what I had read and heard, it seemed to me that by mystical prayer alone could one really reach him.

"Quite right," he said. "Mysticism is the outcome of man's craving for and endless seeking after some way of experiencing actual, ontological, quasi-physical contact with God." And he explained that what feeling was to the body, so was mystical knowledge to the soul.

"It is quite possible," he told me, "that God is drawing you to mystical union with himself. But if so, I warn you that contemplative prayer is about the most crucifying thing that there is. You see, the least wilful distraction, the smallest deliberate relaxation from the incessant all-out effort after perfection will produce a sort of wall between yourself and God which you'll find when you go to prayer."

One other thing he said to me which I still remember.

I had asked him: "Then it isn't wrong to want to be united to God in the same way that the mystics are?"

He laughed. He said: "Good heavens, child, no! Blessed Angela of Foligno declared that the surest and quickest way of reaching it was to go on and on beseeching God to grant it, 'humbly,' 'continually' and even 'violently' ('*The Kingdom of Heaven suffereth violence*', you remember . . .) until he gave it. She even went so far as to say that one could *wrest* that particular grace from God by the intensity of one's desire."

And it was that which first helped me to understand what an enormous amount can be achieved when one concentrates one's whole heart, mind, soul and strength upon "infinite desire".

"*Ce que femme veut, Dieu le veut . . .*"

Especially — as the saints knew well — in spiritual things.

CHAPTER
TWELVE

(1)

Trevelioc was not, of course, the only place I visited while I was in Cornwall. There seems, however, little point in relating my adventures since none of them led to the discovery of either a cottage or a building site near the sea.

It was a pity that shortage of cash made a longer stay in West Penwith out of the question. I determined, however, that later on I would make a second and if necessary a third expedition south of the Tamar and hunt out some temporary abode in which I could lurk until Infinite Desire had wrested what I so desperately longed for from the hands of Providence.

I thought all this out during the long train journey back to London. I had felt leaving the Duchy like a wrench that was very nearly physical: though the intense magnetism relaxed slightly once the train had rattled over Saltash Bridge on to the solid earth of Devon. The change in mentality which one experienced when the enchanted land of spells and sorceries was left behind was really startling. It was curious how, in Cornwall, one had always felt subconsciously aware that something was brewing which, in a world stupefied by civilization, could no longer be experienced. All along the lane that dipped and twisted towards Trevelioc, one had felt the presences and powers that haunt the woods and coves.

Down there, belief in sorceries and superstitions was strong enough to give body to the Things which faded out when disbelieved in. It was useless to try and reason coldly and academically about such notions. In that remote cove, isolated from the outside world by the bulging humps and precipices of the hills and quarries, a secret life was being lived, intense, primeval, pagan. And I remembered one swift and rather thrilling moment which I had experienced just before we finally left the cove when it had seemed to me that just for an instant some bubble out of the prehistoric past had welled up and broken, releasing an atmosphere that was tingling and rapturous.

People up in England would think one crazy if one told them about such things. Well — I reflected — let them! I knew better.

And an almost passionate longing came upon me to get back to Trevelioc, where, in the warm, flower-scented hollow of the hillside I could find solitude and open my soul wide to the secret things that were floating like gossamer spells among the rocks and trees.

But I couldn't help wondering, as the train drew up at Paddington, what Reverend Mother's reactions would have been if she could have glimpsed what was going on inside my mind.

(2)

My admiration for Angela Thirkell, not only as a novelist but as a woman, is such that when at a tea-party in her

London garden, she introduced me to Miss Rachel Ferguson as "my cousin, Monica Baldwin", I was distinctly pleased.

The cousinship, you see, is rather a fragile connexion. Angela's grandmother, Lady Burne-Jones, and my great-uncle's wife, Mrs. Alfred Baldwin, happened to be sisters, so that Angela and I could easily repudiate one another if we chose.

You may possibly wonder what I was doing at her home in Pembroke Gardens.

Let me hasten to explain.

After my incursion into Cornwall, Hove had seemed so intolerable that a kind cousin who owned a bungalow not far from Southwick suggested that I might be happier there.

I accordingly moved in.

During the next few months I worked energetically at my book, read enormously and in my spare moments amused myself with my cousin's exquisite grey Persian cats. I also met the artist Douglas Grey and his wife — both friends of my cousin's — and, as may be imagined, was greatly thrilled when he suggested that I should sit for him.

I thought — and still think — that he has something closely akin to genius, though his Sargent-like habit of stripping all veils from his sitters, invading the back recesses of their personalities and revealing what he finds there by an uncannily clever manipulation of colour and light, suggests a greater esteem for truth than for popularity.

I wish I could have afforded to go up to London to admire my portrait when it was exhibited at the Royal Society of Portrait Painters. It would have roused agreeable feelings of inflation, and might possibly have heped to restore the self-confidence which my years in the convent had so effectively destroyed.

To return, however, to Mrs. Thirkell.

As soon as the pages of my book seemed sufficiently numerous to warrant it, I began wondering about a publisher. It was then that the notion of consulting Angela first came to me.

Our last meeting had been a year or two before I plunged into my convent. She and her husband, newly-wed, had stayed with the Stanley Baldwins at Astley Hall at the same time as I. My recollections were of a lovely and attractive girl who had dazzled and rather alarmed me across the dinner table by the brilliance of her wit.

Her reply to my letter could hardly have been kinder. And not long after, when I met her at the house of mutual friends in Sussex, I liked her so much that I readily fell in with her suggestion that I should stay for a while with her in London and lend a hand with the reopening of the house in Pembroke Gardens after the war.

Some quite interesting pages might be written on the subject of that visit, which in many ways added considerably to my Experience of Life. To be quite frank, however, I found it a little alarming. The intellectual standard of Angela's circle was so much above my level that I soon gave up any attempt to be more than an admiring listener and looker-on. Indeed, apart from my dealings with Angela herself which were always delightful, I think my happiest hours beneath her roof were spent in the society of Me Wang, my newly acquired Siamese cat.

(3)

The story of Me Wang is short and tragic. I mention it because she was the one great love of my post-conventual life.

She was a long-promised present from Wim and Barbara. And when, one day a telegram told me to call for her at South Kensington Station (I was still staying with Angela at Pembroke Gardens), I set out with a green silk pocket-handkerchief to bring her home.

She was hardly larger than a sparrow. Her long, coarse coat suggested goat's hair: the colour deepened from oatmeal to sepia at the ears, nose, paws and tail. Her dazzlingly blue eyes were set in an enormous head rather like something out of a Buddhist monastery, and her short thin tail had a kink as though someone had crimped it with a pair of curling tongs.

I wrapped her carefully in the green silk handkerchief and slipped her into the front of my coat. Upon which, she immediately started to screech at the top of her disproportionately powerful voice, and continued for three days without drawing breath save for those few too brief hours when, from utter exhaustion, she was obliged to sleep.

Her name (I believe it is that of a river in Siam) was bestowed upon her by Angela: and I have reason to think that the creature was no less devoted to me than I was to her. Be that as it may, for three delightful months she filled my rather lonely life with an absurd amount of happiness.

Then came the dreadful day when a hot nose and hideous cough made me realize that things were going ill with her. It was Cat Influenza. And Siamese, for the first few months of their lives, are not robust.

I did what I could for her. But it was of no avail.

Her last gesture (I was kneeling beside the chair on which she lay dying) was to lift herself and, with a supreme effort, creep to my shoulder and push her little black muzzle against my ear.

Since then, I have never had another Siamese.

(4)

I believe it was Oscar Wilde who declared that one should never repeat an emotion. I thought of this as I set out on my second expedition into Cornwall. I need not, however, have worried. It turned out to be even more delightful than my first.

This, I fancy, was partly because I had been steeping myself to the eyebrows in Sir Thomas Malory, and partly because, what with buzz-bombs, pre-invasion of Europe agitation and the just released horror tales of concentration camp atrocities, life north of the Tamar was really becoming a fright.

404

My aim was to find a cottage in which to live while waiting for my summons from Trevelioc. (That it *would* come, in course of time, I was perfectly sure.)

Spring was slowly slipping into summer when I started. My goal was the Lizard, which, so legend declared, was the eastern end of the lost Land of Lyonesse. This would make it an ideal background for a little day-dreaming about Sir Tristram and La Beale Ysoult.

Owing to my long years of enclosure, I still looked on every inch of unknown country with an eye of wonder. It was a thrill when the bus, zigzagging madly down the long green and gold peninsula of the Lizard, passed the turquoise waves at Poldhu, and the white foam that splashed wildly round the savage rocks at Mullion. After that came the long flat stretch of the Goonhilly Downs, where the hot scent of gorse, luscious, heady and nut-flavoured, came drifting from golden hollows and mounds on either side of the road.

If you have ever been to Cadgwith, you will remember how one climbs down from the bus at tiny Ruan Minor, where the tower of the doll's house church is no higher than the village cottages. From there to the cove a steep green lane curves downwards, ablaze with celandine, rose-campion and at least three kinds of lovely fern.

It was at the bend in the lane where the sea comes into sight that I felt the Cornish magic once more beginning to weave its spells. The very air seemed filled with strange and hidden presences. I stood still. (This, of course, was exactly the sort of thing for which I had come to Cornwall.) The oddest sensation started to creep over me. It was as though I had slipped back into contact with some experience that I had undergone in another existence long ago. I felt enraptured. But it was also just a little creepy. And of it some secret instinct warned me immediately to beware.

Shaking myself back into reality, I hurried down towards where the first cottages of Cadgwith clustered at the bottom of the road.

(5)

That night, before getting into bed, I stood for a long time at the window of the cottage in which I was lodging.

A heavenly fragrance of pinks and mignonette floated up from the garden. The world lay in dream, lulled by the soft splash of small waves on the shore. An enormous biscuit-coloured moon hung low above the horizon, tracing a path of palest gold across the sea.

I have observed that moonlight tends to induce a mood of introspection. Or is it only so with older people? Anyhow, as I stood there, a sudden bitter shaft of memory stabbed through me. On just such a night as this I had gazed — let us not enquire how many years ago — into the bland and baffling face of just such another biscuit-coloured moon.

That night, however, I had been wearing a slightly different style of night apparel; and the scrap of sky across which the moon had drifted, had been framed by the narrow window of my cell. By and by, when it finally disappeared from sight, I had crept back to bed and lain there most unhappily, in the darkness, wondering how long it would be before I could finally make up my mind to break with the life for which I now knew myself so unfitted, and go back again to the world.

Which brings us at last to a subject which I now confess I have been carefully avoiding since I started to write this book.

You would be surprised at the number of people who have asked me why it was that I left the convent. What is more, everyone whom I consulted while working on these pages has assured me that unless I give reasons for my exodus, half the interest of the story will be lost. All of which seems to indicate that the repugnance I have always felt for exposing this intimate page of personal history must now be overcome.

A friend of my youth (who had himself whisked in and out of a Dominican noviceship in a praiseworthy effort to test a "vocation" in which no one but himself had ever believed), remarked to me on the subject that he just could not conceive how such a mistake as I had made was possible.

"Why, *surely*," he insisted, "after all those years of probation — six, isn't it? or seven? — with all the hoops they put you through to find out just the sort of person that you are, it *must* be possible to tell for certain whether you really have a religious vocation?"

407

"You'd think so, wouldn't you?" I agreed. "As it happens, my own case is the only one in which I've ever known a mistake to be made."

He sat silent. (I felt sure I knew what he was thinking.) Then he said:

"Of course, one would hate to be — well, indiscreet in any way. But it would be extraordinarily interesting, you know, if you could give one even a hint . . ."

I signed inwardly.

"All right," I said. "I'll confess the awful truth to you. But it *may* sound embarrassingly Group-ish. If so, you have only yourself to blame."

The story I told him began with a Warning, which I fancy it might be well to reproduce.

Should you ever feel attracted to the idea of entering a convent, be sure and test yourself till you know for certain whether your chief motive for so doing is a sincere conviction that it is the Will of God for you. If you enter merely because you feel an attraction for the life, you may expect rocks ahead.

"My failure," I told him, "and the hopeless muddle I've made of everything, was simply because I neglected to do that."

To make this clear, I was obliged to dig up a few personal reminiscences. I give them below in a somewhat condensed form.

I was at a convent school and just seventeen years old when the idea first came to me that I wanted to be a nun. (And please notice that I have deliberately used the word *wanted* instead of *ought to*. Because, later on, all the trouble really hinged upon that.)

I suppose that without realizing it, I must have been ambitious. The things I longed for always seemed too wonderful to be realized. That may have been partly why I was so attracted by the idea of a religious vocation. Here, at last, was a sublime object which really was within my reach. It seemed to me the very highest way of living to which a human being could aspire.

"*La vocation*", as the girls called it among themselves, was discussed in an atmosphere of thrills and trepidation. To feel convinced that one had been chosen especially by God to belong to him alone, was certainly a thought to stir one's being. (Incidentally, it also gave one an indefinable prestige with both mistresses and girls.)

But consecration to God also meant that henceforward one would have to aim unceasingly at a life of absolute perfection. And that gave the idea an element of terror which caused the more earth-bound spirits among us to regard those whom we suspected of "*la vocation*" not so much with envy as with a kind of uncomfortable awe.

Towards the end of the school year, the headmistress — a nun of quite outstanding personality — always chose "*La Vocation Religeuse*" as the subject of one or two of her conferences to the girls. What she said invariably produced a deep impression. She spoke well, and was held in the highest esteem and affection by the girls. It was after one of these conferences that I became obsessed with the idea of becoming a nun. I will not analyse my mental processes during the next few months in order to prove to you exactly where I went wrong. It is enough to say that, when I determined that I would go into a convent, it never occurred to me to ask myself — or indeed, anybody else — whether or no my religious vocation were a genuine affair. I wanted to become a nun: it followed, therefore, as the night the day, that God must have chosen me. Because I wanted it, it *must* be the Will of God for me. It was indeed a supreme example of *Ce que femme veut, Dieu le veut.*

Now, I have always found that to set one's heart stubbornly upon one's own sweet will is apt to blind one. Had I considered, even for a moment, anyone else's point of view except my own, I might have *seen.* For it was my plain duty, as things then were, to remain at home, and, instead of pigheadedly casting myself into a convent, to shoulder my share of certain responsibilities which I dreaded and disliked. What I actually did, however, was to tell everyone — myself included — that I had received a Call which must immediately be obeyed.

Of course, I can't deny that I made great sacrifices when I gave up the world. But — in a certain sense — I *wanted* to make them. Or, to be more exact, the sacrifice of renouncing my longing to enter the convent would have cost me more than the giving up of all the delightful things I knew I should have to leave behind.

It now seems to me that my failure was largely the outcome of arrogance. What I ought to have done was

410

to take advice (instead of merely listening, a little contemptuously, to what people had to say); then, fairly and squarely, to weigh up my faults, qualities and tendencies; and finally, humbly to pray that God would show me whether or no the life I had set my heart on was in reality his Will for me. Instead of which, I simply took the bit between my teeth and galloped onwards. My point of view was that because I so wanted a thing which in itself seemed good to me, it must be right. Besides, in any case, at all costs, and no matter what might happen, a nun I intended to be.

It stands to reason that religious life, which is essentially a life of sacrifice, will never succeed if it is based on selfishness. And I fear (though it deeply humiliates me to confess it) there can be no doubt that selfishness was the foundation on which my own religious life was built. From this the trouble sprang.

It must have been, I think, after about ten years in the convent that I first began to wonder, miserably, whether I had not, perhaps, made a dreadful and tragic mistake.

The idea so disturbed me that I put it aside as a temptation. I dared tell no one. It seemed to me, however, that, mistake or no mistake, I had taken a step from which there could be no withdrawing. The only thing to do was to set one's teeth and go on with it, if not from inclination, then by sheer dogged force of the will.

The intense dislike I felt at this time for the life I had undertaken can really hardly be imagined. From dawn to sunset, almost every detail of it was savagely against the grain. Even now, after all these years, when I look back upon it, my soul is plunged in gloom.

For a time this succeeded. Five — ten — fifteen years dragged past, during which health, circumstances, and my own individual character combined to intensify my already insurmountable difficulties. Try as I would to adjust myself to my surroundings, the conviction grew upon me that I was only becoming more and more different in my ideas and outlook from the rest of the community. (And — believe it or not — were I to tell you about the lengths to which I went in my last years of despairing effort to cling to what I now hardly dared think of as my "vocation", I should probably be considered mad.)

At last came a day when I knew that I could blink the truth no longer. I was no more fitted to be a nun than to be an acrobat. It was then that I finally made up my mind that I must go.

The arrangements made by the Church for the dispensation of nuns who, for valid and adequate reasons, desire to leave their convents and return to the world, could hardly be wiser or more practical. (I may add that in my own case, the kindness and consideration which I received throughout, from everyone concerned, could hardly have been surpassed. It almost overwhelmed me.)

This, briefly, is what happens.

Once your mind is made up, you lay the matter before your Superior. Your case is then examined by the Ecclesiastical Authorities. Through the hands of the Apostolic Delegate (a kind of liaison officer between the Holy See and the Catholic Church in England), it is then dispatched to Rome. Here, it is once again carefully examined: after which, should your reasons be sufficiently sound and convincing, a "rescript" is granted, by which you are dispensed from your Vows and the obligations of religious life. You are thus restored to your former condition of a "secular", with complete freedom to return to the world and live there, according to whatever way of life you choose.

The moral, of course, of all this, seems to be that the actual career which one selects is in itself of only secondary importance. The thing that apparently matters to God is, one's motive for embracing it. A ballet-dancer may be — and I cannot help believing often *is* — quite as pleasing to God as a nun. The important thing is that one should take reasonable means to "fit in" to the jig-saw puzzle of life in exactly the spot where God wants one. If one drifts, or forces oneself into a place for which one was not intended, one not only spoils that particular bit of the picture but defeats the whole purpose in life for which one was made.

And that, as the patient reader will doubtless be relieved to know, is as much as I feel disposed to relate of that melancholy and depressing story.

CHAPTER
THIRTEEN

(1)

When my train steamed in after a long night journey back from my second stay in Cornwall, the queue at Paddington bookstall reached almost into the street.

Something, evidently, had happened.

I bought a paper. The front page displayed a ghastly photograph of the dead body of Mussolini. He was hanging, head downwards, from a rope attached to his ankles, the other end of which had been hitched up to the roof of a garage runway in Milan. A dead woman, also head downwards, hung beside him. Descriptions of the hideous saturnalia following the double murder filled the remainder of the page.

It was clear that I had returned once more to civilization. I felt slightly sick.

My disappointment over having still found no Cornish cottage as a temporary refuge was forgotten in the rush of tremendous happenings which crowded the next few days. The death of Hitler; Germany's unconditional surrender; and on 8 May — Feast of St. Michael the Archangel — VE Day and the announcement that war in Europe was at an end.

The next few months were in some ways rather bleak. Having no home, there really seemed nowhere for me to go. Cornwall, where I intended to settle, had, for the moment, barred its doors against me. And I felt no Inward Urge directing me as to how and where I should mark time.

So that when Lady Anne Lytton — a friend of long years' standing — reappeared rather suddenly on my horizon and whisked me away to beautiful Porlock Weir and the house of friends with whom she herself was staying, I could not have been better pleased.

In that almost forgotten period of history when Anne (who is several years my junior) and I first met, it was she who tended to do the questioning, the answers being laboriously supplied by me. Now, however, the positions were reversed. My attitude was that of the pupil, who, hungry for information, hangs with ears a-prick upon every word that falls from the teacher's lips. Like all the Lyttons, Anne knew how to tell an excellent story. I listened, entranced, to intimate details about the breeding, behaviour and private lives of Arab horses; gasped with admiration at modestly recounted tales of prowess at squash (the record of her championships and "runnings-up" — if that is the proper word for the things — revealed to me my own almost fantastic ignorance of everything to do with sport); and laughed till the tears rolled down at her tales of family, friends and happenings in the years between the wars. Sometimes we gossiped over supper in the pleasant country kitchen; sometimes we wandered through the woods at Ashley Combe. But whether it was by a stormy sea at midnight or an autumn evening when the hunter's moon poured in a surge of silver through the long black branches of the trees, Anne's companionship was always entertaining. What is more, the Experience of Life which I gained from her could not, I think, have been acquired by any other means.

From Porlock I made a third incursion into Cornwall. This time I stopped at a cottage in Trebah Wartha near the Helford River. The estuary was enchanting but it lacked the wild mystery of the Lizard, and Land's End. However, when the kind Vicar of Mawnan and his wife offered me on their glebe land an ideal ex-army hut on an ideal site for an almost incredibly ideal sum, I jumped at it delightedly.

Sad to say, the Commission for Town and Country Planning — if that is the name by which it calls itself — had views on the sacredness of that particular region which were anything but ideal. So once more my hopes were dashed. I returned to Porlock Weir feeling cross, tired, depressed and in the mood to bite off everybody's head.

(2)

I left Porlock on New Year's Eve with a premonition that I was in for a particularly dismal period. And I was right. The world, like the elephant, has a wonderful memory for affronts. Trample it beneath your feet — as I did, when I stepped, rather disdainfully, into my convent — and it will take it out of you when — and if — you have the temerity to return. The waters had closed very definitely over my head in 1914. In 1945, they showed not the smallest sign of opening again.

416

To know that there isn't a corner on earth where you are wanted or even needed, can have an almost influenza-like effect on your morale. And an endless wandering from place to place, camping temporarily in other people's houses, can be quite as tiresome for you as it is for them.

In my case, the difficulty about *doing* anything, or indeed, even making up my mind about what I *intended* to do, was that I simply knew nothing at all about anything. This sounds absurd; but it was literally the case. Even the odds and ends of information that I had picked up on my wanderings since I left the convent were almost more of a hindrance than a help. For instance, immediately I had thought up a line of action, someone invariably remarked: "Ah, yes; but what about so-and-so?" — communicating some vital fact of which I had till then been unaware. This, of course, promptly threw all my values into confusion so that I had to abandon everything and start again to rearrange my universe.

And the more things they told me, the more I realized I didn't know — and must absolutely learn. And yet, of what use was it to try and find out anything about anything, since everything was changing almost from hour to hour? Another cause for headache was that everyone of whom I asked advice immediately urged me to do the opposite of what had just been pointed out to me as essential by somebody else. And this — since I felt that I ought to distrust my own judgment even more than that of other people — led to a mental state of dithering and uncertainty which nearly drove me wild.

My outlook was still that of a twelve-year-old schoolgirl. And the inferiority fixation which resulted

417

automatically from intercourse with my own relations wasn't going to help things one bit.

Two more visits to relatives in Hereford and Sussex convinced me that unless I stopped wobbling to and fro at the suggestion of other people, I should get nowhere. The only way out of the *impasse* was to act for myself. I must be bloody, bold, and resolute; I must hold up my mind by the scruff of its neck and refuse to release it until it had made itself up.

But it needed courage. To fly in the face of all the advice showered on me would mean being condemned as (a) Ungrateful, (b) Pigheaded and — probably — (c) Rude.

In the end, I set my teeth and — did it. And — as usual — the moment I had shaken myself free, the fog began to lift. What was more, I actually perceived, in the depths of my almost atrophied subconscious, the beginnings of another Inward Urge.

In case you may have any difficulty in guessing the direction in which it pushed me, I will tell you.

It was Cornwall again.

(3)

At Porlock Weir I had been told so much about the loveliness of Goran Haven that I decided to go and investigate it for myself.

So, after a preliminary — and rather entertaining — correspondence with a certain Cornish Vicar and his wife, a kind of *au pair* arrangement was agreed upon.

In the mornings, I was to dash round with broom and duster and lend aid where it was required: in the afternoons, they would drive me around with them on their various errands in their car. In this way I hoped to see something of the county, and, just possibly find the longed-for cottage which was to shelter me till the summons from Trevelioc arrived.

Now, when people are terribly, terribly kind to me (and it happens oftener than you might imagine) I always want to go up and proclaim it from the house-top. I have a theory that it makes us all feel better (though quite possibly a little envious) to know just how kind and delightful other folk can be.

So I can't help regretting that (owing to pressure which has been brought to bear upon me by the very persons whom I desire to eulogize) My Lips — alas! — are Sealed.

There really can't be any harm, however, in mentioning that when I at last arrived at Goran, I was in what I can only describe as a thoroughly chewed-up condition. Maybe that was why the impression of really heavenly kindness being showered upon me was so deep. All soreness of heart and mind melted away like snow in sunshine. An inner glow slowly diffused itself throughout my being till I felt like a well-stroked, cream-fed cat, basking comfortably on a cushion in the sun.

I spent the last months of my stay at Goran in a small flat above the kitchen regions. It was known, in my honour, as "The Hermit's Lair". (I may mention that it was lent to me, characteristically, rent-free.)

419

For several reasons, this was an extremely important epoch in my career. One of them was that, since I had left the convent, this was the first time I had "done" for myself.

It was in the Lair that I first experienced the thrill of boiling a kettle; learnt that when you peel and boil potatoes, it is necessary to add salt: cooked a sausage (laying a mine could hardly have provided me with greater excitement) and knew the triumph of having fried my first bacon and egg.

The furniture which my sister had sent me from her flat in London arrived one day, and was installed in my small bed-sitting-room. After that, my happiness was very nearly perfect. I had a Place of My Own at last.

It was a pity there was not a single cottage to be had in the neighbourhood of Goran. Or — was it? Looking back, I think Providence — for once — was right. The coast is magnificent; but the china clay industry has ruined the St. Austell district. I rather doubt whether it and I would ever have become close friends.

(4)

After Goran I spent some time in a seaside bungalow at Trevone, on the north-west coast of Cornwall. It was lent to me by the Lady in the Fur Coat whom I had met, it may be remembered, when I was staying down in Sussex with my aunt.

It was an enchanting neighbourhood. But I think the place which attracted me most was an odd little valley somewhere between Porthcotham Cove and Bedruthan Steps.

I called it "The Little Goat Cove". That wasn't its real name — (I have never yet discovered what that was); I just called it that because it seemed to suit it. Not that there were any goats to be *seen* in it: the point was that although you couldn't *see* them, you felt quite certain that they were there. A narrow stream of silvery, ice-cold water poured down through some fields into the gorge near the mouth of the cove. The sand on either side was rather dirty, and printed with small, cloven hoof-marks, as though it had been recently scampered upon. It was these hoof-marks that fired my imagination. The colour, atmosphere and general *feeling* of the place seemed to belong to another age and nation. And as I picked my way across the stream on stepping-stones, I felt distinctly that unseen eyes were watching me from behind the boulders, and that where the strong, pungent odour of goat was most noticeable, something half-glimpsed, half-guessed at, was observing me furtively. Goats? Satyrs? Fauns? Or simply imagination? All I know is, that to me it appeared as an exciting, half-pagan sort of place, filled with presences which — did one only remain there long enough — would eventually materialize.

(5)

It was about this time that the idea came to me of buying a wooden hut and settling somewhere in the neighbourhood until the day when at last Trevelioc should open its gates to me.

I even got as far as plans and estimates.

And then — suddenly — things started happening in a way which made me wonder what could have caused Providence once more to take an interest in my affairs.

One morning in November I received a letter from a cousin, enclosing a house-agent's advertisement.

"I know," wrote the cousin, "that you've long been looking for a Cornish cottage. What about this?"

This was the description:

"Freehold, vacant possession Jan. Two-roomed granite cottage on cliff-ledge overlooking sea. Electricity and every mod. conven. kitchenette, electric griller: indoor lav. and bathrm. with electric geyser. Stands sheltered from wind in own small cliff garden. Magnificent views. 5 min. village. 15 bus."

"If you are interested", the letter continued, "you had better wire immediately to the agent and, if possible, go down to view it the same day as you get this. Houses these days get snapped up almost before they are advertised."

I turned over the agent's list to see the price and locality of the cottage.

The price would have swallowed all and more than all of my carefully hoarded savings. But the locality was Trevelioc Cove.

My summons had come.

422

(6)

Exactly three-quarters of an hour later, after having wired to the house-agent, I was seated breathless but triumphant beside the driver of the car which, at hideous expense, I had hired to whirl me down immediately to Trevelioc.

My enjoyment of the drive was rather spoilt by a cold fear lest someone might already have rushed in and snapped the cottage up.

The lovely road rushed past us: St. Merryn, with its ancient, secret-looking church; Little Petherick and Trelow Downs, grey-green and smoky lilac in the November sun; Wynnards Perch and the long road leading to St. Columb Major. Scorrier followed. After that, I was inclined to shut my eyes. The hideous, jerry-built cottages of the miners on the way to Redruth are a blotch on the face of Cornwall; and the Camborne houses blight the earth on which they stand. It was a relief to escape on to the long straight road between Hayle and Marazion and to see the frill of foam round the rock-base of St. Michael's Mount. At Penzance the tide was high. We dodged immense green monsters that broke occasionally over the parade. Then up the appalling hill, past Paul turning and on through Sheffield village to where the strange bleak country that heralds the Land's End region first appears. It seemed that there was another approach to Trevelioc — a narrow lane labelled "impracticable to motors". I urged the driver down it. We crept along.

The lovely zigzag led to the dark, rushing stream that flows through the Trevelioc Valley. The bridge took us up past the handful of cottages known as Trevelioc village — down the winding precipice road with the stream on one hand and the brushwood cliff on the other — and so, at last, out into Trevelioc Cove.

It was strikingly different from the way I remembered it two years ago in summer. The sea was grey-green; and immense foam-crested breakers flung themselves in clouds of silvery spray across the ruined pier. The trees were almost bare, so that one could see down into the gorge where the stream, swollen to a roaring torrent, rushed, in a wild series of cascades, down to the sea.

But what struck me most about the change that had come over the place with winter was the appearance of the Stones.

Of course, one had always known that they existed; bits of them had even pushed themselves up between trails of honeysuckle and tufts of flowers. Now, however, they had come out into the open. And no one who had looked on them as they stood there in their stark and savage greyness could doubt the fact that the Stones were *masters* of the Cove.

The cottage was perched on a narrow terrace half-way up the cliff-side. A white gate led into a minute cliff garden, so small as to be almost like a shelf. In the midst of this the house was planted, its long, lean-to roof almost hidden by a windscreen wall whose crenellated top gave it the appearance of a fortress on a Lillputian scale.

"Well, it's certainly small enough," remarked the driver.

It was indeed. In fact, it was the smallest house I had ever been inside. The living-room was simply the frame for an enormous casement window that looked out across the cove on to the sea. Another even smaller room adjoined it, used, apparently, for kitchen, bathroom, lavatory and store. There were no shelves or cupboards anywhere and the "kitchenette" mentioned in the advertisement had apparently been used as the kennel for a dog. The walls of the living-room, instead of being papered, were hung with silken taffeta attached to wooden frames. The design was of a forest glade with bluebells growing beside dark water under shady trees. It made one feel as though one were standing in a fairy forest shut in by trees and flowers instead of walls.

"It's heaven."

I murmured the words rather quietly, in case the driver, who had just returned from examining the drains, should hear.

"They seem Okay," said the driver, without enthusiasm. "But the garden's no larger than a piece of toast."

I followed him into it. It was hardly more than a ledge of granite. Yet it had vast possibilities. At the far end, the cliff rose steeply behind a thicket of blackthorn, continuing like a high wall round the back of the house.

"I like this corner," I said, peering through the blackthorn to where bits of the granite rock-face were still visible. "If all this stuff were cut down, one could strip the cliff and make a marvellous rock-garden."

We returned to the cottage.

"I expect I shall buy it," I announced in a voice which perhaps, in the circumstances, may have sounded over-enthusiastic. The driver's expression of faintly amused disapproval was a little dampening. He said, Well, of course, that was for me to decide. He would not presume to give advice.

After further poking and prying we locked the door and I went round to take a last look at the view from the garden. More than ever my shoe-laces felt as though they were tied to the ground beneath my feet.

"It's like the cell of a medieval hermit," I reflected. "It's my Cottage-in-the-Clouds come down to earth. It's so perfect that it might have been built on purpose for me. In fact, I believe it *was* . . ."

My heart had begun to thump with a strange excitement. Suppose this were to be the end of all my voyagings and ventures? Well — why shouldn't it? After all, the decision lay with me.

We drove back from Trevelioc to Penzance in silence.

In Market Jew Street, I got out and telegraphed to the agent that I would buy the house.

(7)

I moved into my cottage just before midnight at the beginning of February.

Snowdrifts had prevented the furniture van from reaching Goran — (whither I had returned to collect my belongings after leaving Trevone) — till nearly six o'clock in the evening. When we started, it was already dark. I climbed into the seat between the driver and a muscular Remover whose teeth chattered so dismally that he could hardly cope with his cigarette.

It was quite the coldest drive I can remember. There was snow falling and the road opened up in the glare of the headlights like torn linen as we sped along. St. Austell — Truro — Camborne, and then seaward again towards the lights of Marazion and Penzance.

The rattle of the van was so deafening that conversation was impossible. I was glad, because I was tired to death and had drifted into a sort of dream. The noise made by the van was curiously rhythmic. The air, too, seemed full of harmony. Presently it all resolved itself into a sort of symphony in which I myself and everything all round me seemed to be taking part.

But the real music only started as we turned into the lane that leads to Trevelioc. (I can't describe it because it was the sort of music that one hears not with the ears but with the heart. In places it was rather like the "Grand March" in *Aïda* — majestic, full of colour and rhythm and with plenty of tune.) I had the impression that I was entering Trevelioc in a kind of Roman triumph: and that I was doing so after an absence of several thousand years. A white snow carpet had been spread over the last lap of my progress, on either side of which the invisible inhabitants were thronging silently to welcome me. Strange shapes and stranger presences were stirring in the deep gloom among the bushes: the secret life of the place had awakened and was moving to a rhythm older than time.

The climax came at the last bend in the road where the cove springs suddenly upon one. It was black as night except where the moon had let down a ladder of silver over the sea. The driver stopped at the foot of the path which led up the cliff-side to my cottage. And in the silence that filled the timeless instant between the engine's stopping and the noise and movement which inevitably followed it, I heard the music leap up, swift and sudden as a flame — draw all the magic of the night into its harmonies, and sink back, losing itself in the splash of the stream and the waves' roar and the long shiver of the wind among the trees.

In the darkness I stumbled up the narrow path to the little porch that stood half-hidden in the house's shadow.

Then, unlocking the door of my Cottage-in-the-Clouds, I went in.

Other titles published by Ulverscroft:

THE REAL PEAKY BLINDERS

Carl Chinn

In the backstreets of Birmingham after the First World War, Billy Kimber was a feared fighter with an astute mind and magnetic personality. These attributes earned him the leadership of the Birmingham Gang that dominated the highly profitable protection rackets of the racecourses of England. The members of this gang had once been "sloggers" or "peaky blinders", and their rise to supremacy was attributable to their viciousness and to Kimber's shrewd alliances with other mobs. But they soon incurred the envy of the Sabini Gang of London, who fought violently to oust Kimber and his men and take over their rackets. The Birmingham Gang battled back fiercely in the infamous and bloodstained racecourse wars of the 1920s. These were the real Peaky Blinders, and this is their story.

MY LIFE IN HOUSES

Margaret Forster

Margaret Forster takes us on a journey through the houses she's lived in: from the council house in Carlisle where she was born in 1938, to her beloved London house of today — via the Lake District, Oxford, Hampstead, and a spell in the Mediterranean. This is not a book about bricks and mortar, but a book about what houses are to us, and the effect they have on the way we live our lives. It takes a backwards glance at the changing nature of our accommodation: from blacking grates and outside privies to cities dominated by bedsits and lodgings; and houses today being converted back into single dwellings, all open-plan spaces and bringing the outside in. It is also a very personal inquiry into the meaning of home.

THE BUCKET

Allan Ahlberg

In 1938 Allan Ahlberg was picked up in London by his new adoptive mother and taken back to Oldbury in the Black Country. Now one of the most successful children's book writers in the world, here Allan writes of an oddly enchanted childhood lived out in an industrial town; of a tough and fiercely protective mother; of fearsome bacon slicers; of "fugitive memories, the ones that shimmer on the edges of things: trapdoors in the grass, Dad's dancing overalls". Of "two mothers, two fathers and me like a parcel or a baton (or a hot potato!) passed between them". Using a mix of prose and poetry, supported by new drawings by his daughter Jessica and old photographs, *The Bucket* brings to life the childhood that inspired Allan's classic picture books.

BOBBY ON THE BEAT

Bob Dixon

Bob Dixon spent years "on the beat" as a police constable with the Metropolitan Police in the early 1960s, witnessing all manner of incidents, from the serious to the ludicrous. Spending the majority of his time in London's East End dealing with drunks, fatalities on the road, domestic disputes, and even suicides, as well as policing at major public events such as Guy Fawkes night, New Year's Eve, and anti-Vietnam War marches, life was colourful and varied, if not always safe. This memoir of a London copper charts Bob Dixon's experiences as a young police officer before he joined the CID, covering his life before signing up for the force, his rigorous training, and the vagaries of first patrolling the beat, as well as the lighter side of policing.

THE BEST MEDICINE

Georgie Edwards

In 1949, Staff Nurse Georgie Edwards is asked to chaperone medical students undertaking their practical exams, when suddenly the penny drops. Georgie wants to learn to diagnose and treat, too. Against the odds, she wins herself a place to study medicine at London's St Bartholomew's Hospital. Once there, she sets about becoming not a consultant who "sweeps by", but a doctor who listens and cares. Yet Georgie wants to fall in love and start a family as well as have a career. Is this one dream too many for a woman in the 1950s?

THE ZHIVAGO AFFAIR

Peter Finn and Petra Couvee

1956. Boris Pasternak knew his novel, *Doctor Zhivago*, would never be published in the Soviet Union as the authorities regarded it as seditious, so, instead, he pressed the manuscript into the hands of an Italian publishing scout and allowed it to be published in translation all over the world — a highly dangerous act.

1958. The CIA, recognising that the Cold War was primarily an ideological battle, published *Doctor Zhivago* in Russian and smuggled it into the Soviet Union. It was immediately snapped up on the black market. Pasternak was later forced to renounce the Nobel Prize in Literature, igniting worldwide political scandal.

With first access to previously classified CIA files, *The Zhivago Affair* gives an irresistible portrait of Pasternak, and takes us deep into the Cold War, back to a time when literature had the power to shake the world.